P9-DTT-512

The World of
Customer Service

2e

Pattie Gibson-Odgers, Ed.D.

Assistant Professor
Northern Arizona University • Flagstaff, Arizona

SOUTH-WESTERN
CENGAGE Learning

Australia · Brazil · Canada · Mexico · Singapore · Spain · United Kingdom · United States

SOUTH-WESTERN
CENGAGE Learning

The World of Customer Service, 2nd edition

Pattie Gibson-Odgers

VP/Editorial Director:
Jack W. Calhoun

VP/Editor-in-Chief:
Karen Schmohe

Acquisitions Editor:
Jane Phelan

Developmental Editor:
Karen Hein

Marketing Manager:
Valerie Lauer

Marketing Coordinator:
Kelley Gilreath

Senior Marketing Communications Manager:
Terron Sanders

Production Manager:
Tricia Matthews Boies

Production Technology Analyst:
Erin M. Donohoe

Content Project Manager:
Jennifer Ziegler

Technology Project Editor:
Michael Jackson

Manufacturing Coordinator:
Kevin Kluck

Production House:
ICC Macmillan Inc.

Printer:
Edwards Bros.
Ann Arbor, MI

Art Director:
Bethany Casey

Cover and Internal Design:
Chris Miller
C Miller Design

Photo and Permissions Editor:
Darren Wright

For more information about our products,
contact us at:

South-Western Cengage Learning
5191 Natorp Boulevard
Mason, Ohio 45040
USA

Cover Photos: Getty Images, Inc.
Photodisc Red collection, Digital Vision collection

Career Cluster icons are being used with permission of the:

States' Career Clusters Initiative, 2006, www.careerclusters.org.

ExamView is a registered trademark of FSCreations, Inc.

Customer service is a critical element in the success and future of all businesses that compete in today's economy. With global markets more crowded than ever, a major challenge for organizations is to attract and retain customers because more companies are competing for the *same* customer. The secret to getting and keeping loyal customers today comes in creating new business and having a customer-centric approach.

A thriving business lives the mantra that *every* member of its organization is involved in delivering exceptional customer service. As Sam Walton, founder and former CEO of Wal-Mart, so fittingly put it, "There is only one boss—the customer. And he can terminate everybody in the company, from the chairman on down, simply by spending his money somewhere else."

The World of Customer Service, 2e is easy to read, has a user-friendly design, practical customer service tips, and strong critical thinking projects. The text focuses on the role of customer service in helping organizations accomplish their goals, deal with problems and complaints, win new customers, and create loyal customers.

At a Glance

Part 1 introduces the basic concepts of customer service in today's marketplace and identifies the diverse nature of the customer population. Exceptional customer service is also addressed, along with how customer behavior and loyalty have changed.

Part 2 emphasizes the numerous essential personal skills that a customer service representative (CSR) must demonstrate on the job. Attitude and personal approach with customers when dealing with problems and complaints are discussed, as well as how to recover from and win back the angry customer. An overview of the skills CSRs need in managing the customer service role, including problem solving, time management, and stress management, is included.

Part 3 focuses on the communication skills needed for effective customer service. These skills include understanding the essentials of communicating and the importance of customer-focused listening skills, non-verbal communication, dress, and manners. Communicating effectively on the telephone is also discussed.

Part 4 highlights the challenges of customer service in a global world, beginning with the significant impact of globalization on customer service today. It focuses on the importance of technology and the critical need to train, empower, and reward CSRs. It also discusses ways of managing and measuring the effectiveness of customer service in organizations.

New to this Edition

To update and further strengthen coverage of the current research and practices in the customer service field, topics throughout the text are covered in more depth, with an emphasis on the importance of using effective communication and collaboration techniques while applying Internet research and technology skills. A new chapter focusing on the globalization of customer service has been added, as well as a chapter fully dedicated to customer-focused listening skills.

New features in the 2nd edition:

- *Focus On . . .* incorporates real-world customer service issues specifically related to best practices, leadership and management techniques, and career choices.
- *Business in Action* provides examples of actual organizations that demonstrate the use of customer service concepts.

- *Key Terms* call attention to new words and concepts that are introduced in the chapter and serve as a useful review tool to aid student understanding.
- *Remember This* spotlights central issues while serving as a reference tool for solving on-the-job problems at a later date.
- A *Product Website* includes activities and web links to further enhance student learning.
- *Video Clips* with discussion questions, located on the Instructor's Resource CD and the product website, demonstrate real-world customer service issues for better visual understanding of chapter content.

Additional Features

Features designed to attract and hold student attention are found in every chapter.

- *Quotations* introduce each chapter with thoughts from famous people that prompt and focus interest.
- *Customer Service Tips* demonstrate practical suggestions from customer service providers today.
- *Ethics/Choices* pose ethical dilemmas and get students talking about customer service issues in class discussions.
- *Industry Profiles* feature customer service providers who explain their jobs while sharing personal information about attitude, education, and work experience as applied to essential elements of customer service in their field.
- *Let's Discuss* follows each Industry Profile and serves as an excellent activity on the featured industry.

End-of-Chapter Activities

Many projects are based on a simulated company called On-Time Technology Products (OTTP). The applied activities incorporate group interaction and Internet research projects. You will assume the role of a customer service representative for OTTP. As the CSR, you work with five other CSRs, and each of you reports directly to the supervisor, Mary Graeff.

- *Critical Thinking* stretches the student's thinking and poses questions that relate the content to the student's philosophy, value system, and work experience.

- *Online Research Activities* require students to conduct Internet research that supplements chapter topics and customer service in general. Guided instructions assist students in gathering pertinent data for completing these projects.
- *Communication Skills at Work* presents opportunities for students to apply their communication skills to solve customer service problems effectively.
- *Decision Making at Work* allows students to apply their decision-making skills as they think through and effectively solve customer service concerns.
- *Case Studies* reinforce chapter content with real-life scenarios that address important issues in the workplace, including human relations, ethics, and employee attitude problems.
- A *collaborative icon* appears next to the activities that require group interaction.

Supplements Available

- **Instructor's Resource CD** includes the Instructor's Manual, course syllabus, chapter outlines, teaching suggestions, ExamView® testing software and chapter tests, test solutions, and solutions to book projects. The CD-ROM also includes PowerPoint slides that summarize the main topics, issues, and competencies covered in the chapter material, as well as short video clips and JoinIn™ on Turning Point® data files.
- **Product Website** provides links to Internet resources that correlate to the end-of-chapter materials. Go to academic.cengage.com/marketing/odgers and click on the appropriate chapter to find web links and additional activities.
- **eBook** An electronic version of the textbook is available online. eBooks enhance traditional courses by providing material digitally. eBooks are viewed on a computer with a free Adobe® Acrobat® Book Reader™ and look exactly like the printed version—including photos, graphics, and rich fonts. Additional features not available in a printed version include the ability to customize the content by annotating text, highlighting key passages, inserting "sticky notes," and bookmarking pages.

acknowledgments

This textbook has been a living document, undergoing several practical and constructive revisions and ongoing updates. I would like to recognize and thank all those who helped, particularly colleagues and instructors throughout Arizona and California who practice great customer service and who have shared valuable information. Special thanks to the following reviewers of this edition:

Nora Adams
Sinclair Community College
Dayton, OH

W. Russell Brown
Navarro College
Corsicana, TX

Stephen G. Bryant
Antonelli College
Hattiesburg, MS

DeAnn Hurtado
Sinclair Community College
Dayton, OH

about the author

For over 30 years, Dr. Pattie Gibson-Odgers has taught a variety of courses in computer applications and business systems to high school, community college, and university students in Arizona and overseas in West Berlin and Stuttgart, Germany. She received her bachelor's and master's degrees from Arizona State University and her doctorate from Northern Arizona University. She is currently an assistant professor at Northern Arizona University, where she teaches graduate-level adult and higher education classes.

Dr. Odgers owns and operates a successful computer consulting and training business that serves northern Arizona. This experience is invaluable as a means of keeping in touch with what's happening in customer service in the workplace. Earlier in her career, Dr. Odgers worked as a trainer and marketing representative for IBM Corporation on both the East and West Coasts.

A nationally recognized speaker and published author, Dr. Odgers writes journal articles on the information workplace, the training of adult learners through distance delivery, and customer service. She has authored seven textbooks, including *Office Skills* and *Administrative Office Management.* She enjoys traveling, reading, staying active, and spending time with her family.

contents

PART 1

The Customer Service Environment

chapters

PHOTO © MELISSA DEVLIN

Call Centers Profile

by Rob Pasell, Sturner and Klein

In your opinion, how important is customer service today?

Customer service is the single most important aspect of any call center organization, whether its purpose is sales or help desk support, and whether its focus is inbound, outbound, or a combination of both. Customer service is the cornerstone of my company's philosophy, which states, "Quality can never be made up for in quantity."

What are the essential skills that a call center representative should possess to be successful?

One of the most important skills, in my opinion, is the ability to empathize with the customer. Doing this helps put the customer at ease, because more than likely, others have experienced the same problem. Once the caller is comfortable, the rep will have an easier time of proceeding with the nature of the call.

Listening is another essential skill for those working in a call center. A rep must concentrate on what the customer is saying and ask questions until the problem is understood. Once this is accomplished, the rep can take the necessary steps toward solving the problem.

Being able to adapt to situations and solve problems on the spot while maintaining a positive attitude is another very essential skill. Typically, call centers prepare a scripted response to most problems and issues a rep may encounter. Usually, the rep can follow the procedure for that issue, but occasionally will need to think on his or her feet for a creative solution.

What are your thoughts on customer service in the call center industry?

Call centers are growing in number across America. That is, many companies choose to contract out their customer service and sales work to companies such as ours. Today, reliable call centers are in demand from many corporations because often the only contact their customers will have with the company is through a call center. Each contact should result in a positive experience, or those customers may not buy the company's product or use its service again. A favorable first impression is essential. The level of quality and customer service that call center reps provide keeps clients coming back and may result in referrals to other companies that have call center needs.

Industry: Call Centers

Call Center Activities

What are call centers? Call centers are the areas of every company where customers and prospective customers call, make website requests, and correspond through e-mail. Call center areas are where those major customer communications are received and answered.

1. *What industries have call centers?* Research your community, city, and state to determine where call centers are. (Usually, call centers don't hang banners on the door, so you might have to do some investigating.) In the following table, column 1 lists some typical industries that have call centers, and column 2 lists categories or names of companies with call center areas. In column 3, list the companies that have call centers established and operating in your area. You may have to call to confirm some of your choices.

Industry	Examples	Call Centers in Your Area
Telecommunications	Verizon Wireless, MCI	
Financial	Banks and brokerages	
Retail	Sears	
Travel	Airlines, car rentals	
Insurance	Prudential, Farmers	
Reservations/tickets	Ticketron, timeshare condos	
Internet companies	ISPs, e-trade	
Others		

2. *Size and growth of call centers.* Call centers in the United States and offshore (through outsourcing) are growing tremendously. Go to academic.cengage.com/marketing/odgers, find the *Let's Discuss* activity for Part One, and visit the call center websites listed there, or use your favorite search engine to find several call center websites on your own. Provide below three items of information about call centers that you were previously unaware of.

a. _____

_____

b. _____

_____

c. _____

_____

Introduction to Customer-Centric Service

chapter 1

Objectives

1. Define customer-centric service.

2. Contrast traditional customer service with exceptional customer service.

3. Identify required customer service skills and competencies.

There is only one boss—the customer. And he can fire everybody in the company, from the chairman on down, simply by spending his money somewhere else.

—SAM WALTON, FOUNDER OF WAL-MART

Businesses—large or small, industrial or retail, new or established—cannot survive without customers. Customer service is not about fancy products or intricate corporate culture, but about dedicated, trustworthy employees and loyal, satisfied customers. Today, with more and more competitors vying for customers' attention, exceptional customer service is no longer optional—it's essential to staying profitable in business. Although nobody would claim that customer service is simple, the basic foundations and concepts should be.

Service occupations are projected to account for approximately 18.7 million of the 18.9 million new wage and salary jobs generated over the 2004–2014 period. The approach in this book places you in the role of a service provider. If not in your current job, then sometime in the near future, much of your on-the-job success may be influenced by your ability, knowledge, and willingness to provide exceptional customer service.

Part 1 of this text serves as an overview of the key aspects of customer service. Chapter 1 begins by describing what customer service is and how a customer is defined. Discussion then moves to identifying what *exceptional* customer service is and how it has changed. Finally, the goals of customer-oriented organizations and the importance of hiring the right person to perform the role of delivering exceptional customer service are addressed. Chapter 2 is dedicated to exploring the many challenges today in serving a diverse population that varies in terms of personality, generations, ethnicity, gender, and persons with disabilities. In Chapter 3, the critical topics of customer behavior, customer loyalty, and the importance of exceptional service are covered.

Defining Customer Service

Even though every customer is unique, all customers expect three things—a quality product, reliable service, and reasonable prices. In other words, customers want to receive what they feel they have paid for. A customer views *you*, an employee of an organization, as the company, regardless of what your job description says.

Customer service means different things to different people. In reality, however, the only perspective that matters is the customer's perception of good customer service at the time service is needed and delivered. Here are some examples of good customer service:

- For a busy traveling executive, a flight that leaves on time
- For a harried office manager, working with an office supply store that keeps a good inventory of products on hand and delivers dependably
- For a lonely retiree, conversation and kindness from a waitress when frequenting a neighborhood restaurant
- For a college student entering a new school, competent and caring advice from an advisor on the best course of study

Simply stated, **customer service** is the process of satisfying the customer, relative to a product or service, in whatever way the customer defines as meeting his or her need, and having that service delivered with efficiency, understanding, and compassion.

Whether online or offline, customers now have unparalleled power to research and transact with companies exactly when, where, and how they choose. A new worldview is at work that companies must either embrace or ignore at their peril. The **customer-centric service** worldview simply means that business revolves around the customer. Put another way, a customer-centric organization puts customers first, is service oriented, and thoughtfully develops and satisfies a loyal, repeat customer base.

To be customer-centric does not mean being a doormat. It means being respectful to the customer's point of view and letting the customer know that his or her opinion is heard and valued before making the right decision from both the short- and long-term business perspectives. It means listening with care to the customer's concern, then taking the time to respond to that concern reasonably. Companies that focus on creating a good customer experience will succeed far more than those that do not.

> ### customer service TIP
> *It has been said that one way to exceed customer expectations is to promise good but deliver great! In other words, go above and beyond what is expected.*

Mission Statement, Values, and Goals of Customer Service

Organizations, like people, require direction and focus in order to achieve stated goals. How many times have you heard that if you don't have any idea where you're going, you probably don't know where you've been, are confused as to where you are, and most certainly won't know it when you get to where you ought to be? In like fashion, employees who have no idea where they are going flounder aimlessly, trying to get through the day, with no sense of purpose, loyalty, commitment, or urgency. This is not what customers who buy from organizations have a right to expect.

The quality of customer service that a customer receives is greatly influenced by an organization's mission statement and its vision of doing business. As simple as the statement "Good service is good business" can be, it may say all that is necessary to represent a company's mission statement or general values. Another example of a purpose statement is the Ritz-Carlton Hotel's motto: "We are ladies and gentlemen serving ladies and gentlemen." If employees at this hotel follow the motto to the letter, they provide the finest personal service and facilities for their guests, who will always enjoy a warm, relaxed, yet refined hotel experience.

◑ remember this ...

Common Customer Service Myths

Myth	Fact
1. We are providing good service, but a perception exists outside the organization that we are not.	• You may, in fact, already be providing good customer service, but it is not good enough; you can improve it. More important, if you are providing good service but the customer's perception is that you are not, then you have a problem that needs to be corrected; to the customer, perception is reality.
2. You can't improve service without more people and a larger budget.	• Poor service is far more costly to provide than high-quality service. Eliminating long, repetitive customer interactions and responding to customer complaints more efficiently saves time and money.
3. Why all the concern over customer service? If customers don't like the service we provide, they can try getting it elsewhere.	• A "take it or leave it" attitude is unacceptable. If enough customers receive poor service, they will eventually complain to management or an elected official in a way that can be very uncomfortable for you and/or your organization.
4. You can't provide high-quality customer service when the requirements you must implement force you to tell customers "no."	• Quality customer service is not saying "yes" to everything customers request. People can accept a "no" if it is presented in the right way, but they cannot accept loss of dignity and control.
5. Our customers have conflicting objectives; we will never be able to satisfy them.	• You can do only what legal requirements authorize you to do. However, you cannot let what you cannot do be an excuse for not doing all that you are authorized to do. This includes providing warm, friendly, caring service that is responsive, efficient, and accurate.
6. I don't need to worry about customer service because I don't deal with the public.	• You cannot provide high-quality service to your external customers until you provide high-quality service to your internal customers.

FIGURE 1.1

Companies must have planned goals to ensure that daily decisions, actions, and behaviors are totally customer-focused and are designed to be adaptable as needed to changes in customers' needs, desires, and expectations. Many corporations consider Nordstrom's department store as a premier example of superior customer service. When helping customers, top management at this upscale department store has empowered employees with two simple phrases that reflect its core values: (1) use good judgment in all situations, and (2) there will be no additional rules.

In most cases, when companies ask employees to put themselves in the place of their customers, doing so will guide the employees' efforts to provide the same treatment and service that they would expect to receive if they were the customers. If this sounds like the Golden Rule, "Do unto others as you would have them do unto

you," it is. For lack of a stated mission and values statement, many companies use the Golden Rule as a guiding principle when serving customers.

Customer service is not new, but much confusion surrounds its importance and degree of practice in today's marketplace. Figure 1.1 lists some common customer service myths and corresponding facts that speak to an organization's corporate values.

When organizations commit to a way of treating customers by writing down their mission statement, values, and goals, they create a corporate culture that is better understood and lived by all who work there. According to Peggy Morrow, in her book *Customer Service—The Key to Your Competitive Edge*, organizations can take critical steps to create and ensure a customer service culture. Those measures are explained in Figure 1.2.

◑ remember this ...

Keys to Creating a Customer Service Culture within Organizations

1. Management must make the measurement of service quality and feedback from the customer a basic part of everyone's work experience. This information must be available and understood by everyone, no matter what his or her level in the organization. The entire organization must become obsessed with what the customer wants.

2. Be very clear about specifying the behavior that employees are expected to deliver, both with external customers and with their coworkers.

3. Explain why giving excellent customer service is important—not only for the company but also for the world. What does your company do that makes life easier for everyone? What does your product or service add?

4. Create ways to communicate excellent examples of customer service both within and outside the company. Institute celebrations, recognition ceremonies, logos, and symbols of the customer service culture and its values. This is where you want the mugs, buttons, and banners. Seize every opportunity to publicize the times when employees "do it right."

5. Indoctrinate and train all employees in the culture as soon as they are hired. Disney is famous for this. Disney puts all newcomers through a "traditions" course, which details the company history with customer relations and how it is the backbone of Disney. Your orientation program is a key part of the ultimate success of your customer service efforts. Make sure that it contains more than an explanation of benefits and a tour of the facilities.

6. Encourage a sense of responsibility for group performance. Help employees see how their performance affects others. Emphasize the importance of internal customer service. Help everyone see that, if you don't serve each other well, you can never hope to serve your ultimate customer.

7. Establish policies that are customer-friendly and that show concern for your customers. Eliminate all routine and rigid policies and guidelines. Never let your customer service representatives say, "Those are the rules I have to follow; there's nothing I can do about it." There is always a way to satisfy the customer. You must give your employees the power to do so.

8. Remove any employees who do not show the behavior necessary to please customers. Too many companies allow frontline service representatives to remain on the job when they are not suited to a customer service position. Everyone, from the top down, must believe that he or she works for the customer.

FIGURE 1.2   *Source:* Reprinted with permission from Peggy Morrow & Associates, *Customer Service—The Key to Your Competitive Edge,* (Houston, TX: Advantage Plus Publishers, 1995).

External and Internal Customers

To be successful, an organization must first identify its customers and then learn as much about them as possible—including their age, gender, income level, lifestyle, and occupation. This demographic information, once collected, creates a **customer profile** that explains who the customers are and what they want in terms of service. Companies identify their main customers for a very good reason—so they can develop and market the goods and services their customers want.

Most organizations have two main sets of customers: external and internal customers. **External customers** are the customers whose needs we traditionally think of serving, because these customers are the persons or organizations that purchase and use a company's products and services. **Internal customers,** on the other hand, are identified as other people or departments within a company that rely on colleagues to provide the support they need to serve their own internal and external customers. If you work at an organization's computer help desk, for example, your internal customer is anyone who requests your assistance in using the

The external customer buys a company's product or service.

Never take for granted the importance of serving internal customers well.

software packages or hardware components on your company's computer network system.

In many firms, unfortunately, internal customers are often ignored or taken for granted—an attitude that compromises the productive flow of work throughout a company. Employees should respect and serve internal customers as if they were paying clients. Typically, the ways in which internal customers are treated translate into how a company is perceived by its external customers.

Employment Growth—Customer Service Representatives

According to the U.S. Bureau of Labor Statistics, employment in professional and service-related occupations is expected to increase at a faster rate than all other occupations, and these sectors will add the most jobs from 2004 to 2014. Office and administrative support occupations are projected to grow about half as fast as other occupations, while jobs in production are projected to decline slightly.

Beyond growth stemming from expansion of the industries in which customer service representatives are employed, a need for additional personnel in this role is likely to result from heightened reliance on these workers. In many industries, gaining a competitive edge and retaining customers will be increasingly important over the next decade. This is particularly true in industries such as financial services, communications,

and utilities, which already employ numerous customer service representatives.

As the trend toward consolidation in industries continues, centralized call centers will provide an effective method for delivering a high level of customer service. As a result, employment of customer service representatives may grow at a faster rate in call centers than in other areas. However, this growth may be tempered: a variety of factors, including technological improvements, make it increasingly feasible and cost-effective to build or relocate call centers outside the United States.

Prospects for obtaining a job in the customer service field are expected to be excellent, with more job openings than job seekers. Bilingual applicants, in particular, may enjoy favorable job prospects. Replacement needs are expected to be significant in this field because many young people work as customer service representatives before switching to other jobs. This occupation is well suited to flexible work schedules, and many opportunities for part-time work will continue to be available, particularly as organizations attempt to cut labor costs by hiring more temporary workers. Figure 1.3 shows recent employment projections provided by the Bureau of Labor Statistics, reflecting the occupations with the largest job growth from 2004 to 2014.

Understanding the Evolving Role of Customer Service

The Internet and mobile/wireless technologies, which have become fundamental parts of our lives, have caused an unparalleled shift in the balance of power from companies to their customers. Consumers, armed with instant 24-hour access to information, not only are reshaping the products that a company offers and the distribution channels it uses, but also are demanding a higher level and quality of service than ever before.

That power shift from companies to their customers underlies the new **customer economy.** What counts in the new customer economy? American businesses are realizing that the depth of their relationships with customers and the loyalty of those customers to the company are increasingly linked directly to profit margins and, ultimately, to their overall sustained existence.

remember this ...

Occupations with the Largest Job Growth—2004 to 2014

2004 National Employment Matrix Code and Title	Employment Number		Change	
	2004	2014	Number	Percent
41-2031 Retail salespersons	4,256	4,992	736	17.3
29-1111 Registered nurses	2,394	3,096	703	29.4
25-1000 Postsecondary teachers	1,628	2,153	524	32.2
43-4051 Customer service representatives	2,063	2,534	471	22.8
37-2011 Janitors and cleaners, except maids and housekeeping cleaners	2,374	2,813	440	18.5
35-3031 Waiters and waitresses	2,252	2,627	376	16.7
35-3021 Combined food preparation and serving workers, including fast food workers	2,150	2,516	367	17.1
31-1011 Home health aides	624	974	350	56.0
31-1012 Nursing aides, orderlies, and attendants	1,455	1,781	325	22.3

FIGURE 1.3   *Source:* Data from U.S. Department of Labor, Bureau of Labor Statistics.

Traditional versus Exceptional Customer Service

The very nature of customer service has changed dramatically over the last decade. In the past, organizations provided what could be called *traditional* customer service. That is, if customers needed service, they went to the organization's customer service department. The implicit message to the customer was "This department is the *only* place you'll get customer service in this company."

Today's customers, however, expect something more than traditional customer service. They want a company and its employees to exceed their expectations, demonstrate that the organization cares for them, and work immediately and decisively on their behalf. To be precise, customers today demand *exceptional* customer service. To that end, a successful company recognizes that its competitors may easily be able to copy its products, its prices, and even its promotions, but competitors cannot copy an organization's employees and the distinctive and exceptional service they provide.

Each time customers come in contact with an organization, they get an impression of service and the overall products they think they will receive. Everyone in an organization touches customers. The employees'

behavior and attitudes affect how the customer feels about the company. As the **customer service representative (CSR),** or frontline person who deals with customers on a day-to-day basis, you come to signify all that your company stands for—both good and bad. To the customer, you are the voice and personality of your organization. Customers who experience exceptional customer service will come back for more. They will be less likely to shop around as a result of how well you treat them.

customer service T I P

Always strive to improve your overall service by focusing on the small details of each transaction. It will mean a lot to the customer and make a difference in total customer satisfaction.

Multichannel Customer Contact Points

As a customer service representative, you will serve customers in several situations, typically known as **contact points.** For example, customer contact occurs in person, on the phone, through written communications, or online. To the customer, it doesn't matter where the interaction takes place. What does matter is that the frontline employee, the CSR, takes ownership of the problem. The CSR must apply the Golden Rule or other course provided by the organization's values statement and must follow it through to the satisfactory outcome expected by the customer. This is not difficult to do, provided that the CSR has all the knowledge, tools, and authority needed to take care of each customer's problem in a positive way.

A caring, friendly atmosphere and quick resolutions to problems create *positive* points of contact. Clean, neat surroundings—whether in an office, a store, or a restaurant—say, "We pay attention to details because we value them as important to our success." Accurate invoices, prompt shipments, and returned phone calls help convey a positive impression to customers.

On the other hand, examples of *negative* points of contact include letting your phone ring five or six times before answering it, leaving the customer on hold for two or more minutes, and not replying promptly to an e-mail request for information. This translates to the customer as "We don't value your time." Long lines, out-of-stock items, faded signs, and unclean surroundings are other ways to leave an unfavorable impression about the company and its product or services.

Any successful company strives to make sure that all its points of contact with customers are positive ones. In the final analysis, *all* customers deserve exceptional service at each point of contact, regardless of the means they use to seek customer service.

Ethics | Choices

Which of these best reflects your views, in general, of dealing with customer service issues: "I tell the whole truth, all the time" or "I play by the rules, but I bend them to my company's advantage whenever I can."

The Tiered Service System

In years past, most thriving companies gave all their customers special attention, regardless of the size of their purchase. The thinking then was that a customer who makes a small purchase today might make a large

purchase tomorrow. Today, however, the mindset of treating customers differently is based on certain criteria—their actual or potential value, for example. This idea is beginning to make economic sense to more and more businesses. In other words, many companies today are asking themselves, "Why invest the same amount of customer service effort and expense in a one-time customer as we would in a customer who has a multimillion-dollar history with our business?"

This increasingly popular approach to serving customers is referred to as a **tiered service system** and is used with a database of customer transaction records, which have been stored and analyzed with the help of computers and customer relationship management (CRM) software. The concept and use of CRM software will be discussed in depth in a later chapter; however, the underlying principle of CRM is that every interaction with a customer is part of a larger relationship that the company should be able to maximize and use in helping increase customer loyalty.

What does tiered service look like? Whether we realize it or not, we are already being served by this concept each time we choose to fly. Airlines, for example, usually place their customers into three tiers of service: basic, or coach-class; enhanced, or business-class; and premium, or first-class. For the customer, the good news is that a tiered service system has a lot more choices on price, convenience, and comfort. Also, consumers have the option of upgrading if they choose to. On the other hand, companies can invisibly identify individuals who don't generate profits for them and may decide to provide them with inferior service.

Although tiered service exists, customers should never feel that they are getting a certain level of service because they are buying a certain level of business. All customers should feel that they are receiving the same level of customer service when it comes to assistance with problems or the handling of complaints.

Describing the Role of Customer Service Representatives

Superior service doesn't just happen; it is a process. Next to a company's product, excellence in customer service is the single most important factor in determining the future success or failure of a company. Regardless of what products or services a company offers, the company is also in the business of providing customer service.

If you look at companies that are not doing well or have gone under, a common thread is failure to deliver superior customer service. Today's successful companies show that they understand and deliver what their customers want. More important, they are believers in the value of hiring the right people and providing customer service training not only for frontline employees, but for management and all other support workers as well.

Top organizations carefully select people to fill the position of customer service representatives. CSRs are trained well and are provided a supportive working environment because CSRs *count* in these companies. A customer service representative can work in a variety of settings and have any number of job titles. For instance, a CSR might work in a telephone call center, at a help desk, with customers at a counter face-to-face, on the phone in the role of telemarketing, or on the Internet, providing hospitality and technical information to both internal and external clients. Regardless of the setting or job title, the CSR's role, in general, is to answer questions, solve problems, take orders, and resolve complaints.

Ethics / **Choices**

Assume you are answering a customer's inquiry about a product. After an amicable conversation with you, the customer realizes she cannot afford your product and thanks you. You know that a competitor offers the same product in her price range. What do you do?

Required Customer Service Skills and Competencies

Although the responsibilities of a CSR are many and varied, most companies write the job description to include the following duties:

• Provides in-house support for salespeople whenever a customer requires information or assistance

• Provides communication between levels of management and customers

• Represents the customer's interests, rather than those of a department within the company

• Helps develop and maintain customer loyalty

• Handles customer complaints and strives to have the company set them right

• Alerts upper management to trends or any conditions within the company's products or services that lead to customer dissatisfaction and recommends solutions to problems

The fundamental service skills needed by all customer service professionals involve knowing how to

• build rapport, uncover needs, listen, empathize, clarify, explain, and delight customers.

• handle customer complaints, irate customers, and challenging situations.

• avoid misunderstandings, manage expectations, and take responsibility.

• work in teams and build internal cooperation and communication within the organization.

• show a positive customer service attitude.

Hiring the Right Person

The CSR's task is always to resolve the customer's problem as quickly and completely as possible. This requires three critical skills: (1) exercising judgment, (2) possessing knowledge of the product, customer history, company information, and competitive data, and (3) using that judgment and knowledge, along with common sense.

When hiring customer service professionals, companies should look for a helping attitude. You can teach anyone almost anything, but the feeling of customer service has to come from within a person. First-rate CSRs sense what irritates their customers. For example, seemingly minor issues such as the way a carton is labeled or type of packaging *are not minor,* if they bother the customer.

The most important task in hiring CSRs is to select individuals who fit in with the company's customer service culture and have a demonstrated skill and interest in working with the public. Companies look for a variety of character traits, abilities, and experience levels for customer service jobs. The profile for an exceptional CSR includes the following characteristics.

INITIATIVE Takes the initiative to resolve issues before they become problems; ensures that customer needs are met

RESPONSIVENESS Looks for speedy solutions to problems; goes the extra mile to please the customer; responds quickly and effectively

RELATIONSHIP BUILDING Is friendly and courteous; easy to talk to; tactful and diplomatic; respectful and considerate

SENSITIVITY Shows an understanding of and an interest in customers' needs and concerns

OBJECTIVITY Is open-minded; is respectful to others; treats others equally and fairly; tolerates different points of view

RESISTANCE TO STRESS Works effectively under stressful conditions; remains calm; copes well under pressure

RESILIENCE Is open to criticism; feelings are not easily hurt; tolerates frustration well

PROBLEM SOLVING Provides appropriate solutions to problems; capably handles customer requests; finds positive resolutions to problems

POSITIVE ATTITUDE Is optimistic; maintains a cheerful attitude; looks for positive resolutions to problems

The Workplace Environment

Not too long ago, most customer service representatives worked at retail stores or corporate headquarters. Today, if you work in customer service, you might be located in a retail store or an office, but CSRs are just as likely to work at a remote call center, at a help desk for a computer software company, or for a web-based company. As the number of web-based companies grows almost daily, a need for more CSRs to professionally and accurately take orders, answer questions, handle complaints, and track customer information is growing steadily. You might be called by any of the following job titles: customer service representative, customer care representative, client services representative, customer service specialist, account manager, account service representative, call center representative, claims service representative, help-desk assistant, telesales representative, telemarketer, or by another job title.

A **call center** is a location where groups of people use telephones to provide service and support to customers. Increasingly, this area is also referred to as a

---

focus on Career

Review the following job description for a Customer Service Manager. Then ask yourself, "Is a management position in my future?"

Manages multiple teams of customer service associates and coordinates a large segment of a customer service function. Responsible for staffing as well as CSR training and development. Establishes policies and procedures and monitors for compliance. Implements changes to enhance efficiency and high-quality customer interactions. Involves processes and procedures for fulfilling internal and external customer needs related to products and services offered through a multi-channel contact center environment. Monitors e-mail and call volume levels and trends in order to maximize efficiencies and makes recommendations for improvement. Performs all aspects of management including leadership, performance planning/evaluations, expense planning and control, initiating process improvements, and interacting with customers and associates at all levels. Ensures scheduling and forecasting are completed in a timely manner and schedules communicated to customer service representatives.

---

contact center, because it uses more technologically sophisticated devices when interacting with customers. Contact center representatives don't only answer the phones; they also respond to customers' e-mail messages and participate in chat sessions via a chat room set up for the purpose of live customer interaction.

Call centers can be inbound, outbound, or both. That is to say, some call centers handle only inbound calls, such as customer orders and questions or complaints about service issues. Others are outbound centers, where CSRs call customers to promote products or services or to conduct polls about anything from product testing to opinions about recent purchases. Some call centers perform both inbound and outbound functions.

At a **help desk,** customer service representatives answer customer questions by phone, fax, e-mail, and the Internet. **Help desk software** automates the help desk and is available to assist CSRs in quickly finding answers to commonly asked questions about particular products and services. Typical functions of this software include call management, call tracking, knowledge management, problem resolution, and self-help capabilities.

The Customer Service Challenge

Customer service begins with putting the right people in place. Teaching customer service skills to employees who don't have a service-oriented attitude is difficult. As the workforce changes, identifying the specific skills employees need to learn about serving customers becomes more important. For instance, simple acts of kindness that we used to take for granted—such as smiling and saying "thank you"—may now have to be taught. A major challenge of customer service today is the shortage of customer-oriented employees.

An additional challenge most companies face is finding and training staff that can keep up with the technology in the industry. Consider the changes in technology that CSRs have seen in the past few years: e-mail, text-based Internet chatting (the ability to hold a real-time conversation over the web by typing back and forth), voice-over Internet protocol (the ability to have a real-time verbal conversation over the Internet), and push technology (the ability to send a specific image over the Internet directly to the customer's computer screen).

With the growth of the Internet and online companies, CSRs must be able to manage digital contacts effectively. Quick, accurate, and appropriate responses by e-mail that adequately address customer concerns can prevent the risk of losing customers to a competitor in seconds with just a few clicks of the mouse. If call center representatives aren't familiar or comfortable with instant messaging, chat rooms, and customer-friendly e-mail responses, they may be left behind in these critical skill areas.

Is it any wonder that customer service training—especially with the new generation of workers—is taking on greater importance? The new breed of CSR will need to be able to handle not only the latest technology, but also the most complex customer interactions—those requiring

extensive problem-solving and negotiating skills. Making matters even more challenging, these CSRs will have to be able to communicate both verbally and in writing. Increasingly, companies are realizing that the most significant investment they can make is not in purchasing their databases or computer systems, but in making the best decisions when hiring their customer service staff. Moreover, once customer service representatives are hired, often the challenge is to keep them trained and ready to do their jobs in this technology-driven society.

BUSINESS in action

T-MOBILE

When Sue Nokes joined T-Mobile as the Senior Vice President of Customer Service, the cell-phone company, based in Bellevue, WA, had a big problem. Lousy customer service was driving T-Mobile users crazy. When calling with a question or complaint, they were often placed on hold for what seemed like eons and then spoke with customer service reps who weren't very helpful. J. D. Power's customer-satisfaction surveys ranked T-Mobile dead last in the industry, trailing Verizon, Cingular, Nextel, and Sprint. Nokes launched a total overhaul. The first step was getting T-Mobile's human resources people and its marketing department to sit down and talk. The idea was to revamp the company's hiring practices, thus increasing the odds of picking customer service staffers willing and able to follow through on the marketing mavens' promises. Sounds like common sense, doesn't it? But surprisingly few companies do it.

Source: "For Happier Customers, Call HR," *Fortune* (November 28, 2005): 272.

Concluding Message for CSRs

Marshall Field, founder of the Chicago-based department store Marshall Field and Company, said, "Those who come to me with a complaint teach me. Right or wrong, the customer is always right." He was saying that a complaint gives a service provider the chance to show just how good he or she can really be. Field wasn't saying that the customer is truly *always* right; some customers are very wrong. What Field meant was that, in dealing with complaints, you're dealing with people's perceptions. Although a customer's perception of a problem may be shortsighted or distorted, in the customer's eyes that perception is right. Most people who complain truly feel they have a legitimate concern.

A customer service representative is often the customer's first impression of the competence, quality, and tone of the company. The CSR serves as the company's first line of defense against an unhappy customer. Further, customers are more likely to listen to reason and to a different perspective of their problem if frontline providers have product knowledge, express understanding, and treat each customer as if he or she were unique. To a consumer, that human touch of being treated as a valued individual is often more important than price.

Summary

- Customer service is the process of satisfying a customer relative to a product or service, in whatever way the customer defines his or her need, and then delivering that service with efficiency, understanding, and compassion.
- The power shift from companies to their customers underlies the new customer economy, in which the depth of relationships and loyalty to customers are critical to an organization's success.
- Regardless of the setting or job title, the customer service representative's duties are to answer questions, solve problems, take customers' orders, and resolve complaints.
- One of the most important tasks in hiring CSRs is selecting an individual who has a service-oriented attitude and a demonstrated skill and interest in working with the public. The new breed of CSR will need to be able to handle the latest technology and the most complex customer interactions—those requiring extensive problem-solving and negotiating skills.

KEY TERMS

call center	customer service	help desk
contact center	customer service representative (CSR)	help desk software
contact points		internal customers
customer economy	customer-centric service	tiered service system
customer profile	external customers	

CRITICAL THINKING

1. Give two examples of a customer's concept of good customer service.

2. Why do organizations' mission statements for customer service differ from one another's?

3. In your opinion, which type of customer is more important in the long run to an organization—external or internal customers? Explain.

4. Describe the ways traditional customer service varies from exceptional customer service.

5. Name two advantages to organizations of providing customers with multichannel contact points.

6. If you owned your own business, would you provide your customers with a tiered service system? Why or why not?

7. List five critical skills and competencies a customer service representative must possess.

8. Of the various working environments presented in this chapter, which one would you prefer to work in and why?

Project 1.1 Outstanding Customer Service

Assume you are doing a report on the top outstanding customer service organizations in the United States. Use the Internet to research and specifically locate the publications within the past six months from only .com domains. As a result of your search, outline three items (including the URLs) of current information you might use in your report.

Project 1.2 Customer Service Training Topics

Assume Mary Graeff, your supervisor at On-Time Technology Products (OTTP), has asked you to conduct online research to locate at least three outside sources that OTTP can use to provide training on customer service. Consider all types of training materials as possibilities. For example, consider videos on customer service, bringing in an outside consultant to train in-house, and subscribing to magazines that focus on customer service issues.

Use the information from this chapter to evaluate the information on each resource you discover. Fill in the table below with the data you collect.

Source or Website URL	Description of Training Topics	Cost	Advantages
1.			
2.			
3.			

Project 1.3 Customer Service Culture Task Force

Assume you have been asked to participate on a company task force with two co-workers at On-Time Technology Products. The three of you have been asked to come up with ways to improve the customer service culture at OTTP. Using the list of eight items from Figure 1.2 on page 8, prioritize and reach a consensus about the top five methods you feel would represent the approach your company should follow.

Working in small groups, discuss the issue, reach a consensus, and complete the table below.

Methods	Reasons for Supporting Each Method
1.	
2.	
3.	
4.	
5.	

DECISION MAKING AT WORK

Project 1.4 Tiered Service—a New Approach

Collin MacGibson, President of On-Time Technology Products, recently returned from a Manufacturing Technology Conference in downtown Chicago. As a result of talking with leaders of other companies, he is now considering establishing a tiered service system, an idea he shared with Mary Graeff. Mr. MacGibson's basic thought is to reward the customers who give On-Time Technology Products $100,000 worth of business an end-of-year "thank you payment" that reflects a 5 percent discount on all yearly purchases. In addition, those customers would receive a commitment to next-day turnaround time on the resolution of all customer service problems. Moreover, the customers who purchase $500,000 or more annually would receive a 10 percent discount and a commitment to a four-hour resolution of customer service problems.

Prior to responding to Mr. MacGibson's idea, Ms. Graeff has asked you and the other five CSRs your opinion, because she has some customer service concerns about this new proposal.

1. As a CSR, what is your initial reaction to this new tiered service recommendation by Mr. MacGibson?

   _____

   _____

   _____

2. What would be some advantages of going to a tiered service approach at On-Time Technology Products?

   _____

   _____

   _____

3. What would be some disadvantages of going to a tiered service approach at On-Time Technology Products?

_____

_____

_____

CASE STUDIES

Project 1.5 Customer Orders Are Perfect or They Don't Pay

Thunderbird Technology Products president, Darrell Williams, stormed out of his office and said, "Customers' orders are perfect or they don't pay." At first, those in earshot thought he must be kidding, but the seriousness with which he made that statement and his demeanor said differently. Give some thought to this pronouncement and be prepared to discuss the following three questions in a class discussion.

1. In your opinion, can a company literally afford to live by this statement? Why or why not?
2. Can you think of any situations in which an organization may have difficulty honoring such a customer pledge?
3. What are some hidden and actual benefits to the company of setting such a standard?

Project 1.6 Customer Service Job Description

Because sales have been increasing over the past few months, On-Time Technology Products is planning to advertise for an additional customer service representative position. As a result, your supervisor has asked you to review the following draft of a job description, which will be printed in the local newspaper early next week. Your opinion has been requested as to its wording and appropriateness in attracting the right applicants for a new CSR at OTTP.

We are currently seeking to hire a superior customer service representative. The ideal candidate must be familiar with technology and computers. In addition, a postsecondary degree or certificate in information technology is a plus. Those who apply should possess an enthusiastic personality, have excellent problem-solving skills, and work well under pressure. As part of the team, responsibilities involve dealing with customers over the phone, providing pricing, technical, and order-processing information. Strong communication and interpersonal skills are a must. Contact Ms. Graeff at (312) 555-0111 for more information.

1. What is your first reaction to the wording of this job announcement?
2. What recommendations to improve the intent and wording would you suggest?

Serving a Diverse Population of Customers

chapter

2

Objectives

1. Describe diversity in the workplace relative to the needs of a business enterprise.

2. Identify the four personalities of customers and distinguish among them.

3. Contrast customer service activities among the four generational groups.

4. Learn how to communicate effectively with disabled persons.

The customer perceives service in his or her own terms.

—STEW LEONARD, FOUNDER OF A CONNECTICUT DAIRY AND GROCERY STORE

To communicate effectively with other people, we must know them as individuals—their unique backgrounds, personalities, preferences, and styles. Customer service interactions can be complex under the best of conditions. When you add issues of language, race, gender, religion, age, or disability into the mix, otherwise competent employees can be found acting in ways ranging from mildly inappropriate to inexcusably rude.

The customer demographics for most organizations are changing in such a way as to increase the diversity and uniqueness of the populations that are served. This trend makes it imperative that CSRs be aware of how customers perceive their service. Further, how CSRs perceive the needs of customers may depend on their own cultural and generational perspectives as well as their personalities.

Ethnic and Cultural Diversity

Diversity in the United States has evolved since the 1960s. Diversity was first based on the **assimilation** approach, with everyone being part of the "melting pot." Compliance, in the form of affirmative action and equal employment opportunity, is important in diversity. Key legislation such as Title VII of the Civil Rights Act of 1964, the Age Discrimination in Employment Act of 1967, and the Americans with Disabilities Act of 1990 has been an effective tool for change. Today, however, the force behind workplace diversity is that of inclusion. **Inclusion** involves embracing and leveraging differences for the benefit of the organization. The collaboration of cultures, ideas, and different perspectives is now considered an organizational asset—bringing forth greater creativity and innovation. As a result, many companies are focusing more on corporate diversity initiatives to improve organizational performance.

The shift in purchasing power in the United States provides further evidence for the importance of workplace diversity. According to the Selig Center for Economic Growth, the purchasing power of minorities in the United States will quickly outpace that of whites. In 2009, for example, the combined buying power of African-Americans, Hispanics, Asian-Americans, and Native Americans is expected to exceed $1.5 trillion, more than triple the 1990 level by a gain of $1.1 trillion, or 242 percent. In contrast, the buying power of whites will increase by 140 percent.[1]

Diversity in the Workplace

Creating and sustaining a diverse workforce and a diverse customer base are competitive advantages. Diverse ideas come from diverse people, and diverse revenue streams come from diverse customers. It does not matter whether the diversity involves race, age, gender, sexual orientation, ethnicity, physical ability, religion, education, appearance, or any other characteristic.

Ethics / Choices

Suppose you and several of your coworkers received a racially slurred e-mail joke from another coworker. It was meant to be "funny" but is very offensive in content. Would you ignore it and simply delete it, talk about it with the sender or others who received it, or take a copy of the e-mail message to management? Explain.

Creating and encouraging a diverse workforce is good for employees and the organization.

A significant point for understanding diversity is to recognize that it is reciprocal. That is to say, if someone is different from you, then you are different from him or her. Accepting the diversity of others is expressing your desire for others to accept your diversity. Companies accept diversity as an organizational value, not because it is the politically correct thing to do or even a nice thing to do, but because it is the *smart* thing to do to remain competitive.[2]

Not only the workforce, but the nation's customer base, too, is becoming increasingly diverse. Customers are asserting their differences, and they expect the people with whom they do business to respect diverse backgrounds. Here are some ways the typical customer is changing radically:

- *Hispanics* According to recent United States Census data, Hispanics are the largest minority group in the country. U.S. Hispanic income and buying power is growing stronger and is expected to reach over $1 trillion by the end of the decade. The U.S. Hispanic population has exploded 75 percent in the last decade, reaching 39 million, while the general population increased just 14 percent, to 283 million.[3]
- *Asians* Asians are even more culturally diverse as a group than are Hispanics. In fact, no one Asian subgroup makes up more than 25 percent of the

[1]Nancy R. Lockwood, "Workplace Diversity: Leveraging the Power of Difference for Competitive Advantage," *HR Magazine* (June 2005): 35.

[2]Stephanie Wood, "Leveraging Diversity: A Customer Service Strategy," *American Water Works Association Journal* (January 2005): 47.

[3]Terry Beltran-Miller, "So You've Targeted the Hispanic Market, But Can You Service It?" www.marketingprofs.com.

total U.S. Asian population, and each has a more distinctly different set of cultural values, beliefs, and attitudes than is typically the case for individuals from Latin America. Thus, Asian consumers are more difficult to target as a separate shopper segment. As a group, however, Asians tend to have more education and higher incomes than the general population.

- *African-Americans* Although most African-Americans share a common cultural heritage, they are, by definition, native citizens and make up part of the broader culture of the United States. Many inner-city black communities, however, have undergone several of the same cultural disconnects from mainstream markets as have some immigrant groups. These neighborhoods are united by a common experience that creates its own sense of community, pride, style, and identity. These factors all affect purchase decisions.[4]

Businesses often make the mistake of assuming far more commonality exists within a given culture than might actually be the case. To the contrary, in many instances, some differences between individuals from the same culture may be more significant than their differences with individuals from other cultures. For example, Puerto Ricans and Mexicans are both Hispanic, but their cultural cues and product preferences differ in many ways. Conversely, individuals of similar income and education may be far more alike than their diverse ethnic backgrounds might suggest. In other words, it's not only ethnicity, but also a whole range of life experiences that forms a customer's culture, behavior, and attitude.

Cultural Values and Workplace Communication

Too often, English language skill is the only communication issue considered within the context of cultural diversity. However, language barriers and cultural misunderstandings can get in the way of effective communication and create complexities in customer situations. **Culture** is defined as a system of shared values, beliefs, and rituals that are learned and passed on through generations of families and social groups. Most individuals' cultural makeup is simultaneously shaped by several different elements such as ethnicity, family, religion, and economic status. Culture affects a person's perception of the world and, during customer interactions, often defines acceptable and unacceptable behavior.

Our cultural values provide an unconscious worldview that we use to function and interact with others. We begin to learn this worldview at a very early age, even before we acquire language skills. It guides our reflexive behavior by providing us with guidelines on how to respond in a wide range of situations—how formal to be, how close to stand to someone, what physical contact is appropriate, how much eye contact to maintain, how to demonstrate respect, and so forth.

One's own culture is often taken for granted, unexamined, and accepted as the norm. This means we are often not aware of the filter we are looking through. People from different cultures encode and decode messages differently. These differences increase the chances of misunderstanding, especially relative to nonverbal behaviors and concepts of time and space, which are particularly troublesome during customer service encounters.

NONVERBAL BEHAVIORS Cultural differences in nonverbal behaviors are a common source of misunderstandings and conflict in the workplace. For instance, many Westerners like to make eye contact, interpreting it as an indication of interest and honesty. They also show friendliness through relaxed body language. If these behaviors do not happen, a person's attitude can be interpreted as shifty, cold, and disinterested. However, in some cultures, averted eyes and reserved behavior are signs of courtesy and respect. Being aware of these nuances will help you to reduce negative impressions in intercultural communications with customers. Low-context cultures like those in the United States and Canada tend to give relatively less emphasis to nonverbal communication. This does not mean that nonverbal communication does not happen or that it is unimportant, but that people in these settings tend to place less importance on it than on the literal meanings of words themselves. In high-context settings such as those in Japan or Colombia, understanding the nonverbal components of communication is relatively more important to receiving the intended meaning of the communication as a whole.

[4]Joseph Tarnowski, "Assimilate or Perish," *Progressive Grocer* (February 1, 2006): 93–94.

CONCEPT OF TIME The perception of time is a central difference between cultures. In the West, time tends to be seen as quantitative, measured in units that reflect the march of progress. It is logical, sequential, and present-focused. In the East, time is treated as though it has unlimited continuity, as an unraveling rather than a strict boundary. For example, for the Japanese, time is not such an important criterion when it comes to schedules and timelines. They often will extend discussions and negotiations beyond what Westerners are comfortable doing.

CONCEPT OF SPACE Another variable across cultures has to do with ways of relating to space. Crossing cultures, we encounter very different ideas about appropriate space for conversations and negotiations. North Americans tend to prefer a large amount of space. Europeans tend to stand more closely with each other when talking and are accustomed to smaller personal spaces. The difficulty with space preferences is not that they exist, but with the judgments that get attached to them. If someone is accustomed to standing or sitting very close when talking with another, he or she may see the other's attempt to create more space as evidence of coldness, condescension, or a lack of interest. On the other hand, those who are accustomed to more personal space may view attempts to get closer as pushy, disrespectful, or threatening. Neither is correct; they are simply different.

Organizations and their employees who are aware of these cultural value differences have a competitive advantage. Understanding the customer and strategically aligning products and services to meet these needs will reap benefits. Understanding that the meaning of "good service" has different connotations in different cultures is particularly important. The more service providers know about their customers and culture, the better customer relations will be.

What role does culture play in customer service? CSRs will interact with people of diverse cultural backgrounds every day. Although knowing about every element of a person's culture is impossible, each customer should receive the same courteous, professional, and knowledgeable service. Some additional information to ensure sensitivity to cultural differences follows:

- Use a variety of communication methods (written, visual, verbal) to get your message across.

- Err on the side of formality. Most cultural groups value formality, and it will demonstrate respect on your part.
- Make an effort to pronounce names and titles correctly. If you are not sure about proper pronunciation, ask.
- Respond to what is being said, not how it is said.
- Never make a derogatory comment about any culture.

Serving Diverse Customers Well

As companies expand across the globe, challenges in customer service grow. To avoid cultural collisions with customers—when emotions, habits, or judgments taint service efforts—a CSR needs to be aware of how culture plays a role in the service encounter. One suggestion is for CSRs to identify their own cultural differences and be conscious about not stereotyping any customer. **Stereotyping** happens when people categorize individuals or groups according to an oversimplified standardized image or idea. Because stereotyping can lead to misunderstandings and prejudgments, it strongly hinders positive customer service encounters.

Customers with accents generally know they have an accent, but the responsibility for understanding what is being said still rests with the CSR. When serving customers from a different culture, apologize to them when you don't understand what they are saying. Be sure to speak to them slowly and clearly. Repeat back, or **paraphrase,** what they have said to you, using other words for clarification. Or, if necessary, ask them to repeat what they have said. This gives you another chance to develop "an ear" for the accent.

Attempting to understand a heavy accent is as important for a listener as making strides toward improving English skills is for the other person. Because some cultures consider feedback or criticism damaging to one's reputation, CSRs might paraphrase often.

Sensitive companies that provide a good cross-cultural employee training program find it to be very helpful. The content of this training program might include an explanation of the differences between cultures, as well as formal manners and etiquette to follow when serving international customers.

Analytical   Driver

Amiable   Expressive

© GETTY IMAGES/PHOTODISC

Examples of the personality types CSRs serve.

Customer Personalities

Today we know more about basic human personality types than ever before. We also know how each personality type needs to be handled. Only when CSRs apply this knowledge on a regular basis will customers feel they have been treated sympathetically and properly.

People often feel they don't belong to any one personality group, but each of us has one dominant personality style that defines our behavior. Although every customer is different, most can be categorized into one of four groups: *analytical, driver, amiable,* and *expressive.* Here are some basic characteristics of personality styles, along with suggestions for how best to serve each.[5]

The Analytical

People with an **analytical personality** are known for being systematic, well organized, and deliberate. They value numbers and statistics, love details, and tend to be introverted. These individuals appreciate facts and information written and presented in a logical manner. They enjoy completing detailed tasks and take the time to analyze and compare their choices before making a purchasing decision. Analytics believe the more thought they put into a decision, the happier they will be with it. Others may see the analytical person as being too cautious, overly structured, and someone who does things "by the book."

Because people with this personality type often work with numbers and technology, they seek careers in engineering, computer science, finance, purchasing, quality control, and accounting. When working with analytical customers, a CSR needs to provide facts and work with them in step-by-step fashion to understand customer service issues.

The Driver

Those with a **driver personality** want to save time, value results, and love being in control and doing things their own way. They are extroverted and may show little or no emotion. They are called Drivers because they're the people who make things happen—they take tremendous pride in getting tasks and objectives completed. Drivers thrive on the thrill of the challenge and the internal motivation to succeed. They are practical people who can do a lot in a relatively short amount of time. They usually talk fast and get right to the point. Others often view them as decisive, direct, and pragmatic. Business owners and doctors often fall into this personality category. These dominant risk takers quite often end up at the top of an organization.

As customers, Drivers will tell you exactly what they want, and they don't want to hear a lot of "fluff." When you tell them what you will do for them, they expect you to follow through and do it quickly.

The Amiable

The **amiable personality** type wants to build relationships, loves to give others support and attention, values suggestions from others, and fears disagreement. This

[5]Peter Urs Bender, "How to Deal with Difficult Customers," *Professional Selling,* http://www.peterursbender.com/articles/difficult.html.

remember this ...

Personality Characteristics

Analytical	Driver	Amiable	Expressive
• controlled	• action-oriented	• patient	• verbal
• orderly	• decisive	• loyal	• motivating
• precise	• problem solver	• sympathetic	• enthusiastic
• disciplined	• direct	• team player	• convincing
• deliberate	• assertive	• mature	• impulsive
• cautious	• risk taker	• supportive	• influential
• diplomatic	• forceful	• considerate	• charming
• systematic	• competitive	• empathetic	• confident
• logical	• independent	• persevering	• optimistic
• conventional	• determined	• trusting	• animated
	• results-oriented	• congenial	

FIGURE 2.1   *Source:* "If You Only Understood Your Customer's Personality Style," *Internet Marketing Tips* (July 14, 2005).

personality type tends to display a lot of emotion. Amiables are dependable, loyal, and easygoing. They like things that are nonthreatening and friendly; they dislike dealing with impersonal details and cold hard facts. Often described as warm and sensitive to the feelings of others, they can at the same time act wishy-washy.

Amiable people gravitate toward professions such as nursing, teaching, and jobs that require teamwork. They like to work in teams, are very family-oriented, and resist sudden changes. Amiables want sincerity from a salesperson and appreciate a stable buying environment. One of their worst fears is to buy from a fly-by-night operation and be taken advantage of.

CSRs will find that this personality tends to be the most challenging because the cautious nature of these people keeps them from getting too enthusiastic about anything. They tend to be factually driven, so when working with these clients, give them a lot of information and don't pressure them to make a decision. Remember, when serving this personality type, be vigilant about keeping appointments, staying on schedule, and honoring commitments. Amiables like everything to be predictable and planned; they want to know how things are going to be handled.

The Expressive

The person who has an **expressive personality** values appreciation and a pat on the back, loves social situations and parties, likes to inspire others, and is extroverted, readily showing emotion to others. A person of this type is usually identified as "the life of the party" and is very outgoing and enthusiastic, with a high energy level. Expressives can be great idea generators but may not have the ability to see an idea through to completion.

Often thought of as talkers, overly dramatic, impulsive, and manipulative, expressive people are great communicators and are attracted to professions such as sales and marketing. They are comfortable with people and spend a fair amount of time "shooting the breeze" in order to develop trust. They tend to be disorganized and dislike details. More often than not, they are slow to reach a buying decision.

Figure 2.1 recaps in table form characteristics of each personality type.

Generational Differences

Having an awareness of a customer's generation and knowing that generation's service preferences are two steps that lead to excellent customer service. At no time in our history have so many and such different generations been asked to work shoulder to shoulder, side by side, cubicle by cubicle. The once linear nature of power at work, from older to younger, has been dislocated by changes in life expectancy and increases in longevity and health, as well as changes in lifestyle, technology, and knowledge base.

Each generation has been influenced by different formative events, so each brings a unique set of core values, skills, and expectations to the job. These generational differences can result in a synergistic explosion of productivity or a downward spiral of miscommunication and misunderstanding. Knowing generational information is tremendously valuable; it often explains the baffling and

confusing differences behind the unspoken assumptions underneath our attitudes.[6]

Good service must be seen *from a customer's point of view*. In service interactions, what you do, how you do it, how well it must be done, and proving you can do it again are all based on who the customer is. To that end, each generation tends to have its own definition of service. What might seem like excellent customer service to one person might be offensive to another, especially if they are from different generations.

Understanding these generational differences is critical to CSRs who are willing to adapt their personal styles to meet their customers' needs. These understandings have the promise of creating harmony, mutual respect, and joint effort, where today there is often suspicion, mistrust, isolation, and employee turnover. The following is a description of the four generations in today's population, which includes the Mature Generation, Baby Boomer Generation, Generation X, and Millennial Generation.

customer service T I P

By examining customer service through the perspectives of the different generations, we know what kind of customer service techniques will be successful in each generation's context.

Mature Generation

Presently some 300 million people live in the United States. The oldest of these groups are referred to as the **Matures.** Matures currently comprise some 63 million people within the U.S. population.

The Matures grew up in the midst of wartime shortages and economic depression. They have always worked hard and tried to do the right thing by others. Even in better times, they have continued these ways simply because this is the ethic they feel most comfortable with. Matures tend to perform best with clear direction and reinforcement for doing a good job.

[6]Ron Zemke, Claire Raines, and Bob Filipczak, "Generations at Work," AMACOM (1999): 14.

This generation grew up learning that "a penny saved is a penny earned" and that you needed to "put something away for a rainy day." Even now, they remain conservative spenders, opting to do without rather than spending impulsively. When they decide to purchase an item, they generally save up the money to pay for it in cash. Matures come from an era that taught them duty to country and community, and they have applied these values to the workplace as well. They feel rewarded by a job well done.

Baby Boomer Generation

Baby Boomers came of age in the midst of tremendous economic expansion, learning to use all the convenience-oriented products that came on the market during their youth. Because of their generation's size, some 77 million strong, Boomers have a significant influence on every aspect of society. Baby Boomers currently make up the majority of the political, cultural, industrial, and academic leadership roles in the United States.

Boomers have always put in long hours because of how closely they associate their occupations with their identities. Even as they edge into retirement, predictions are that most of them will still "live to work." Baby Boomers were the first credit-card generation. Unfortunately, many have experienced the devastating power of credit-card usage and have huge debts they will be forced to pay down in their later years.

Generation X

The U.S. Bureau of the Census estimates **Generation X** to be some 50 million strong. They "work to live," not "live to work" as the previous generation does. Because many of them were latchkey kids—with both parents working—they have been the most unsupervised generation and have developed into self-sufficient adults. They were the first generation to expect diversity as a fact of life and to fully accept women in positions of power in the workplace.

Gen Xers operate as people "who walk the talk." They are verbal, globally aware, street-smart, process driven, and technically adept. They want loyalty in relationships, respect for their expertise, and products that are modern.

Having watched their Baby Boomer parents put in long hours, Generation Xers have developed a different perspective about work. They do not necessarily equate productive work with long hours. Instead, they look for ways to work smarter, resulting in fewer hours but greater output.

The Gen Xer views training and development as a means for enhancing his or her versatility in the marketplace—as an investment in the future with *any* employer, not just the present organization. This generation believes that a job is a contract, and the burden is on the organization to keep them engaged and growing. If that doesn't happen, then all bets are off, and they will happily move to the next job.

Having come of age after the chaos of the sixties and seventies, coupled with watching their parents spend extravagantly, Gen Xers have chosen the more conservative path of saving and spending prudently. They value time off, which provides the work–family balance they seek. Finally, they look for an enjoyable atmosphere where work is not taken too seriously.

Millennial Generation

The **Millennials** are the current generation and number about 81 million. This generation is the most unique of the groups we've discussed. They have been highly nurtured by family and others, and the Internet is their medium for communicating, entertaining, and learning.

The Millennials are displaying spending habits remarkably similar to the Baby Boomers, having come of age in the era of credit cards rather than cash. Although many of them have learned to spend substantial amounts of money at an earlier age than previous generations, their attitudes about spending in general are viewed as troubling by many.

Millennials are coming of age in an era of technology and rapid change. Many of them honestly wonder why machines don't do many of the mundane tasks they are asked to perform in entry-level positions. As this generation matures into the workforce, some of these perceptions will change. But this group will also alter society's interpretation of the work ethic. As the leading edge of the Millennials has entered the workforce, employers have discovered that "fun" and "stimulation" seem to be the operative words for rewarding this generation. Employers embracing these desires have been

remember this ...

Generational Differences

Mature Generation	Born prior to 1946, this generation is patriotic, loyal, fiscally conservative, and has faith in institutions. These customers tend to struggle with technology and typically need more attention than others.
Baby Boomer Generation	Born between 1946 and 1964, this generation is idealistic, competitive, questions authority, desires to put its own stamp on things, and challenges institutions. These customers are independent, with a "can-do" attitude. They like to dig in and overcome obstacles all on their own.
Generation X	Born between 1965 and 1981, this generation is resourceful, self-reliant, distrusts institutions, and is highly adaptive to both change and technology. These customers have very strong opinions and are very in tune with issues regarding relationships, community, and the environment.
Millennial Generation	Born after 1981, these confident and ambitious customers are very technologically savvy. They can be impatient and need information quickly, as evidenced by their use of multiple techno-gadgets and their ability to multitask with ease.

FIGURE 2.2   Reprinted with permission of Emily McRobbie

able to maintain lower turnover rates and higher productivity.

As customers, Millennials are usually known as those that need instant gratification. Once they decide they want something, they usually make a pretty quick decision to get it—especially with technology purchases, as they are very techno-savvy.

Figure 2.2 recaps in table form characteristics of each generation.

Serving the Different Generations

A major challenge is to serve multiple generations all at the same time. Specifically, when serving the newest generations of customers, Gen Xers and Millennials, some unique service reminders are in order. These groups are unforgiving about poor customer service, expect 24/7 service, and are prepared to negotiate service relationships. When getting their needs met, they believe that if you don't ask, then you don't receive.

On the whole, the younger generations prefer to conduct business and make purchases online or by phone instead of face-to-face. Because they are in constant communication with others, using cell phones, personal digital assistants (PDAs), and other electronic devices, they have high consumer awareness and know how to work the system to obtain what they need or desire.

The concept of customer service can take a different twist when working with the senior market consisting of

the older Mature and Baby Boomer generations. These consumers are typically more loyal, but simultaneously more demanding. They want less noise and fewer visual stimuli in their on-ground shopping experiences. In addition, they want to travel shorter distances to shop and to visit smaller stores. Wellness, energy, travel, and experience will all drive consumer demand.[7]

Many seniors are not computer literate and are uncomfortable with directions such as "See our home page" or "Access your account on the Internet." Companies must be prepared to provide materials in writing and to offer printed versions of information that is now only available online.

Customer service representatives should be sensitive to the special needs of some seniors. Many retirees struggle with hearing and vision loss. Their mobility may be restricted, they may be in pain, and it may take them a bit longer to do things.

In addition to physical challenges, countless retirees may suffer emotionally from a lack of significant social contact. Although no one expects CSRs to be therapists, they must understand the importance of spending a little extra time with senior customers. Service providers should not brush off seniors or cut off conversations with them. They must keep in mind that a senior's trip to the bank or the store may provide his or her only social

---

[7]Carl Steidtmann, "Gray Matters," *Progressive Grocer* (April 15, 2006): 109.

contact for the day. It takes so little to be kind to others and it can mean so much.

> ### customer service **T I P**
> *In delivering great customer service, create a customer experience that is unique to a person and isn't the same as the next customer's.*

The Disabled Customer

A **disability** is a condition caused by an accident, trauma, genetics, or disease, which may limit a person's mobility, hearing, vision, speech, or mental function. Specifically, an individual with a disability is a person who has a physical or mental impairment that substantially limits one or more major life activities; has a record of such an impairment; or is regarded as having such an impairment.[8]

Discrimination against customers with disabilities is often unintentional. It may stem from a general lack of awareness many of us have about disabilities. Consequently, companies must plan ahead to meet the requirements of their customers with disabilities. Wherever necessary and reasonable, service providers should adjust the way they provide their services so that physically challenged people can use them in the best way.

In all cases, ensuring that the dignity of people with disabilities is respected when services are provided is important. Consulting with them about how they might best be served is perfectly fine. Often, minor measures that are embedded in common sense work wonderfully. One example is to practice patience and allow more time to deal with customers with disabilities.

Understanding Disabilities

The Americans with Disabilities Act and the efforts of many disability advocacy organizations have made strides in improving accessibility in buildings, increasing access to education, opening employment opportunities, and developing realistic portrayals of persons with disabilities in television programming and motion pictures. However, progress is still needed in communication and interaction with people who have disabilities.

© STOCKBYTE

When in doubt, ask a disabled customer what he or she needs to make the shopping experience more enjoyable.

Nondisabled individuals are sometimes concerned that they will say the wrong thing, so they say nothing at all—thus further segregating themselves.

Serving People with Disabilities

Etiquette considered appropriate when interacting with people with disabilities is based primarily on being respectful and courteous without being condescending. Outlined below are several lists of tips to help service providers when communicating with persons who have disabilities.

COMMUNICATING WITH PHYSICALLY DISABLED PEOPLE

- When introduced to a person with a disability, offering to shake hands is appropriate. People with limited hand use or who wear an artificial limb can usually shake hands. (Shaking hands with the left hand is an acceptable greeting.)
- If you offer assistance, wait until the offer is accepted. Then listen to or ask for instructions.
- Don't be afraid to ask questions when you're unsure of what to do.

COMMUNICATING WITH VISUALLY IMPAIRED PEOPLE

- Speak to the individual when you approach him or her.
- State clearly who you are; speak in a normal tone of voice.
- When conversing in a group, identify yourself and the person to whom you are speaking.

---

[8]http://www.eeoc.gov/types/ada.html (accessed August 20, 2006).

- Never touch or distract a service dog without first asking the owner.
- Tell the individual when you are leaving.
- Do not attempt to lead the individual without first asking; allow the person to hold your arm and control her or his own movements.
- Be descriptive when giving directions; verbally give the person information that is visually obvious to individuals who can see. For example, if you are approaching steps, mention how many steps.
- If you are offering a seat, gently place the individual's hand on the back or arm of the chair so the person can locate the seat.

COMMUNICATING WITH HEARING IMPAIRED PEOPLE

- Gain the person's attention before starting a conversation (by tapping the person gently on the shoulder or arm).
- If the individual is lip reading, look directly at him or her and speak clearly (in a normal tone of voice), keeping your hands away from your face. Use short, simple sentences. Avoid smoking or chewing gum.
- If the individual uses a sign language interpreter, speak directly to the person, not the interpreter.
- If you are telephoning, let the phone ring longer than usual. Speak clearly and be prepared to repeat the reason for the call and who you are.

COMMUNICATING WITH MOBILITY IMPAIRED PEOPLE

- If possible, put yourself at the wheelchair user's eye level.
- Do not lean on a wheelchair or any other assistive device the customer may be using.
- Do not assume the individual wants his or her wheelchair to be pushed—ask first.
- Offer assistance if the individual appears to be having difficulty opening a door.
- If you are telephoning, allow the phone to ring longer than usual to allow extra time for the person to reach the telephone.

COMMUNICATING WITH SPEECH IMPAIRED PEOPLE

- If you do not understand something the individual says, do not pretend that you do. Ask the individual to repeat what he or she said, and then repeat it back.
- Be patient. Take as much time as necessary.

- Try to ask questions that require only short answers or a nod of the head.
- Concentrate on what the individual is saying.
- Do not speak for the individual or attempt to finish her or his sentences.
- If you are having difficulty understanding the individual, consider writing as an alternative means of communicating, but first ask the individual whether this is acceptable.

COMMUNICATING WITH LEARNING DISABLED PEOPLE

- If you are in a public area with many distractions, consider moving to a quiet or private location.
- Be prepared to repeat what you say, orally or in writing.
- Offer assistance completing forms or understanding written instructions, and provide extra time for decision making. Wait for the individual to accept the offer of assistance; do not over-assist or be patronizing.
- Be patient, flexible, and supportive. Take time to understand the individual and make sure the individual understands you.

Ethics / Choices

If you saw a coworker bend down to pet and talk to a guide dog that was assisting a blind person, would you react in any way? Explain.

Service Animals

Over 12,000 people with disabilities use service animals. Although the most familiar types of service animals are guide dogs used by the blind, service animals assist people who have other disabilities as well. Many disabling conditions are invisible. Therefore, a person who is accompanied by a service animal may or may not look disabled. A service animal is not required to have any special certification.

A service animal is *not* a pet. According to the Americans with Disabilities Act, a **service animal** is any animal that has been individually trained to provide assistance or perform tasks for the benefit of a person with a physical or mental disability that substantially limits one or more major life functions.

Remember, when serving a person who is accompanied by a service dog, you should not touch the service animal or the person it assists without permission. In addition, do not make noises at the service animal, as it may distract the animal from doing its job. Finally, avoid trying to feed the service animal, as it may disrupt his or her schedule.

BUSINESS *in action*

WONDERLIC, INC.

Wonderlic, Inc. has more than 65 years of experience helping employers and schools of all types and sizes select the best people. They tout on their website, "Measure and manage people according to person/job fit." One product they offer is the Comprehensive Personality Profile® (CPP®), a personality test that is particularly effective for positions requiring significant client interaction, such as customer service, telemarketing, and sales.

Used in employment screening, CPP assigns a personality type to each candidate and suggests ways to improve employee motivation. The CPP provides a 37-page report that describes a candidate's personality in terms of job-related strengths and weaknesses. The CPP measures seven primary personality traits: emotional intensity, intuition, recognition motivation, sensitivity, assertiveness, trust, and good impression. A Summary Profile identifies candidates as one of four common personality types.

Concluding Message for CSRs

Listening carefully and responding appropriately help CSRs meet the requirements and expectations of the diverse group of customers who consume products and services in the global and large-scale marketplaces. To put it briefly, when serving *any* customer—regardless of his or her culture, personality, generation, or disability, remember these points:

- Greet all customers and make them feel comfortable.
- Respect personal differences.
- Evaluate how the customer wants to be served.
- Adjust your approach to match the customer's needs.
- Always thank customers for their business.

Summary

- Creating and sustaining a diverse workforce and a diverse customer base are competitive advantages to a business enterprise.
- To serve customers best, identify which personality types they are, and then deal with each individual as he or she would like to be treated. The four personality types are analytical, driver, amiable, and expressive.
- Understanding generational differences allows service providers to adapt their personal styles to serve customers with respect to each customer's individual set of core values and expectations. The four generations in today's marketplace include the Matures, Baby Boomers, Generation Xers, and Millennials.
- Whenever necessary and reasonable, service providers should adjust the way they provide their services to customers with disabilities so that people who are challenged can still receive the best possible service.

KEY TERMS

amiable personality	disability	Mature Generation
analytical personality	driver personality	Millennial Generation
assimilation	expressive personality	paraphrase
Baby Boomer Generation	Generation X	service animal
culture	inclusion	stereotyping

CRITICAL THINKING

1. Why is diversity in the workplace deemed advantageous to businesses that sell products and services? In what ways can it be challenging to an organization?

2. In your own words, give a simple, one-sentence description for each of the four personality types.

3. If you were a guest service agent at a fine hotel in your area, how would your personal service approach be different when serving each of the following generations of customers: Matures, Baby Boomers, Generation Xers, and Millennials?

4. Describe an experience you have had or have heard about where a person with disabilities was served in an exemplary fashion.

ONLINE RESEARCH ACTIVITIES

Project 2.1 Culturally Oriented Marketing Plans

Assume you are doing a report on marketing plans for Hispanics and Asians. Use the Internet to locate examples of published information from business journals and business-oriented websites. List the results of your search, including the URLs, for current information you might use in your report.

_____

_____

_____

_____

_____

Project 2.2 Techno-Gadgets for Baby Boomers and Gen Xers

On-Time Technology Products' (OTTP) sales manager, Mr. Brown, feels that not enough is being done to meet the needs of the generations of buyers. He plans to survey how the Baby Boomers and Gen Xers respond to innovations, especially in techno-gadgets and communication devices.

Go to Barnes and Noble's website and locate three published books on the two generations of customers that you feel would best answer Mr. Brown's concerns. List the books that you would recommend, along with a brief description of each, in the table below.

Title and Author	Price	Brief Description of Book
1.		
2.		
3.		

Project 2.3 Communication Styles among Generations

Younger generations seem more detached in their communication styles. A great deal of the differences among communication styles can be attributed to the development of electronic technology.

Jot down some quick ideas as you answer the following two questions. Then, be ready to discuss in class your ideas about the importance of serving all generations of customers well.

1. What impact are variations in communication styles having on the workplace?

    _____

    _____

2. How should employers deal with these differences effectively?

    _____

    _____

DECISION MAKING AT WORK

Project 2.4 Free Personality Test for CSR Position

Many employers look for specific personality types to fit certain roles. For a CSR position, for example, they might look for someone who is an Amiable and has these general tendencies: cautious, gentle, and thoughtful; hesitant until he or she knows people well, then affectionate and caring; very literal and aware of the physical world; uncompromising about personal standards; diligent and conscientious, organized and decisive.

What is your personality type? Go to academic.cengage.com/marketing/odgers and find the web links for Chapter 2. Visit any of the websites listed there for a free assessment of your personality type. After you have determined your personality type, do the following:

- Link the results of it to one of the four types most fitting you that were covered in the chapter.
- With that personality type in mind, assume you are a CSR interacting with each of the following personality types in a customer service situation: analytical, driver, amiable, and expressive.
- Using the information covered in the chapter, decide how you will react, based on your own personality type, to each of the personality types in a customer situation in which the customer is returning a faulty product and wants cash back, not credit toward a future purchase. Your company's policy gives you the authority to make that decision.
- Prepare a one-page synopsis in which you summarize these four situations. Be prepared to discuss your ideas in class, if directed, before you submit your report to the instructor.

Here is an example: You are the CSR and you are an Expressive. Your customer is an Analytical. As an Expressive, you really want to understand your customer as a person. You like to get enthusiastic about things—but that's the wrong approach with an Analytical. You will need to be as systematic, thorough, deliberate, and precise as you can in your approach. Provide analysis and facts.

CASE STUDIES

Project 2.5 A Complaint from a Disabled Customer

At On-Time Technology Products, customers seldom complain because customer service is a top priority. However, recently the president of the company, Mr. MacGibson, received a complaint in writing from a person who is disabled. Mr. MacGibson knows that he not only must respond, but also perhaps change policy and procedures in the company relative to serving the disabled in more appropriate ways. Mr. MacGibson has asked for a focus group to be formed to give him advice on handling the complaint and what steps the company should take at this time.

In part, the complaint read,

> Today I was at your store and wanted to purchase a new laptop computer. I never write companies when small incidents occur (relative to my disability of being in a wheelchair), but I feel that today's behavior by your sales staff was over the top and warrants this letter. I chose to inform you, the president, so that others in my circumstance at your place of business will not be so offended.
>
> I felt very patronized when, after asking questions of your service/sales representative Joanne, she responded in an almost childlike voice—not once, but three times! Then she proceeded to lean on my wheelchair as she was demonstrating the laptop to me. I felt it would have been more appropriate for her to use a chair, but when I suggested she do so, she said, "Oh, this will only take a minute or so more" and then continued to lean over me for another five minutes!
>
> I am incensed enough to write this letter! By the way, after leaving your store I purchased my laptop from another store within the hour.

Analyze the case and determine: (1) whether the customer has a legitimate complaint, (2) what Mr. MacGibson's response should be to the customer, and (3) what recommendations as far as training, policies, and procedural changes you might make to Mr. MacGibson. Be ready to participate in a group discussion, as directed by your instructor, or to submit a case analysis if requested.

Project 2.6 Adapting to Electronic Technology

As electronic technology has evolved over the past 40 years, each successive generation has become more dependent on it in daily life. That is one of the reasons that On-Time Technology Products has been so successful. Now the company finds itself in a unique situation. As part of an employee recognition plan, it would like to discount by 50 percent the newest and most up-to-date handheld PDA to every employee. But there is dissention in the ranks—some employees would rather have money than the PDA. OTTP management is in conflict because it not only wants to do this for the sake of recognition, but also the thinking is that those who use the products can better sell and answer questions about their features, functions, and the benefits of their use. It seems that the younger a person is, the more he or she seems to embrace electronic technology. Thirty percent of the employees are over 55 years old.

Be prepared to discuss your views of the situation in class relative to the two questions that follow. Bring your information and reasoning to class for this discussion, as directed by your instructor.

1. How do different generations view the role of these devices in their lives and in the workplace?

    _____

    _____

    _____

    _____

2. What should OTTP do about the recognition program now—keep it? Modify it? Or just forget about doing it?

    _____

    _____

    _____

    _____

chapter 3

Customer Behavior, Customer Loyalty, and Exceptional Service

Objectives

1. Describe customers' buying behavior relative to their basic needs.

2. Distinguish between customer satisfaction and customer loyalty.

3. State the relationship between customer expectations and customer perceptions.

4. Describe methods companies use to measure customer satisfaction.

It's the little things that make the big things possible. Only close attention to the fine details of any operation makes the operation first-class.

—J. WILLARD MARRIOTT, FOUNDER, MARRIOTT INTERNATIONAL

In a business sense, customers can be considered as assets. Most companies regard assets as items that must be protected and whose value must be maintained and even maximized over time. From the customer's viewpoint, virtually all customer service activities, from billing accuracy to courtesy and accessibility of personnel, are prime components of excellent customer service. The trend in customer behavior and attitude is to expect that excellent customer service will be provided during all customer contacts.

Because recent data show that 40 percent of even satisfied customers will defect to a competitor, companies that are intent on retaining customers must cultivate loyalty by establishing a common ground and showing concern for customers through listening and using humor.[1] Contrary to popular belief, increased technology isn't the way to create customer loyalty. In fact, the more high-tech the business world becomes, the more challenging it is to build customer rapport. Despite their obvious conveniences, e-mail, voicemail, fax machines, PDAs, and other technological devices take

---

[1] Laura Michaud, "Beyond Customer Satisfaction," *Expert Magazine* (August 14, 2003): 15.

attention *away* from customers. These gadgets eliminate the human touch needed to build long-term customer relationships.

Understanding Customer Behavior

The primary objectives of perfect customer service are to experience repeat business and to increase business from current customers. These goals require specific knowledge about customers' behavior—*why* they buy, *how* they buy, and particularly *what* causes them to return and increase their purchases over time. Thinking like a customer isn't easy. In fact, many companies are unable to do it. Today's customers want choices, but they want them to be relevant to what they need to accomplish.

Although the reasons consumers buy vary considerably, they are derived from four basic needs that each of us has, regardless of our industries or businesses.

1. *The need to be understood.* Emotions, customs, and language barriers can get in the way of properly understanding the needs of customers. Every effort should be made to work with these challenges.

2. *The need to feel welcome.* That first impression a customer gets from service professionals is critical. Anyone who is made to feel like an outsider when doing business with a company will probably not return for future goods and services.

3. *The need to feel important.* Little things mean a lot. Acknowledgment, name recognition, and eye contact make a person feel important and appreciated.

4. *The need for comfort.* People need physical comfort—places to wait, rest, talk, or do business. They also need psychological comfort—the assurance and confidence they will be taken care of properly and fairly.

Organizations that understand customer behavior and make the transition to customer-centric service are characterized in two ways: (1) the organization is regarded by customers as easy to buy from or deal with, and (2) the organization depends on systems and processes (not speeches and slogans) to see that its service fits the customer's needs at a price the customer is willing to pay.

Ethics **/ Choices**

If you were being verbally "beaten up" by a customer for an issue you knew was caused by a colleague who was just fired last week, would you tell the customer who caused the problem? Explain.

In various industries, excellent service is often driven by customer behaviors and needs. Some examples are:

1. *The retail business.* A customer-oriented retail organization provides a wide variety of merchandise, convenient shopping hours, parking, reasonable policies on returns and exchanges, and availability of trained, courteous sales and service professionals.

2. *The consumer direct-marketing or mail-order business.* The nature of this business requires a high degree of customer trust and, in general, centers on immediate access to advertised products, prompt delivery, a liberal exchange and return policy, and hassle-free dealings that occur from a distance.

3. *The banking and financial services business.* This area has shown tremendous advances in customer service recently, with its automatic teller machines, interactive phone systems for handling account queries, and increased availability and higher skill levels of customer service personnel. In addition, customers receive faster turnaround on loans and quick

Our basic needs drive our decisions to buy from certain companies, while not buying from others.

resolution of money problems through immediate access to the financial institution's website links.

Earning Customer Loyalty

The customer is king. This phrase has become something of a mantra for retailers during the last several years, but many fail to support it with their behaviors or policies. Customer-centricity has become the new, challenging, competitive battlefield. The only way to survive in the current marketplace is by building a wide base of loyal customers, and the only way to do that is by tailoring the shopping experience to customer wants and needs as much as possible.

In companies across America, a disconnect between intentions and reality may be driving away customers. Often, companies do not live up to customer expectations. Incredibly, the disappointments that customers experience are frequently the result of expectations that the company has set up for itself. For example, customers are routinely surprised because many businesses fail to meet their own promised deadlines, fail to back up their products adequately, provide only limited availability of their advertised products, or provide inconsistent product service and support after the sale. Clearly, customer loyalty is not earned in these ways.

How Loyalty Is Earned

Profound changes have transformed the business world. Ask most managers what is different in today's economy, and they will tell you that markets are more crowded with global competitors, and attracting and retaining customer attention is harder than ever. An increased capacity to produce products and information has created an overcrowded marketplace, as more and more companies compete for the *same* customers.

Interestingly enough, a momentous shift has occurred: we have, in effect, entered an age of *customer scarcity*. The end result of this shift is that customers have become the most precious of all economic resources to businesses. Earning and keeping their loyalty, therefore, is tremendously valuable to successful companies.

Many companies today are maximizing the loyalty and the purchasing behavior of their customers by

Companies that have earned customer loyalty get the results they want—increased and consistent sales revenues.

offering customer rewards programs. The popularity of loyalty programs among today's consumers is evident in multiple industries in the United States. According to an October 2004 poll commissioned by Maritz Loyalty Marketing, nearly 90 percent of Americans actively participate in some type of loyalty program, including credit card, retail store, and airline rewards programs, and most consumers are enrolled in more than one. Further, research indicates that more than half of those surveyed are more loyal to companies that offer rewards programs.[2]

Customers tend to stay with organizations that enable them to experience positive, meaningful, and personally important feelings, even if an organization cannot always provide everything customers want or cannot solve all their problems. Most people shift from one supplier to another because of dissatisfaction with service, not price or product offerings. The service provider's responsibility is to manage the emotions in customer service exchanges.

According to Technical Assistance Research Programs, Inc. (TARP), a Washington, DC, consulting firm, 68 percent of customers who go elsewhere do so because of a perception of indifference.[3] Indifference in this

---

[2]Gail Sneed, "Do Your Customers Really Feel Rewarded?" *Target Marketing* (September 2005): 41.

[3]Joan Fox, "How to Keep Customers from Slipping through the Cracks," *The Small Business Journal* (May 2001): 2.

remember this ...

Tips to Earn Repeat Business from Customers

• Ask questions	Never make assumptions about what customers expect in terms of quality and service.
• Be honest	For long-term success, honesty is not just the best policy—it's the only policy.
• Fix the problems	When a mistake occurs, give your customers two things: an apology and a fix to the problem at no expense to the customer.
• Learn from the competition	Pay attention to the service provided by competitors; then try to improve on that level when you are dealing with your customers.
• Back up your company's promises	Nothing ruins credibility more than when customer service representatives promise what their company cannot deliver.
• Offer one-stop service	Customers don't like being passed along from one person to another. Always try to take care of the problem up-front and immediately.
• Build on emotion-friendly service culture	To deal effectively with customers' emotions, employees must be aware of the full range of their own emotional states—both positive and negative.

FIGURE 3.1

regard means that customers believe their loyalty is wasted on a company that doesn't care whether they remain customers. Thus, they vote with their feet and walk out the door, seldom or never to be seen again. Establishing lasting customer relationships can be extremely difficult, because one bad experience—or even a mediocre one—can cause a customer to take his or her business to a competitor.

An equation for keeping customers—not exactly a secret, considering the multitude of books on the topic—goes as follows: Take a good, first reaction with the customer; add in reliability, a quick response time, quality services and products, plus empathy; and you end up with a satisfied customer. Take away any of these factors and customer loyalty will begin to wane. Figure 3.1 lists some tips that are useful to earn repeat business from customers.

There is a cost benefit of building customer loyalty. Companies that frequently and periodically survey their customers to find out how happy they are and what suggestions they have to offer to improve products and services are doing the right thing. Some corporations and retailers that have taken these steps and, thus, have earned the right to experience deep customer loyalty are GE, Microsoft, Intel, Yahoo!, Home Depot, Wal-Mart, Nordstrom's, L.L. Bean, and Amazon.com. These are some companies that actively seek out from their customers better ways to serve them. Ultimately, the entire purpose of improved service is to honor customers by caring enough to meet their needs. Loyalty is earned when intentions and reality blend and become one. Customer-centric organizations do whatever it takes to avoid any type of customer turnoff.

Customer Turnoffs

Attracting replacement customers is an expensive process, because research indicates that it costs five times as much to generate a new customer as it does to keep an existing one. Unfortunately, few companies even track customer retention rates, much less inquire about what issues might be driving their customers away. Could it be fear about discovering the answers that prevents businesses from ever asking the question "What turns you off as a customer?"

If asked, customers would probably cite three categories of turnoffs, illustrated in Figure 3.2.

1. *Value turnoffs.* When a customer says, "I didn't get my money's worth on this product," this is a value turnoff. Value turnoffs include inadequate guarantees, a failure to meet quality expectations, and high prices relative to the perceived value of the product or service.

2. *System turnoffs.* These irritations arise from the way a company delivers its products or services.

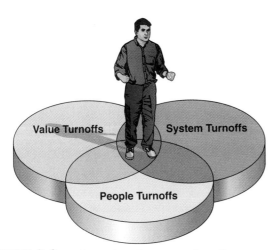

FIGURE 3.2   *What Drives Customers Away?*

fulfilling a key function are symptomatic of system failures. So are voicemail menus that are unnecessarily complicated. Slow service, lack of delivery options, cluttered workplaces, unnecessary or repetitious paperwork requirements, poor product selection, and inadequate reordering processes are additional examples of system turnoffs.

3. *People turnoffs.* These are the turnoff occurrences most often associated with poor customer service. Examples include showing lack of courtesy or attention, using inappropriate or unprofessional behavior, and projecting an indifferent attitude. In short, any behavior that conveys a lack of appreciation, care, or consideration for the customer is a people turnoff.

When transactions are unnecessarily complicated, inefficient, or troublesome, customers experience system turnoffs. For example, employees who lack the knowledge to answer customer questions and organizations that have just one person capable of

According to Jill Griffin and Michael Lowenstein, co-authors of *Customer WinBack*, customers defect from an established relationship for seven primary reasons. Figure 3.3 itemizes these reasons and goes on to suggest approaches companies can take to reduce customer defections.

remember this ...
Why Customers Defect and Approaches to Reduce Defections

Why Do Customers Defect from Established Relationships?

1. They don't know where or how to complain to the supplier.

2. They are too busy and can't, or won't, take the time to resolve concerns they have.

3. They consider complaining to be an annoyance that they would rather avoid.

4. They don't believe the company will do anything about it anyway.

5. They don't see any direct value or benefit to them from complaining.

6. They fear some post-complaint hostility or retaliation on the part of the company.

7. They can get what they want from a competitor, so switching is easy.

Steps to Reduce Defections

1. Make it easy for customers to complain.

2. Train CSRs to use good questioning techniques to uncover complaints.

3. Get resolution to customer problems more quickly.

4. Positively acknowledge every complaint as soon as possible.

5. Enforce a closed-loop complaint management system in which complaints are routinely gathered and analyzed for insights.

FIGURE 3.3   *Source:* Jill Griffin and Michael Lowenstein, *Customer WinBack* (Jossey-Bass, 2001).

Offering Exceptional Customer Service

Exceptional customer service is in the eye of the beholder—the customer. How does the customer determine whether a company has provided exceptional customer service? It usually depends on two factors: the customer's expectations and his or her perceptions. **Customer expectations** are what a customer wants *before* a transaction. Typically, a customer forms expectations from several sources: advertising, previous experience, word of mouth, and the competition.

Customer perceptions, in contrast, are created *during and after* a transaction. A customer's perception is based on how actual service measures up to his or her expectations. If customers get more than they expected, the end result is **exceptional customer service.** However, if customers get anything less than they expected, they perceive a performance gap; in that gap lies customer disappointment. Disappointed customers will leave an organization and take their business elsewhere, and poor customer service is responsible for much of the disappointment experienced by customers.

In practice, what does exceptional customer service really mean? Perhaps it happens when a company seriously tries to determine what makes it truly unique and what makes its customer experience better than that of its competitors. Keep in mind also that when you define what better customer service means for your customers, that definition is based on how they feel *now;* this doesn't necessarily mean that the definition won't change in the future. In other words, defining exceptional customer service is an ongoing, fluid process.

focus on Best Practices

Ritz-Carlton is the only service company to have won the prestigious Malcolm Baldrige National Quality Award twice—in 1992 and again in 1999. Receiving this industry-honored distinction was certainly not by accident. Every day at the chain's 57 hotels, all 25,000 Ritz-Carlton employees participate in a 15-minute "lineup" to talk about one of the basics. For example, Basic #14 states, "Use words such as 'Good morning,' 'Certainly,' 'I'll be happy to,' and 'My pleasure.' Do not use words such as 'O.K.,' 'Sure,' 'Hi/Hello,' 'Folks,' and 'No problem.'" The lineup ritual makes the hotel one of the few large companies that sets aside time for a daily discussion of its core values.

Further, if you are employed by Ritz-Carlton, the hotelier will spend about $5,000 to train you. First, you'll get a two-day introduction to the company values (it's all about the service), including the credo (again, service) and the 20 Ritz-Carlton basics (you got it—service!). Next comes a 21-day course focused on job responsibilities, such as a bellman's 28 steps to greeting a guest. Each employee carries a plastic card imprinted with the credo and the basics, as well as the "employee promise" and the three steps of service.

Step 1: "A warm and sincere greeting. Use the guest's name."

Step 2: "Anticipation and fulfillment of each guest's needs."

Step 3: "Fond farewell. Give a warm good-bye and use the guest's name."

For those reasons, strong organizations stay in touch with their customers on a regular basis and are not afraid to receive negative comments. In fact, they welcome negative comments that help them improve. Complaining is not only appropriate, but necessary. Why? Because it lets businesses know where they have room for improvement. When businesses know what they should improve and then make these improvements, they bring in more customers, resulting in more sales. Good companies fully recognize that it is infinitely better to have customers tell their complaints to the company's service representatives than to tell them to someone else.

The Value of Exceptional Customer Service

Exceptional customer service matters. Customers who experience world-class customer service return for more products and services and are less likely to shop around. Knowing what is on the customer's mind, therefore, is the smartest thing a business can do. Successful companies focus on what the customer is saying and then tailor their products or services to meet customer needs.

Profits and customer service go hand in hand. The value and economic effects of exceptional customer service are realities businesses are recognizing. According to a myriad of customer service surveys and resulting statistics, on average,

- Most people tell 10 other people about great service they have received (and are willing to pay more just to have), but will tell up to 20 people about poor service they have gotten.
- Depending on the industry, it costs between 2 and 20 times more to gain a new customer than it does to satisfy and retain a current one.
- Ninety-five percent of the customers whose problems are fixed quickly continue to do business with the company.

Paying attention to the finer points throughout a buying transaction is that special touch that makes a company stand out from the crowd. Some of the most effective extras are really very basic concepts of conducting good business, although customers are often surprised when these actions take place. Little details that contribute to exceptional customer service include:

- Treating customers respectfully and courteously at all times.
- Greeting customers by name and promptly answering their questions. (If you can't answer promptly, get back to the customer with an answer as quickly as possible.)
- Standing behind your product or service and doing whatever it takes to right a customer service concern in a manner that is fair to both sides.

Moment of truth is a term coined by Jan (Yon) Carlzon of Scandinavian Airlines Systems (SAS) in turning around his company as a result of a tremendous loss of profits in 1981. Simply put, a **moment of truth** is an episode in which a customer comes in contact with any aspect of the company, however remote, and thereby has an opportunity to form an impression. This moment of truth happens in a very short time period, from 7 to 40 seconds. That is the amount of time you, as a CSR, have to make a good impression on your customer. This impression will guide the rest of the encounter.

If the moment is favorable, the whole interaction will be pleasant. If it is not, a positive customer relationship has been tarnished. Carlzon's idea is that, if his company's 10 million passengers had an average contact with five SAS employees, the company had 50 million unique, never-to-be-repeated opportunities, or "moments of truth." With these moment-of-truth events, the company recovered from an $8 million loss to a profit of $71 million in two years.

customer service **T I P**

Customers with high expectations— sometimes referred to as tough, demanding customers—make a business better. The secret is to use these situations as opportunities to maximize customer retention and improve customer services.

Critical First Impressions

According to an old saying, "You never get a second chance to make a first impression." Nowhere is this more applicable than in business situations, whatever the industry, because how you initially communicate with people is key to your overall and continued success. In general, most consumers prefer to spend their money where they are treated well.

Research suggests that when two individuals meet for the first time, they take only four minutes to decide whether to continue the relationship. Evidently, this decision is based on certain assumptions. Perhaps the scariest truth of all is that this initial impression usually lasts a lifetime. If the first interaction with a customer is poor, even if a fairly good relationship ensues, the brain remembers that very first impression.

Successful companies examine and evaluate their customer service program regularly in order to establish a baseline standard for serving customers. A **baseline standard** is the minimum level of service it takes to satisfy customers under ordinary circumstances. Here are some examples of practices that constitute a baseline:

- Greet all customers just after entering your business.
- When possible, use a customer's name.
- Ask a customer about his or her visit.
- When asked, walk the customer to the product and place the item in his or her hand.
- Return voice and e-mail messages within 12 to 24 hours of receipt.

Positive first impressions are critical. Several types of communication can be used to create a positive first impression: in person at the physical place of business (both the environment and the way in which people are greeted); by telephone, voicemail, and e-mail; through printed materials; and by the way you present yourself and your company outside the office. First impressions are also influenced by a customer service representative's personal habits. When a CSR's hair is groomed, hands and fingernails are clean, clothing is appropriate and clean, and general actions reflect professionalism on the job, these practices send a positive impression to those who do business with your company.

Indicative of our age of quick response time, returning calls promptly, delivering products or services quickly, and using modern technology to decrease response time are also smart business moves. Each of these actions helps to create superior first impressions, because customers simply are not willing to wait. Beware of using on-hold time to deliver information about your business. A waiting customer can easily take offense at being forced to endure your advertising or your taste in music. If at all possible, have enough phone lines (and enough people to answer them) so that callers don't get a busy signal or get put on hold for longer than 45 seconds.

In making a favorable first impression, a good rule of thumb is to consistently exceed customer expectations. Keep in mind, however, that a positive first impression isn't going to do much good in the long run if a subsequent negative experience eclipses it. The best way to maximize the value of a positive first impression is to reinforce it with extraordinary approaches to customer service and other favorable experiences throughout the course of future interactions. Empowering employees to solve customer concerns is a critical component to making a great first impression.

Empowerment

Empowerment, defined as giving somebody power or authority, must follow a top-down model that conveys authority through the ranks to frontline staff members. It enables them to make administrative decisions based on corporate guidelines. It means that employees should never have to tell a customer "no." When an employee can do whatever he has to do on the spot to take care of a customer to that customer's satisfaction, not to the company's satisfaction, that is empowerment, because if the customer doesn't win, the company loses.

One significant benefit of empowerment is the elimination of nearly all multilevel problem solving that involves management. Scores of managers talk about empowerment, but many more have difficulty putting it into practice. Too often, they don't really understand what empowerment is. To many managers, empowerment is giving employees the authority to make a decision to take care of the customer—as long as the action they take follows the rules, policies, and procedures of the organization. Some would interpret this to mean there actually is no empowerment. True empowerment means employees can bend and break the rules to do whatever they have to do to take care of the customer.

customer service T I P

Undeliverable promises can do more harm than saying "no" to a customer.

Empowerment is an important aspect of legendary customer service for any business. Having a team of empowered employees who are afraid to make a decision is as bad, if not worse, than not having an empowerment program at all. When employees make a customer-related decision, the greatest concern for many of them is that they will be reprimanded—or worse, fired—for making what management sees as a bad decision.

For empowerment to work, employees should know they won't be fired if they make an error and that it's okay to make mistakes in the process of working to win customer satisfaction. Once empowered, customer service representatives have the responsibility to exercise that authority when the need arises. Ultimately, an empowered staff reduces the amount of time customers spend reaching satisfactory conclusions and has far-reaching effects in keeping a customer who would consider going elsewhere for your product or service.

Ethics / Choices

Time after time, when entering the employee break room, you overhear other CSRs talking about how bad the management is at your company—specifically, your manager. What is your reaction to this situation? Would you enter the discussion to express your personal views, ignore the discussion, or try to reason with your coworkers and advise them against spreading negative thoughts? Explain.

Extraordinary Approaches to Customer Service

To go beyond client satisfaction, make every effort to exceed your clients' expectations, every time. An age-old rule that is followed by customer-savvy organizations is to "under promise and over deliver." For example, if you think it will take two months to complete a project, quote a two-month time frame. If you get the job done a week or two early, you have under promised and over delivered. Tactics such as these empower people in the organization by giving them freedom to act in customers' best interests, and they yield enormous dividends for the company.

Stellar customer service is a mindset that defines each company's culture. It is pervasive, visible to others, and everyone's responsibility. Obviously, this unity of purpose begins with hiring and training the right people, but it also requires organizations to keep the basic company functions in superior shape, so that CSRs do not get bogged down by the grind of cleaning up problems, correcting errors, or being on the defensive with customers. The following six actions can help improve performance and apply extraordinary approaches to customer service.

1. *Decide who you are and what you can deliver.* It's important to know what you can and cannot provide. Make sure you are true to your company's mission. Decide who you want to provide exemplary service to. Decide what you want to deliver and deliver it well.

2. *Decide who your customers are and what they want.* What you think customers should value might not be what they really value. Make sure you are in sync with customer interests and concerns.

3. *Deliver more than you promise.* Make sure you give your customers more than they request, but, when doing so, ensure it is something they will value.

4. *Review your rules.* Look at both formal and informal rules. Some rules might have evolved from previous customer encounters in your company. Examine which rules obstruct serving your customers' needs and get rid of them, if possible. Make every effort to favor the customers' needs over internal needs.

5. *Celebrate your diversity.* Some employees might be difficult to work with, but they might be the best fit with some customers. Empower them. They might become your best employees.

6. *Treat your employees as you expect them to treat your customers.* Treat your employees with respect. Put yourself in their shoes. Make them feel special. Make time for them. The result will be that they will treat customers the same way. In business, this idea is referred to as the **mirror principle,** which says, your employees won't treat customers better than you treat your employees.

In this discussion about what exemplary customer service is, it is perhaps prudent to examine what service *is not.* Service is not easily managed, because so many factors make it unpredictable and difficult to control fully. The following characteristics of service contribute to this complexity; therefore, when focusing on serving customers in the best way, remember these realities, which can cause dilemmas for CSRs:

*   Customer service happens instantaneously and right in front of the customer.

- Customer service is created and delivered at the same time.
- Service must be individualized for each customer; it cannot be standardized or routinely applied universally.
- The perception of the customer may not be the same perception as that of the service providers.
- Often, customer requests are complex and unique, and cannot be speedily resolved.
- Different customers have different needs; further, the needs of the same customers change constantly.
- Complete customer service requires others in your organization to support you; it requires customer service teamwork, with everyone committed to the same goal.

customer service T I P

If a company doesn't take care of its customers, some other company will.

Measuring Customer Satisfaction

The case for maximizing customer satisfaction is a strong one, because a customer base will remain if it is built on trust, quality, timely service, and product excellence. Although superior customer satisfaction is the goal, it is difficult to measure. Satisfaction, like quality, is in the eye of the beholder. What is the best way to measure customer service and satisfaction? The answer is simple—ask your customers. Having customers tell you specifically what you are doing right, what you are doing wrong, and how you can improve critical areas of your business is the single and most accurate means of determining how well you are meeting their needs.

Benefits to the Customer

Several ways exist to gather customer feedback: surveys and assessments, focus groups, and interviews. When conducted at six-month and yearly intervals, these are all first-rate methods for generating qualitative and quantitative information for sound decision making and appropriate changes to the way a business operates. Customer feedback can help companies increase service quality, innovation, and most important, customer retention. This feedback meets one or any number of the objectives that follow:

- Finding and acting on the issues which lead to innovation, employee or customer turnover, or other key outcomes
- Motivating and guiding change efforts and identifying the most promising opportunities for improvement
- Recording a baseline from which progress can be measured
- Creating a consensus on priorities or issues to be dealt with
- Providing a two-way communication with employees or customers

The traditional methods to gauge customer satisfaction are to conduct periodic customer surveys via telephone, direct mail, the Internet, and e-mail. Some problems inherent in the use of these approaches are that they are often slow, expensive, imprecise, and not always helpful for getting at the root of deviations in customer satisfaction. In a perfect world, customer satisfaction data should be reliable, viewed in real time, tied to specific CSRs, and cost a fraction of traditional third-party surveys.

A faulty belief exists in the marketplace that the mere collection of data will result in improvement. That's probably because, in years past, just the act of conducting a survey had some positive impact on customer satisfaction and loyalty, but the bar has been raised. With a smarter base of customers who have greater expectations of service, companies can no longer ask whether customers are satisfied without acting in a personalized way on the responses they receive. The process of asking customers to set the standards for the level of service they expect from a company

- Helps the company set realistic goals and monitor trends.
- Provides critical input for analyzing problem areas.
- Assists the company in monitoring progress toward improvements.
- Keeps the company close to its customers.

Benefits to the CSR

You cannot change what you don't measure, understand, and acknowledge. Customer service representatives and their managers, therefore, pay more attention to performance standards that are measured because they then know what to expect. Customer-focused measurements are needed because they explain reasons for lost sales, retention problems, time-consuming and costly complaints, and cost redundancies.

Without measurable performance standards, employees are left to guess what good service is. When that happens, customers become disappointed. The following are some examples of measurable customer service standards that good companies implement:

- Answering telephones by the third ring
- Serving hot food at a temperature of at least 140 degrees
- Smiling and greeting all guests within 10 feet of you
- Responding to each shopper so that he or she does not stand in line more than two minutes
- Offering bellman or concierge service to every hotel guest
- Speaking professionally to clients and avoiding the use of slang expressions

How do you ask customers if your service goals are in line with their service expectations? The easiest way is to have a customer response system in place. You can use several methods, such as comment card surveys, post-episodic surveys, automated call surveys, or mail surveys, to name a few.

COMMENT CARD SURVEYS Hand the card to the customer at the end of the transaction. Ask the customer to please take a moment to complete the survey, as it will be useful to your company in determining how well you are meeting his or her needs.

POST-EPISODIC SURVEYS A new feedback concept gaining popularity with perceptive companies is the post-episodic survey. **Post-episodic surveys** gather information from customers after they have completed a business transaction such as opening a new account or getting a car serviced at a dealership. Essentially, this is a satisfaction survey dealing with just one service episode. Surveys are usually conducted by phone within 24 to 48 hours of the transaction. Post-episodic surveys are valuable when you want to measure improvement in customer service, develop further insight into the needs and expectations of your customers, or identify best practices.

AUTOMATED CALL SURVEYS This survey uses specific software that is integrated with the customer call center's system. After the caller has elected to bypass self-service and speak with an agent (usually by pressing "0"), the caller is asked to participate in a survey after the call. Typically, they are instructed to press "1" for "yes" and "2" for "no."

Callers respond via entries on the touch-tone pad. Some systems accept verbal responses. Usually, between 5 and 10 percent of callers will agree to participate in the survey.[4]

MAIL SURVEYS Include a cover letter explaining the reasons for your survey. Address a short survey to the person who interacted with your company and include a postage-paid return envelope.

OTHER METHODS Electronic surveys, in-store shopper surveys, and onsite interviews can also be effective. In addition, create a forum for customer service representatives to provide anecdotal, subjective feedback from customers about product features, functionality, and pricing.

Finally, nobody knows what customers are thinking better than CSRs do. Examples of customer response methods are shown in Figure 3.4.

FIGURE 3.4 *Two methods that survey customers' expectations and satisfaction with products and services.*

[4]Dick Bucci, "The New Best Way to Measure Customer Satisfaction," *Call Center Magazine* (November 2005): 44.

BUSINESS in action

BEN & JERRY'S

The consumer services manager at Ben and Jerry's Homemade, Inc., describes how "euphoric service" can move customers from mere satisfaction of purchasing their ice cream into passionate loyalty like this: "Customer satisfaction is only a feeling—an attitude—that does not predict future customer performance, because satisfied customers will still purchase from your competitor. Customer loyalty, on the other hand, is a behavior. When you make a personal connection with your customers and let them know that you hear what they're saying, and then prove it by being responsive to their needs, you're building loyalty that influences behavior. Loyalty is always going to be based on relationships, and that's what you want."

Concluding Message for CSRs

To be sure, it takes more than "the customer is always right" rhetoric to satisfy today's diverse customers. Customers are not always right, but customers are always emotional. They always have feelings—sometimes intense, other times barely perceptible—when they make purchases or engage in business transactions. When unhappy CSRs in an organization are out of touch with their own feelings, they cannot provide emotional competence or use emotional connections to increase customer loyalty.

If you want loyal customers, don't just stop at customer satisfaction, because basic service delivery isn't enough in today's marketplace. Here is something to

think about: when a company loses a customer, it does not lose one sale, but a lifetime opportunity of profitability with that individual. The question becomes "What could that customer have been worth?" To determine the average lifetime value of customers, first estimate how much they will spend with your company on an annual basis, and multiply it by the number of years they could potentially use your products and services. For example, if an average customer spends $100 a month, 12 months a year, for 10 years, their average lifetime value is $12,000. Now add on the value of all the new customers that your loyal customer will refer to your company. You can easily see how increasing customer retention and loyalty translates into huge increases in profitability and long life to any company.

Summary

- The primary mission of perfect customer service is to experience repeat business and to increase business from current customers.

- Earning customer loyalty is critical, because today's economy has an increased capacity to produce products and information; therefore, an excess in the marketplace is inherent as more and more companies compete for the same customers.

- Customer expectations are what a customer wants before a transaction; customer perceptions are created during and after a transaction.

- In terms of making a favorable first impression, a good rule of thumb is to exceed customer expectations consistently, because first impressions are formed within the first four minutes of customer contact.

- Because of a smarter customer base that has greater expectations, companies can no longer use survey techniques to ask whether customers are satisfied, without acting on the responses they receive.

KEY TERMS

baseline standard	empowerment	moment of truth
customer expectations	exceptional customer service	post-episodic surveys
customer perceptions	mirror principle	

CRITICAL THINKING

1. In what ways do the four basic needs described in this chapter relate to the reasons people buy from certain companies?

2. Describe an experience you have had or have heard about that demonstrates excellent customer service.

3. Are customer satisfaction and customer loyalty the same in meaning? Why or why not?

4. Of the three types of customer turnoffs—value turnoffs, system turnoffs, and people turnoffs—which do you feel is the most often violated by organizations? Why?

5. In your own words, explain the relationship between customer expectations and customer perceptions.

6. Do you agree with the statement "You never get a second chance to make a first impression"? Why or why not?

7. Are the reasons customer service is difficult to manage just excuses for poor customer service or are they reasonable? Explain.

8. If you were the president of a retail organization, what methods would you use to measure customer satisfaction? Why?

ONLINE RESEARCH ACTIVITIES

Project 3.1 Measuring Customer Satisfaction

Assume you are doing a report on surveys that measure customer satisfaction. Use the Internet to locate examples of published information from business journals and business-oriented websites. List the results of your search, including the URLs, of current information you might use in your report.

_____

_____

_____

_____

_____

Project 3.2 Customer Loyalty and Retention

The big push at On-Time Technology Products is to increase sales by doing whatever it takes to retain customers and increase customer loyalty. In the technology business, however, Vice President Woo, who is in charge of customer relations, realizes that because of many good ideas and outstanding competitors, it might be prudent to do some research on the Internet. He specifically wants to survey how customer loyalty is achieved—especially as it applies to the technology industry.

Go to the Amazon website and locate three books on customer loyalty and customer retention. Enter your findings in the following table to inform Mr. Woo which recently published books are available and those you would recommend, along with a brief description of each.

Title and Author	Price	Brief Description of Book
1.		
2.		
3.		

COMMUNICATION SKILLS AT WORK

Project 3.3 Moment of Truth Examples

A moment of truth is an episode in which a customer comes in contact with any aspect of the organization, however remote, and thereby has an opportunity to form an impression. In other words, a moment of truth

- Consists of any interaction with a customer.
- Determines a customer's perception of your service.
- Requires judgment, skill, and understanding by the CSR.
- Occurs in less than 40 seconds.

Look at the list of customer-oriented industries in column 1. In column 2, write down specific actions a customer service professional can make to improve a moment-of-truth experience as it relates to each industry. For informal research, ask another adult if they have had a moment-of-truth experience in the past week and if so, have the person describe it. Be prepared to share your findings and written ideas as part of a class group discussion.

How to Create Positive Moments of Truths for Customers (for example, Smile)

1. Hotel	• • •
2. Restaurant	• • •
3. Retail store (for example, Wal-Mart)	• • •
4. Airline (for example, Southwest Airlines)	• • •

DECISION MAKING AT WORK

Project 3.4 Customer Turnoffs Discussion

You are sitting in the lunchroom at On-Time Technology Products with two other CSRs, Rosie and Doug. It's Friday and everyone is looking forward to the weekend, but Doug is relating a customer problem he has just experienced and is asking how you and Rosie would have handled it. You discuss it, then the discussion moves to other examples of situations that turn customers off and how each of you would handle those situations. Listed below are three major customer turnoffs, which are not specific to the technology industry.

1. Waiting in line while the CSR is chatting with a coworker
2. Red tape—such as refunds, credit checks, and adjustments on account
3. A company's failure to stand behind their products or services

Pair up with a classmate and role-play each of the given situations that can turn customers off. In a class discussion, be prepared to state how you, representing a specific company, might address each scenario in a positive way.

CASE STUDIES

Project 3.5 The Mirror Principle

Helen Harrison, marketing director of a major manufacturing plant on the east coast, was driving back from a noon chamber of commerce meeting and was reflecting on a statement made by the luncheon speaker. The speaker described the mirror principle by saying, "Your employees won't treat your customers better than you treat your employees." Given the increasingly fragile employee morale, decrease in sales, and increase in customer service complaints at the plant over the past six months, Helen is wondering whether this is what is happening in her company.

1. If you were Helen, in what ways would you translate your feelings into an action plan for improvement?

    _____

    _____

    _____

2. What steps would be included in your action plan to turn these problematic customer service issues around?

    _____

    _____

    _____

    _____

Project 3.6 Customer Service Satisfaction and the Budget

It is budget time at On-Time Technology Products, and Mr. MacGibson is seeking input from employees in order to develop a realistic budget for next year. One budgeting change he is considering is to increase the amount of money allocated to the customer service department by 8 percent. Sam Brown, Vice President of Sales, has advised him that just committing more resources to customer service will not necessarily increase customer satisfaction and loyalty. Nonetheless, Mr. MacGibson needs more input and has asked you and the other CSRs to respond to the following three customer service situations in order to acquire more information as he prepares the budget.

Set up a class panel discussion to address these questions:

1. In what ways could a higher budget assist On-Time Technology Products to make credits and adjustments to customer accounts easier?

    _____

    _____

    _____

2. In what ways could a higher budget assist On-Time Technology Products in providing information and answers to customers in a more timely way?

    _____

    _____

    _____

3. Can allocating more money to a department really solve customer service problems? Why or why not?

    _____

    _____

    _____

Action Plan

Based on your study of Part 1, think about the qualities a customer service representative (CSR) should possess in order to provide exemplary service and retain loyal customers, and then complete the following activities.

Activity 1

Divide a sheet of paper into four columns and create the following list in column 1: Provides Customer-Centric Service, Serves Diverse Populations, Aware of Generational Differences, and Promotes Customer Loyalty. Label column 2 *Strength*, column 3 *Needs Improvement*, and column 4 *Method of Improvement*.

Give some thought as to how you would rate yourself on each item in column 1. How do you measure up? If there is a skill that you feel especially strong in, put an X in column 2 next to that item, showing it as a strength of yours. If it is a skill that you may need to work on in some way, place an X in column 3. Finally, in column 4, indicate how you might improve on those skills you've identified in column 3.

Activity 2

Work together as a class and assign one person to write on the whiteboard or chalkboard. Break the writing space into four areas: Provides Customer-Centric Service, Serves Diverse Populations, Aware of Generational Differences, and Promotes Customer Loyalty. Devote some class time to brainstorming about each of the four areas on the board. When class members respond, they should use the sentence stem, "Remember to . . ."

Finally, each student should select from each group two reminders that the student feels have the most relevance to him or her and place those items on note cards to be posted in a workspace or at home.

P A R T

2

Customer Service and Essential Personal Skills

chapters

PHOTO © LESLIE CONNELL

Hospitality and Tourism Profile

by Leslie Connell,
Flagstaff Convention
and Visitors Bureau

How did you begin in the hospitality industry?

I began my career in the hospitality industry cleaning rooms in a small resort ski town in the Canadian Rockies. I hadn't intended to make this my lifelong direction, but little did I know that I had begun a career I would grow to love.

Unfortunately, in those days customer service was not taken too seriously. Small, busy resort towns can sometimes have an attitude about their attractiveness to visitors. The thought was, if customers were unhappy, there would be someone in line behind them ready to fill that space.

I left the industry for a few years and spent some time walking in the shoes of those visitors I used to serve. By the time I returned, it was with a whole new perspective. I joined Marriott, a company that already knew the importance of customer relationships and great service, and I spent 17 years in management positions with that chain.

What are some qualities that are critical when working in the hospitality and tourism industry?

Experience has taught me some inevitable truths. The hospitality industry is not for everyone, attitude is everything, and hiring great associates who take superb care of the guests makes management much easier. I learned to look for the applicants who had the right "people-person" qualities, people who could interact well with guests and other employees. They had to have the "spirit to serve" and exhibit the ability to work well in a team environment. As far as I was concerned, everything else was something they could be trained to do.

How important is it to give exemplary customer service to guests?

As a manager, I felt that great customer service could not be stressed enough. I empowered my staff to make immediate decisions to fix a situation, instead of having to wait for management authority. Overall, we had very happy guests. From time to time, we encountered someone who was almost impossible to please, but we kept trying. It's important to provide quality training to staff, so that they can perform to a level where mistakes are few, but I think it's more important to provide the type of training that will enable employees to fix something that goes wrong, because Murphy's Law guarantees that at some point, something will.

Customer expectations are high and ever on the rise. In order to compete in today's marketplace, a company must pay attention to how it treats its customers. Customers remember the business that provides consistent service, and return business is almost guaranteed. Gone forever are the days when someone will automatically appear to take the place of an unhappy customer. Companies are getting wise to this fact.

What advice do you have for those seeking a career in customer service?

Now is a great time for people who are assessing their goals in life to take a look at the hospitality industry. This career requires flexibility, patience, humility, and a good sense of humor. Some of these attributes I possessed when I began down this long road, and some were acquired along the way. As difficult as it is, I couldn't have picked a better career path. It has been rewarding and, most of all, fun.

Industry: Hospitality and Tourism

Hospitality and Tourism Activities

1. Think about your total experience the last time you stayed at a hotel and respond with "yes" or "no" to the following questions:

    _____ Did the guest service agent (GSA) greet you with a smile and say, "Welcome to _____ Hotel"?

    _____ Did the GSA acknowledge guests who were waiting in line?

    _____ Did the GSA use each guest's name frequently?

    _____ Was the GSA knowledgeable regarding the property?

    _____ Did the GSA make frequent eye contact throughout the interaction with you?

    _____ When you checked out, did the GSA ask you, "Did you enjoy your stay?"

    _____ Did the GSA invite you to return by saying, "We look forward to seeing you again?"

    _____ How would you rank customer service at this hotel (1 = poor; 5 = superior)?

    Explain in a few words why you evaluated the hotel as you did.

    _____

    _____

    _____

2. Briefly describe a situation at a restaurant in which you or someone you know returned a meal because of dissatisfaction.

    How did your server handle the complaint?

    _____

    _____

    What attempts were made to retain you as a satisfied customer?

    _____

    _____

3. Assume you are a director for a tour company that serves more than 500 tourists to Arizona's Grand Canyon per week. In that role, what are three time factors and three stress factors that you would need to manage and ultimately master to serve customers well?

    _____

    _____

    _____

Attitude, Angry Customers, and Relationship Building

chapter 4

Objectives

1. Describe a customer-oriented attitude.

2. Recognize situational examples that elicit rage reactions in customers.

3. Identify actions CSRs can take to ensure delivery of comprehensive customer services.

4. Describe the customer service benefits of the teamwork approach in organizations.

An optimistic, positive mind is far more likely to come up with creative solutions than a mind that dwells on setbacks and difficulties.

—ZIG ZIGLAR, MOTIVATIONAL SPEAKER AND AUTHOR

Customer expectations have a power in and of themselves. Learning to define, meet, and exceed those expectations is essential to customer satisfaction. As all the management and quality consultants will tell you, "The customer is king," because the customer remains the final judge of quality. The customer sets the standard for excellent service. The customer keeps a business in business.

All customers—internal and external—place different values on service, attitude, and performance. Therefore, find out exactly which areas are most important to the customer you are currently serving. Customer expectations must be realistic and attainable. Being able to define, meet, and exceed those expectations on a regular basis is the key to personal service performance, business growth, and customer satisfaction.

Part 2 focuses on the many essential personal skills that customer service representatives must demonstrate on the job. The four chapters in this section discuss customer conflicts and complaints, as well as how to recover from and win back the customer who is angry. Skills you will need in managing the customer service role, including problem-solving, time management, and stress management skills, are also discussed.

A Customer-Oriented Service Attitude

Think about the last time you visited a restaurant. What do you remember about it? Is your strongest memory of the food or of the service you received? Most of us say the service, even though we consciously believe we are going to a restaurant to get a good meal.

Management guru Peter Drucker put it best when he said, "The purpose of business is to create a customer." The logic follows that business is not about making sales, or even making profits. Those come naturally when you create customers—and keep them. Employees who give exceptional customer service have a positive, can-do attitude. They treat customers honorably and know it's essential to their success.

The **American Customer Satisfaction Index (ACSI),** established in 1994 by the Business School at the University of Michigan, tracks trends in customer satisfaction and provides valuable benchmarking insights of the consumer economy for companies, industry trade associations, and government agencies. In the first quarter of every year, the ACSI measures customer satisfaction with the quality of products and services in energy utilities, airlines, express delivery, U.S. Postal Service, hospitals, hotels, fast-food restaurants, cable and satellite TV, and telecommunications services. After nudging upwards the previous quarter, the ACSI rose to 74.1 in the first quarter of 2006, its largest jump since 2003.[1]

Ethics / Choices

Carolyn, a CSR you work with, is having a difficult day. You have overheard her on two occasions sounding short with customers on the phone and are aware that your company is randomly monitoring customers' calls. Would you pull Carolyn aside to talk with her about your concerns?

The Power of a Positive Attitude

It may sound simplistic, but the first step toward creating an appropriate customer-oriented attitude is to begin thinking positive thoughts about yourself and others. What we see depends more often than not on what we look for. The second step is to reflect those thoughts in positive self-talk. **Self-talk** happens inside us, whether we are aware of it or not. We all talk to ourselves, and this self-talk can have a tremendous effect on our attitudes. Positive self-talk can help each of us build a positive, winning attitude.

Conversely, negative self-talk can do just the opposite. For example, we become our own worst enemies by telling ourselves things like "I'll never be any good at this" or "I look terrible today." We feel better if we replace those thoughts with statements such as "I'm sure I can do this with just a little practice" or "I look and feel great today."

A positive attitude is not necessarily something you are born with. Even if your attitude is negative from time to time, you can change and create a positive customer attitude that is helpful and dedicated to being outstanding. Today's customers perceive good service as added value. In other words, you need to add something extra to the product or service that is delivered.

Customers can sense positive energy, and the result is that they too come away feeling positive. The late Dr. Norman Vincent Peale had this to say about positive thinking: "You can make yourself sick with your thoughts, and you can make yourself well with them. A positive emotion is created by positive thoughts and images."

A positive attitude is not only about choosing to have a good outlook through good times and bad, but also about learning to love what you do. Think of the successful people you know and you may agree that most are passionate about what they do, are rarely affected by negativity, and tend to enjoy their work. Having a positive attitude will help you make the best of almost any situation.

It's true that you can never have absolute control over what occurs in your company and in your personal life. But the attitude with which you choose to greet the day, approach your work, and respond to the people around you is fully within your control. A positive workplace attitude is reflected when you believe in your company, its products or services, its people, and in yourself. It should culminate in making the customer feel your belief from your words and actions.

---

[1]"Consumer Willingness to Spend Beyond Means May Exceed Ability, According to American Customer Satisfaction Index," (May 16, 2006). www.theacsi.org.

The Customer's Attitude and You

In the real world, CSRs serve customers who display a variety of attitudes. For example, some customers are

1. *Comfortable.* Customers who believe their needs and expectations will be met.
2. *Indecisive.* Customers who cannot make up their minds or may not even know what they want.
3. *Insistent.* Customers who make demands and require you to take immediate action.
4. *Irate.* Customers who are angry and need to blow off steam before you can begin to work with them.

Your attitude toward a customer is not the only factor that can affect the outcome of that customer contact. When some other aspect of your life is bothering you, it can affect the way you interact with others. Whether your negative thoughts are based on something that happened to you earlier that day or on your negative expectations regarding a particular customer, replace them with positive ones, such as "I'm eager to help" or "Problem solving is something I'm good at." Sometimes, on "off days," we say things we later regret. Figure 4.1 describes seven statements you should never say to customers.

The following list offers some survival tips to help keep your attitude up:

- *Engage in positive self-talk.* Practice healthy thinking. Do not clutter your mind with negatives.
- *Get a calming object.* Use a photo, cartoon, small stuffed animal, or positive notes in your work area that remind you "this too shall pass."
- *Focus on successes rather than negatives.* Track the things that go right.
- *Use your break time effectively.* Do something to keep yourself going, something that relaxes you and clears your mind. For example, listen to music, take a short walk, do some yoga stretches, or read. Do not use your free time for complaining to others.
- *Develop a buddy system at work.* Learn from each other and share the load.

remember this ...
Seven Statements You Should Never Say to Customers

Statement	Reason
1. "We don't offer that."	It's fine to say "no"; however, how you say "no" is all-important. For example, when you have to turn away a customer, recommend where the product or service can be found.
2. "All sales are final."	Your business should have a reasonable return policy and warranty plan. This sends a clear message to customers that you believe in what you are selling.
3. "I don't know who does that."	Business is lost, and this type of response frustrates customers. Employees must be familiar with who does what at a business or at least have immediate access to people who do have this knowledge.
4. "Sorry, that's our policy."	Customers faced with this statement will be annoyed at the lack of creativity a company shows in resolving their problems. Be flexible and helpful with customers who deserve a break.
5. "Tell us what you think."	Unless you are prepared to react to all varieties of feedback, be careful with this statement. A survey to assess customer satisfaction can be designed by companies to handle complaints as well as compliments.
6. "It will be ready tomorrow."	Unless you are sure it will be ready as promised, don't make this commitment. It is smarter to under promise and over deliver.
7. "I don't know."	Don't use that phrase unless you follow it with the phrase "but I will find out for you." Admitting you don't have the answer is fine and can actually improve your credibility, as long as you make an effort to get the answer for the customer.

FIGURE 4.1

As a CSR, do whatever it takes to avoid customer rage confrontations.

- *Keep in mind your overall goals.* When the details of work or a particular customer situation are getting you down, step back and look at the big picture.
- *Be kind to yourself.* Exercise, volunteer, spend time with friends and family, and do other things that add value to your life.
- *Take your sense of humor to work.* Take your work seriously, but don't take yourself seriously. Learn to laugh at yourself.

Ethics / Choices

Do you feel that service professionals have a choice whether to be rude or kind to others? Explain.

Customer Rage

Imagine these scenarios:

- Driving to work one morning, someone cuts you off in traffic. A little while later, you can't get someone to wait on you in a store when you run in for a pack of gum. Finally, you call your insurance agent but are unable to get a live person on the phone to answer a question. Before you know it, you're behaving rudely to somebody else.
- More than 25 times over the past couple of weeks, you've dialed your cell phone provider's customer service department, asking for help. Each time you had to ensure that the cell phone was fully charged, you would not be interrupted, and you had the time available to complete the call. Even after you were placed on hold for more than 20 minutes, no one responded to your call.
- When calling the bank, you provided your account number at the time of the automated phone greeting by using your touch-tone phone. You were passed off three times to another live agent, who asked you for the same information you'd already given.
- A CSR told you that she understood and sympathized with your problem and that she would refund your money (or fix the product) if she could, but unfortunately, she was powerless to do so. The computer system wouldn't permit her to help you. Then she said, "You are the tenth person with this problem today. We've asked management to fix this, but they never listen to us."
- You buy a software program hoping it will save you time, but it doesn't work. After combing the company's website for 10 minutes to find a telephone number, you call, only to be greeted by the company's seven-layer voicemail system. Once you finally get someone on the line, he insists that you are the one who created the problem and puts you on hold while finding someone who might be qualified to answer your questions.

Many frustrating situations can lead to customer rage. With **customer rage** comes an increasing number of irritated consumers who are taking out their anger on the CSRs they are dealing with. According to a customer rage survey released in November 2005, 15 percent of shoppers surveyed who received unsatisfactory service actually sought revenge for their suffering. Luckily for frontline customer service representatives, just 1 percent reported actually exacting vengeance (the details of which were not divulged in the study). A more composed 33 percent admitted to raising their voices, while 13 percent said they used profanity when interacting with CSRs.

The findings of the report, conducted by Customer Care Alliance in collaboration with the W. P. Carey School of Business at Arizona State University, show that the relationship between sellers and shoppers is rocky at best. Of the 1,012 survey respondents, 70 percent experienced customer rage, relating that their most serious consumer problem in the past year made them "extremely" or "very" upset. Most consumers characterize the service they get as "acceptable" or "average," and according to the report, more people say it is getting worse instead of better.[2]

[2]Dayana Yochim. "Customer Rage Is on the Rise," *The Motley Fool* (November 3, 2005).

Providing customer service seems as if it should be a matter of common sense. But many different things can go wrong. Although no one condones over-the-top behavior that sometimes accompanies customer rage, many of us have witnessed it as the unfortunate result of poor service.

Customers don't become dissatisfied because of problems. Customers become dissatisfied with the way problems are handled. Dealing ineffectively with a complaint can ruin brand or company loyalty. Putting the wrong person in front of a customer is ineffective and bears enormous costs. Add the loss of the lifetime value of a customer to the cost of hiring and replacing an employee, and your bottom line becomes affected. What can you do? Develop a real plan for problem resolution. Put the right people in place, make sure they are well trained to listen and offer apologies when appropriate, and give them the authority to offer solutions. These actions show customers that you have a trained staff ready to help them.

Some companies give employees the authority to make customers happy. With these guidelines, customer care representatives are empowered to make decisions on the spot—to give exchanges, credits, or refunds, or even to get a customer something else by having a "no-hassle" policy whereby customers can return products at any time for any reason.[3]

Delivering Comprehensive Service

Serving customers well is not a case of "us versus them," but rather a win–win situation. When common goals with your customer are established, you are both working toward something you agree is worthy. When you reach those goals, you are both satisfied. Moreover, if you don't reach them, the customer feels that at least you tried and gave an honest effort.

When a customer complains, you need to take corrective action as soon as possible. If the customer complains directly to you, avoid being defensive or judgmental. Do not attempt to explain why the problem occurred. The customer is not particularly interested in reasons for poor service or who is to blame. Customers want to know they are being heard and that their comments are valued. Most of all, they want the problem resolved. Remember, when a customer perceives that he or she is not being served well, that is the customer's reality.

> ### customer service **T I P**
> *If a word or a phrase isn't common knowledge, don't use it with a customer. Always speak distinctly, or you risk failing to connect with the customer.*

Delivery of Services

Often, customer service representatives have to deal with customers who perceive services they receive through a **filter,** or screen. Such a frame of reference can depend on one or more factors.

- How the customer feels that day
- Experiences the customer has had that day
- Experiences the customer has had in the past with the CSR or the company
- Experiences the customer's friends or family members have had with employees in the company
- The setting, environment, and circumstances of the current interaction

All things being equal, there is little difference between one organization's product over its competitor's. Customer service is the variable. One small action can make all the difference to a customer on a particular day. In the case of customer service, we can look at delivery of services similar to those in Figure 4.2. The concept of delivery of services can be represented by two circles—one within the other.

The inner circle is made up of the basic services and products an organization and its competition provide. Customers *expect* the services shown in the inner circle: convenient hours of operation, accurate and timely billing processes, adequate computer systems, convenient locations, and shipping services. In contrast, the outer circle allows a company to showcase its organization, to set itself apart from the competition by providing elements that *exceed* customers' expectations: customer follow-up, guaranteed appointment times, personal services, repeat customer incentives, and assistance taking products to the car.

Outer-circle service is extremely important. This is where you can separate yourself from the competition. Your inner circle may be perfect because you do everything

---

[3]Elaine Appleton Grant, "Top 10 Ways to Fail at Customer Service," *Momentum*, the Microsoft® newsletter (December 1, 2005).

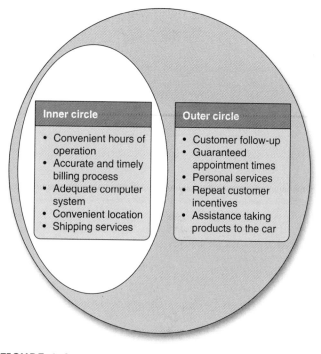

FIGURE 4.2 *When delivering services to customers, the inner and outer circles of service characterize an organization.*

the customer expects, but what you do might not be enough to guarantee that the customer will come back on a regular basis. Without strong outer-circle service, you may not be offering the customer anything *special enough* to set you apart from the competition.

Service, a critical business function, is driven primarily by the mindset, perspective, and abilities of the people who perform the activities. Granted, you can provide people with better tools, improved systems, enhanced delivery methods, improved facilities, and all the rest. But the bottom line is simple—good people get good results, better people get better results, and superior people get superior results. Only accomplished service providers can turn the correct phrase, make the proper decision, take ownership of problems, and go out of the way to do the right thing. And, in the final analysis, those are the things that determine long-term business success—or failure.[4]

CSRs and the Adversity Quotient®

Paul Stoltz, author of the book *Adversity Quotient @ Work*, states that companies should hire customer service representatives who have a high adversity quotient (AQ®). An **adversity quotient** is a precise, measurable, unconscious pattern of how people respond

to adversity. According to Stoltz, companies need to hire customer service representatives who are not only nice but also resilient and who have high AQs. Unless CSRs learn how to maintain control and be energized by tough problems, adversity will take its toll on them and negatively affect the services they provide to customers. The core elements of an adversity quotient, according to Stoltz, are control, ownership, reach, and endurance.

CONTROL CSRs who have a high AQ perceive that they have influence over adverse customer service situations. For example, if the company has a product recall, CSRs remain calm, project a positive attitude, and reassure customers that the problem will be remedied. On the other hand, low-AQ CSRs become stressed and overwhelmed by adversity.

OWNERSHIP CSRs with a high AQ hold themselves accountable for solving customers' problems. Conversely, low-AQ CSRs are likely to say, "It's not my fault."

REACH High-AQ CSRs refuse to allow negative situations to reach into other areas of their work lives. For instance, if a customer threatens to defect to a competitor, they focus on earning back the customer's loyalty, remaining upbeat no matter what. Conversely, low-AQ CSRs view the situation as hopeless and allow their feelings to have an impact on other aspects of their job.

ENDURANCE High-AQ CSRs can see beyond difficulties and retain their optimism. This gives them the endurance to hang on during adverse encounters with customers. In contrast, low-AQ CSRs reason, "Why try to endure this? It's only going to end in disaster!"[5]

Star CSRs have a number of skills and personal characteristics in common. In today's competitive marketplace, you need to do all you can to differentiate yourself in terms of providing excellent customer service. Assume the role of the CSR you want to become and answer each question in Figure 4.3 to determine how well you might stand out compared with other service providers.

Customer Service Rules and Guidelines

When you work for any organization, you must follow some rules and guidelines. To distinguish among these rules, we'll refer to them as red and blue rules. **Red rules** are very prescriptive, because they must be followed exactly as specified. An example of a red rule is a legal

[4]Bill Brooks, "It's All about People—All the Time," *Agency Sales* (September 2005): 35.

[5]"Forget the Smile Training—Consider Boot Camp!" *Managing Customer Service* (April 2001): 8.

remember this ...

Do You Stand Out from the Competition?

Yes	No	Question
☐	☐	1. Do you spend 60 to 70 percent of your time listening while a customer talks?
☐	☐	2. Do you smile more often than most other people?
☐	☐	3. Are you better than others at recognizing and responding to customer questions and problems?
☐	☐	4. Are you highly effective at identifying and prioritizing customer needs?
☐	☐	5. Do you tend to recommend additional products or services that meet a customer's specific needs?
☐	☐	6. Do you explain procedures in clear, concise terms?
☐	☐	7. Are you highly enthusiastic about attending customer service training seminars and classes?
☐	☐	8. Do you listen to motivational tapes and read inspirational books in your leisure time?
☐	☐	9. Do you regard yourself as generally upbeat and positive?
☐	☐	10. Do you enjoy the work you do?
——	——	Total

FIGURE 4.3   *Note:* If you answered "yes" to nine or ten questions, you already have many habits of highly successful CSRs. Eight is an average score. Seven or fewer indicates that you can improve your performance.

obligation to follow particular procedures exactly as outlined. Another red rule might involve safety issues federally mandated by the Occupational Safety and Health Administration (OSHA). Every employee in an organization must follow red rules.

Blue rules are optional and can be bent or modified based on the circumstances. Statements such as "We don't work after 5:00 p.m." and "Late fees cannot be waived" are examples of blue rules. They play into the old saying, "There is an exception to every (blue) rule."

Sometimes the most reasonable and prudent action is to bend the rule because it makes sense and is for the greater good of the situation and for the customer involved. In a customer-centric organization, you must clearly define both the red and blue rules, and give individual employees the discretion to change blue rules on a case-by-case basis. CSRs are empowered when working for customer-centric organizations to use their best judgment.

Building a Teamwork Approach to Customer Service

What do you think of when someone mentions the word *teamwork*? Sports teams most often come to mind, but

other situations involve teamwork as well. For example, consider the movie industry. Every time producers make a movie, they have to put together a new team that includes actors, sound and light crews, makeup artists, clothes designers, and directors, among others. All the members of the team are needed to create the finished product, a movie. In order to accomplish that goal with positive results, all the members must work together as a team.

Similarly, taking a team approach to customer service means working together as a group with common expectations and goals. Although companies focus thousands of dollars on external customer service in hopes of wooing and retaining customers, little attention is being paid to the effect poor internal customer service has on customer satisfaction. It all starts within the organization. Sooner or later the ripple effect reaches out to customers.

Internal customer service refers to service directed toward others within the organization. It refers to the level of responsiveness, quality, communication, teamwork, and morale. To help strengthen internal customer service orientation, CSRs should follow these basic rules.

- Employees should never complain within earshot of customers. It gives them the impression your company isn't well run, shaking their confidence in you.

focus on (**Best Practices**

FedEx Corp. is ranked among the best 100 companies to work for by *Fortune* magazine. The Memphis-based FedEx, which has been on the list for nine consecutive years, ranked 64th and was noted as one of the most diverse companies. In addition, FedEx was ranked No. 1 in job growth, based on number of new jobs.

Frederick W. Smith, chairman, president, and CEO of FedEx, said that the ranking was a testament to "our belief in the value of our employees. Every day, their passion allows us to deliver an exceptional experience for our customers." To determine the best places to work, *Fortune* and the Great Place to Work Institute conducted anonymous employee satisfaction surveys and analyzed the company's policies, culture, demographics, salaries, and benefits. With annual revenues of $31 billion, FedEx Corp. employs about 30,000 in Memphis and more than 230,000 around the United States and the globe.

Source: Memphis Business Journal (January 11, 2006).

Customers feel special when service providers work as a team.

Teamwork Communication

Communication is one of the most important elements of a successful team. For a team to be effective, its members must communicate with each other so everyone can stay informed. Whenever a team is put together, issues such as different personalities, management styles, and company hierarchies arise. Many times, exchanging honest, open feedback is more difficult with someone you work with than with your customers. This might be because the message you have to share with a fellow worker is not a positive one.

To maintain good working relationships, any negative feedback you offer a coworker should be focused on a specific task, not on his or her personality. Also, to be constructive, any criticism you offer should be accompanied by a positive suggestion on how to improve the task. By the same token, if a teammate is doing something well, be sure to mention it. Again, focus your comments on the task. An effective customer-centric environment fosters forthright feedback and values honesty.

- Employees should never complain to customers about another department's employees. Who wants to patronize a company whose people don't get along with each other?
- Employees at every level should strive to build bridges between departments. This can be done through cross training, joint picnics, off-site gatherings, or creative meetings, as well as day-to-day niceties.

What does teamwork show customers? A good team approach shows that the company is organized and that everyone is moving toward a common goal of satisfying the customer. Because of shared ownership, no team member will allow the failure of one member, because the entire team will fail. When team members are accountable to each other, customers know that the final objective of the team is their satisfaction.

Ethics / Choices

Your company encourages employees to work in teams. Brent is a fellow CSR you have worked with before. On numerous occasions, you have noticed that he has a poor attitude. To you, it appears that he is always angry and seems to put others down without realizing his words may be upsetting to others. Most of your coworkers simply ignore Brent and try to have as little to do with him as possible. What would be your approach with Brent?

Benefits of Teamwork

When customer service is built with organizational teamwork as its foundation, many benefits result. One of the most important benefits is that teamwork helps break down walls that can sometimes exist between departments within organizations. Teamwork can also provide new ideas and a new slant on customer problems. Finally, teamwork can create a more effective method for delegating work and any follow-up actions that must be taken.

Because no one is an expert on everything, people need to gather knowledge from others. People who work together tend to learn things faster and retain information longer than do individuals who work alone. Teamwork creates a **synergy,** which means that the combined effect of the efforts of many individuals is greater than the sum of their individual efforts. With synergy, problem solving becomes more effective, and better decisions tend to be made. Figure 4.4 provides some strategies that team members can adopt to provide exceptional customer service.

◐ remember this ...
Teamwork Strategies That Promote Customer Service

1. *Support your teammates with information.* Share what you know freely with your coworkers. Use huddles—brief, informal meetings—instead of formal meetings, when time is limited.

2. *Discuss new policies.* Discuss any new policies with your team and jointly create a way to explain changes to your customers in a positive way. Sometimes, using a script can ensure that everyone is consistently following the same plan.

3. *Identify areas for improvement.* Let the ideas flow without judgment in a brainstorming session. The craziest ideas sometimes turn out to be the ones that work best.

4. *Show pride in yourself and your coworkers.* Celebrate others' successes. Let the customer know you are proud of yourself, your coworkers, and your organization.

FIGURE 4.4

BUSINESS in action

FORRESTER RESEARCH

Forrester Research, an independent technology and market research company, has reported the 2006 Customer Advocacy Rankings in Financial Services. Based on a survey of nearly 5,000 consumers, the rankings rate 32 leading U.S. financial services firms according to the key driver of customer loyalty. Customer advocacy is the perception on the part of consumers that their financial services firm does what's best for its customers, not just for the firm's own bottom line.

For the third consecutive year, United Services Automobile Association (USAA) retained the top spot in Forrester's rankings, followed by credit unions, GEICO®, AAA, State Farm, and Vanguard. Rounding out the bottom of the 2006 list were Bank of America, Morgan Stanley, National City, Citibank, and JP Morgan Chase. The report concludes that firms with high customer-advocacy rankings are best positioned to grow in the coming years, as intense competition forces firms to focus on selling more to their existing customers rather than growing by merger and acquisition.

Source: www.forrester.com.

Concluding Message for CSRs

Companies sometimes make painful compromises by hiring people with less than stable work histories and less than acceptable customer service attitudes. Employers want service providers who make a commitment to getting to work on time and who are energetic, knowledgeable, kind, and efficient with customers.

Customer care representatives can provide service more consistently if four important guidelines are followed: View all customers positively; establish an emotional connection with customers by giving them your undivided attention; listen actively to all customer concerns; and take action to resolve any problems.

Summary

- The customer is the one who sets the standard for service excellence.
- When a customer complains, corrective action should be taken as soon as possible to prevent customer rage.
- The adversity quotient is the precise, measurable, unconscious pattern of how people respond to adversity.
- A good team approach shows that the company is organized and that everyone is moving toward the common goal of doing whatever it takes to satisfy the customer.

KEY TERMS

adversity quotient	blue rules	red rules
American Customer Satisfaction Index (ACSI)	customer rage	self-talk
	filter	synergy

CRITICAL THINKING

1. How would you describe the best customer-oriented attitude you've encountered relative to services you've received over the past month?

2. Name four ways that customer rage can be prevented or reduced.

3. Describe a business you've encountered in your city where you feel both its outer- and inner-level elements of customer service are excellent.

4. Do you agree that the way people handle adversity in their lives affects their service and work attitudes? Explain.

5. What are two benefits to a CSR of contributing to team efforts at work? Why do you think some service professionals prefer to work alone rather than in a team?

ONLINE RESEARCH ACTIVITIES

Project 4.1 Customer Rage

Assume you are doing a report on the risks of customer rage to the customer service person. Use the Internet to search for information on this topic. As a result of your search, list three items and their URLs you might include in your report.

_____

_____

_____

_____

_____

Project 4.2 The Adversity Quotient

In the lunchroom one day at On-Time Technology Products, someone left the book *Adversity Quotient @ Work* on one of the tables. Several CSRs picked it up and started talking about the usefulness of AQ when applying these concepts in the world of business. You said you felt it could apply to any aspect of our lives, including how we work, play, learn, and interact with others. Doug, on the other hand, said he felt that AQ applied only to the business world, and Ruth said that if educators could help students achieve higher AQs, then school environments would be less violent.

Use your favorite search engine to locate and read additional information about applying the adversity quotient in other venues. With a broader understanding of its multi-application, supply responses that provide information on ways that a high adversity quotient can positively influence each of the following life situations.

Life Situation	Benefit of Applying High AQs
1. In business, in general	
2. In call centers for CSRs	
3. In the home or family	
4. In schools (K–12)	

COMMUNICATION SKILLS AT WORK

Project 4.3 Action Plan for Improving Your Attitude

Supervisor Mary Graeff has asked each CSR at OTTP to develop an action plan to improve employees' attitudes when working with customers. Give some thought to each of the situations in column 1 and respond in column 2 with an activity that would work for you.

What Can You Do to...	
1. Convey interest in your customers?	
2. Keep your attitude positive?	
3. Remain energized and enthusiastic on the job?	
4. Learn more about the organization you work for?	
5. Take initiative when helping a customer?	

DECISION MAKING AT WORK

Project 4.4 How to Motivate the Unenthusiastic Teammate

During a weekly team meeting at On-Time Technology Products, you notice that one of your coworkers is quieter than usual. He acts as if he does not care to be involved in the team's brainstorming session.

Respond to each of the following statements with an example of what you might say to a team member who suffers from a lack of motivation.

1. Acknowledge your teammate's value.

    _____

    _____

2. Get to the source of the problem.

    _____

    _____

3. Stress the importance of team harmony.

    _____

    _____

CASE STUDIES

Project 4.5 "Deal with It!"

On the first day of a four-day holiday weekend, Samantha was having a problem with her phone and needed to use her neighbor Tim's phone. When she finished talking to the customer service representative at the phone company, she was quite shocked by the service she had received. She told Tim that the CSR said she would just "have to deal with the inconvenience until Tuesday morning." Samantha ranted and raved to Tim for 20 minutes. After answering the following two questions, discuss how the conversation should have gone.

1. Does Samantha have a legitimate reason to be upset with the phone company?

    _____

    _____

    _____

2. If this happened to you, what steps would you suggest to the phone company for improving its customer service?

_____

_____

_____

Project 4.6 "If There's a Rule, I'll Follow It"

Doug, a CSR for On-Time Technology Products, recently experienced a very frustrating brush with civil law concerning boundary lines between his property and a neighbor's. Everyone at work recognizes that as a consequence of this negative legal experience, Doug is a bit strict when it comes to following rules. However, the situation is beginning to affect his work, because his narrow-minded attitude is being reflected in how he treats customers.

1. In what ways do situations in someone's personal life spill over and affect attitudes on the job? Describe some examples you've observed or experienced.

_____

_____

_____

2. If you were Mary Graeff, Doug's supervisor, how would you explain to him the best way to interpret which rules he is required to follow to the letter and which ones allow him some flexibility?

_____

_____

_____

3. If Ms. Graeff were to ask you what steps you would take to help Doug overcome this attitude and get back on track with customers, what would you recommend that she do (simply talk to him, reprimand him, enroll him in training, . . .)?

_____

_____

_____

5 chapter

Resolving Customer Problems and Complaints

Objectives

1. Describe the activities involved in proactive problem solving.

2. List reasons that customers complain and describe the process for handling those complaints.

3. Discuss approaches to use when handling angry customers.

Pursue excellence in what you do and contain mistakes so the customers don't have to experience them.

—TOM REILLY, AUTHOR, *VALUE ADDED CUSTOMER SERVICE*

Everyone has tales of very bad service, often so bad the story becomes comical. Customer service seems so simple—treat customers with dignity and respect, and they will reward you by using your product. Handling a complaint becomes a moment of truth in maintaining and developing long-term customer relations. Customers indicate that getting a fair resolution during a product or service dispute is a reason for continuing to do business with a company. For example, L.L. Bean built an empire on the simple rule that "no customer should have a product that isn't completely satisfactory."

Customer service is a hard job. We expect service and support representatives to have diagnostic skills, zeroing in on problems from thousands of possibilities based on brief discussions. We ask them to make judgments about how and when to apply policies, and to handle each customer interaction with courtesy and efficiency. Data from the Service and Support Professionals Association (SSPA) tell us that 82 percent or more of the cost of delivering service and support is incurred when actually resolving customer issues and that the cost of handling a single incident is now more than $55.[1]

---

[1] Mark Angel, "Treating Service as a Business," *CRM Today*. http://www.crm2day.com.

Customer complaints can be viewed as opportunities, because dealing effectively with them can not only appease an unhappy customer but also build loyalty. In many cases, a business's most loyal customers are those who have had a bad experience made right. In the eyes of many customers, whether a company gets it right the first time is not what matters most, but how it reacts to and corrects its mistakes.

Solving Customer Problems

If you can't put your finger on a customer's problem, you can't solve it. Worse, you will waste time and lose credibility. Solving problems is one of the primary goals of any customer service professional. When we think of problem solving, however, we generally think of dealing with problems *after* they arise—a sort of crisis-management approach. This is the traditional view of problem solving; however, to exceed customers' expectations and provide exceptional service, successful companies try to anticipate and solve problems *before* they occur. This process is called **proactive problem solving.**

Proactive Problem Solving and Customer Self-Service

Proactive means taking the initiative by *acting* rather than *reacting* to events. When you solve customer problems proactively, you attempt to manage customer expectations and clarify incorrect assumptions the customer may have about the product or service. As you work with your customers, try to anticipate any problems that could arise. For example, at the time of the sale, educate and inform buyers about extra costs and possible delays.

Customer self-service (CSS) is a new proactive technological approach in customer service that empowers customers to go to a company's website and initiate most of the queries and functions that normally go through a call center. These might include finding information, viewing a bill, analyzing usage, comparing rate plans, ordering new products and services, or executing another type of account transaction. CSS does not limit other person-to-person service options, but it offers customers a convenient alternative.

Done correctly, customer self-service organizes appropriate data and integrates relevant systems so that all the resources and information are available through one easily navigated web interface. One of the most important items it contains is an accurate and well-written **knowledge base.** The knowledge base is created when a customer submits a question about a service issue. The question goes to a live CSR, who responds to it and adds it to the computerized knowledge base.

Access to quick responses and common questions makes the website a natural starting point for a customer's support needs. Customer self-service includes well-written FAQs (frequently asked questions), a robust and accurate knowledge base, and secure access to customer accounts so that they can manage their interactions. The requirements for effective customer self-service success include these:

1. *Access to billing and account data.* Interactive access to detailed account data is required to answer the most common questions and establish the self-service site as the first place to go for answers.

2. *Customer-driven functionality and design based on the most frequently asked questions.* The most successful customer self-service implementations provide easy-to-understand capabilities to address customers' most common service needs. For most service providers, these inquires are billing and account related.

An important benefit of self-service is freeing reps from answering basic questions so focus can be devoted to more difficult questions. When answering these difficult customer concerns online, CSRs must have good writing skills so they can answer customers' questions quickly and accurately. Sending clear and easily understood e-mail responses is different from addressing the same question over the phone. During a phone call, an agent can ask follow-up questions to get more information or determine how to resolve the problem. With e-mail, however, the customers' questions might be unclear, or customers may provide incomplete information. The agent has to read between the lines to know what the customer is asking in order to provide a solution to the problem. Here are some techniques for writing clearly understood service-related e-mails.

• *Restate the customer's question in the opening paragraph of the e-mail.* This technique helps the CSR focus on the customer's question and gather all necessary information. Seeing the question restated reassures the customer that the correct problem is being addressed.

- *Use headings to organize the e-mail.* Many customers send complex e-mail inquiries that include several questions or require several actions for resolution. Headings allow the CSR to highlight the response to each action the customer must take. In addition, headings make scanning easier so customers can find the answers they need.

- *Make the e-mail brief by linking to detailed information online.* When responding, provide links to detailed information online, such as frequently asked questions and knowledge-base items. This lets the CSR write a concise answer while providing access to the details that the customer may need.

- *Use consistent formatting to indicate procedures or instructions.* Make it easy for customers by offering easy step-by-step instructions. Use numbers to indicate ordered steps in a procedure; use bullets to highlight nonsequential points.

- *Write for easy reading and comprehension.* Write and format e-mails so that customers can understand them easily. This means writing short sentences and paragraphs, and using bullets instead of dense paragraphs.[2]

> **customer service T I P**
>
> *The best time to deal with a customer's criticism is while the complaint is happening.*

First-Call Resolution

Endless customer service e-mail loops and phone tag are frustrating for customers and costly for companies. The result is that dissatisfied customers take their business elsewhere. Calls to service reps that are completely resolved on that first call are referred to as **first-call resolutions (FCR)**. If the customer does not call back about the same problem for a certain period of time, the resolution is considered successful. Because nearly 80 percent of the time and cost of providing customer service is spent on service resolution, efforts toward FCR have a positive effect on the bottom line.

A 2004 study on first-call resolution by research firm Ascent Group revealed that more than 90 percent of companies measuring FCR performance reported from 2 to 23 percent improvement in that performance. Today, companies are recognizing that being able to deliver a high-quality customer experience and first-call resolution through enhanced agent productivity is of major strategic value to the organization.[3]

Beware of the Quiet Customer

Should you settle for the old axiom that "no news is good news"? Just because a company isn't hearing complaints doesn't mean the company has satisfied customers. Whereas some customers shout, many customers just leave quietly. Silent attrition is deadly because companies get no opportunity to remedy problems and retain customers.

Quiet customers are the ones who don't make a fuss about problems—they let their complaints build up to the point that they think it's easier to simply leave than to attempt to fix all that's wrong. Quiet customers usually fit into one of these five categories:

1. *The Satisfied Client.* This is what we'd like to assume we have when we don't get complaints—that service is fine and customers are happy. There may, however, be fewer people in this category than we think.

2. *The Accumulator.* These customers allow problems to mount up. Then something sets them off and they erupt, listing a string of wrongs that have been building up since their first purchase.

3. *The Thinker.* These customers are the ones who say to themselves, "They [the business] must know this already so I'm not going to say anything."

4. *The Runner.* These are the people who hate conflict and will do anything to avoid it. For them, it's easier to run away and find a new vendor than to tell you about a problem.

5. *The Busy Bee.* These customers use the excuse that pointing out a problem will take up too much of their time and energy. They tell themselves, "I'm too busy. I'll find the easiest way out."[4]

[2]Marilynne Rudick and Leslie O'Flahavan, "One-and-Done Customer Service E-Mail," *Contact Professional.* http://www.writingworkbook.com/pdf/one-and-done.pdf.

[3]Keith Dawson, "First-Call Resolution Is the New Service Level," *Call Center Magazine* (April 2005): 6.

[4]Andrea Obston, "Getting Customers to Complain," *Entrepreneur* (October 14, 2004).

Resolving Customer Complaints

Unhappy customers are bad news for any company. It only takes one unsatisfied person to shatter a perfectly good day at work for everyone and to steer many more prospective customers away from you. Unhappy customers have their reasons for being discontent. Some may not feel well, some have unrealistic expectations, and others may just have angry dispositions.

Customer complaints can be a real challenge. Because businesses are complex, it simply isn't possible to do everything right all the time. Many things can go wrong, and some issues, such as weather, are beyond a person's control.

One approach before offering to remedy a customer complaint is to ask the customer how he or she would prefer the problem be resolved. A customer may be agreeable to the simple solution of your replacing an item or redoing the work at no charge. If a customer will only accept a full or partial refund, it may be in your best interest to honor the request, even when it is not written in your guidelines to do so. Your willingness to do this might squash any bad word-of-mouth advertising that could affect future sales.

Unarticulated complaints manifest themselves in many negative ways: unpaid invoices, lack of courtesy to frontline service reps, and negative word-of-mouth. With the Internet, an unhappy customer can now reach thousands of would-be customers in a few keystrokes. Be proactive—head off bad press before it happens by making it easy for customers to complain, and then treat those complaints seriously. Establish firm guidelines regarding customer response times and stick to them.

According to the Customer Rage survey published in 2005, after having a product repaired or service issue fixed, the overwhelming majority of those surveyed don't want something free or other compensation. Instead, they want an explanation for why the problem occurred (69 percent), assurance that it won't happen again (69 percent), an apology (54 percent), or a chance to vent (54 percent).[5]

Why Customers Complain

Customers complain for a host of different reasons. Most often, however, the overriding reason is because the expectations they have when purchasing a product or service are not met. In the findings from a 2005 Accenture study of mobile phone users, the top 12 reasons that consumers changed providers were:

1. Poor service or product quality
2. Lower prices elsewhere
3. Service representative's lack of knowledge
4. Lack of customized solutions
5. Company policies that create bureaucracy
6. Technologies that delay or stop service
7. Desire for a one-call resolution or not being forwarded to multiple reps
8. The inability of reps to solve problems
9. Reps trying to sell other services or products
10. Inflexible service
11. Slow responses
12. CSR not being personable[6]

Technology, which has done so much to make nearly all aspects of business easier and more efficient, has created problems for customer service. A recent survey by the technology consultancy Gartner found that two-thirds of customers who try to get service online give up and use the phone instead. But those voice menus aren't much better. When you put a customer into a voice-response system, you've effectively passed control to the customer, who may end the call at any time. In another study conducted in 2004 by the market research firm Harris Interactive, 37 percent of people who reach an automated voice-response system press zero immediately in an effort to reach a live person.

Yet despite the risk of alienating customers, businesses have little choice but to automate. It all comes down to the bottom line: A call involving a live agent is at least

---

[5] Scott M. Broetzmann and Marc Grainer, *First Results of the 2005 National Customer Rage Study* (November 2, 2005): 25.

[6] "Talk About Service Advocates, Top 12 Reasons That Consumers Switch Providers" (February 18, 2006). http://edhorrell.com/advocates/resources.shtml.

five times as expensive on average as one handled by a voice-response system, according to Gartner.[7]

Disagreement versus Conflict

When dealing with customer complaints, distinguishing between disagreement and conflict is important. In general, disagreements occur between people who have different opinions about something. Disagreements don't necessarily have to be resolved. You can, for example, agree to debate for the fun of it or even agree to disagree.

A conflict with a customer, on the other hand, is more serious. It can jeopardize productivity, relationships at work, and dealings with customers. The basis of a **conflict** is, "If you get what you want, then I can't get what I want." Although most of us dislike being exposed to conflict situations, we must realize that good can sometimes be brought about by conflict. Conflict can

- produce changes for the better.
- result in gains and innovations.
- foster unity and understanding.
- bring about positive and meaningful changes in behavior.

Not all conflict, however, is good. If conflict escalates with customers, you may end up with accusations and threats, with parties getting angry and blaming each other. Two possible events resulting from conflict are

- General issues replace specific issues as the problem goes from a person being angry over a specific behavior to wanting to sever the relationship completely.
- Concern for self turns into retaliation, and the primary interest becomes hurting each other or getting even.

The Complaint-Handling Process

The foundation for maintaining customer goodwill in organizations is the existence, promotion, and practice of a sound **customer relations policy.** Any complaint-handling system is structured from this customer relations policy and must operate simply, effectively, and quickly to everyone's mutual benefit. A customer relations policy should encourage customers to communicate their concerns and demonstrate a strong commitment to customer satisfaction.

In addition, the policy should spell out how, when, where, and by whom complaints and questions are handled. One person within the company should have the ultimate authority and responsibility for customer relations, although *all* employees should know the guidelines as stated in the policy and how to implement them.

What should a company do to get customers to complain? The answer rests in making it easy for customers to give honest, regular feedback and then making sure they receive meaningful responses in return. Treat every complaint as the key to developing a better way of doing things, and allow customers to feel safe enough to complain in a timely manner. Respond to all customer complaints directly and in a professional and courteous manner.

In addition, give specific and realistic feedback about what the next steps will be in response to a customer's complaint. For example, will you research why the problem happened and how it can be resolved? Will you discuss it with your staff to prevent it from happening again? When will you get back to the customer? Will it be in writing, by phone, or by e-mail? Set a reasonable time frame for the resolution, and be sure to thank the customer sincerely for helping you improve the way you serve customers.

Customer complaints are never easy to hear. If a shift is made from being defensive to opportunistic, however, complaints can become advantageous. Thriving companies take basic steps to completely and systematically process customer complaints.

SCREEN AND LOG IN INFORMATION Start the procedure by screening the call, electronically logging in the date the complaint is received, and recording all pertinent customer information.

LISTEN A disgruntled customer wants to know that someone is willing to listen. Being quiet, paying attention, and listening carefully to what the customer is saying—without being distracted or sounding impatient—are important. Try not to interrupt, as doing so may cause the customer to argue, withdraw, or simply hang up or walk away. At an appropriate time during this initial contact, remember to thank the customer for bringing the problem to your attention.

EMPATHIZE After having the opportunity to express dissatisfaction, the customer wants to know that someone understands and cares about the situation. Listen and

---

[7]David H. Freedman, "What's Next: Service with a Smile. Really." *Inc. Magazine* (October 2005): 75.

respond with empathy to acknowledge the customer's feelings (upset, frustrated, disappointed). If possible, tell the customer how long it will take to satisfy the complaint, especially if a delay might occur.

SOLICIT FEEDBACK Try to get the customer to explain how the problem happened. By asking the customer for feedback on how the problem occurred, you convey concern and a willingness to understand the problem in order to arrive at the best solution. Another way to get feedback is to ask, "What do you think would be fair in this situation?" It will appeal to the customer's sense of justice and feeling of involvement in trying to resolve the problem.

APOLOGIZE The customer wants to hear that you are sorry about the problem or inconvenience, even if you are not necessarily the one to blame. You can apologize without accepting blame by saying, "This situation is unfortunate, and I apologize for it." A genuine apology is often the key to healing wounds. An immediate, sincere apology defuses hostility, no matter how grievous the injury. An apology is not only an expected social politeness but also a practical step that helps open the door to further communication and possible resolution of the complaint.

DELIVER BAD NEWS POSITIVELY There may come a time when you must tell a customer that you will not be able to take something back, that the item he or she ordered is out of stock, or that he or she must pay in advance. The following list offers some suggestions for delivering un-avoidable bad news to a customer:

1. Look for an alternative first.
2. Inform the customer as early in the process as possible. Even though this part of the job is unpleasant, do not put it off.
3. Inform the customer over the phone or in person, not by letter.
4. Get to the point quickly. You can warn the customer that bad news is coming in a kind way by saying something like, "You're not going to like hearing this, but...." This can sometimes soften the subsequent distress.
5. Treat the customer fairly. Customers remember your courtesy and professionalism long after the actual problem has been forgotten.

TAKE OWNERSHIP AND FORMULATE A SOLUTION If there is one thing that will frustrate a customer, it is **"ping-ponging,"** being passed from one employee or department to another. Ping-ponging occurs when you come into contact with a customer service rep that either isn't given the authority to resolve issues, isn't trained properly, or both. If the problem can be fixed on the spot, take care of it. If not, call your supervisor or transfer the customer to the appropriate person who can address the situation. Take ownership of the problem and make sure that it is handled appropriately and immediately. Any solution should conform to your established customer relations policy and take into account contractual and warranty obligations, customer expectations, your company's expectations, and your ability to deliver on your decision.

COMMUNICATE A SOLUTION When you respond, make sure your message is clear and appropriate. Try to avoid technical jargon. A respectful explanation of even an adverse decision can often preserve customer goodwill.

FOLLOW UP Following any action that has been taken, contact the customer to ensure that the matter has been resolved satisfactorily. Ask for a second chance by saying, "We hope we'll have a chance to serve you again."

In a published article, Bernice Johnston, author of **Real World Customer Service,** offers suggestions to customer service professionals on what to say when customers complain. Figure 5.1 provides real-world examples submitted by service representatives to Ms. Johnston and the responses she recommends they give.

Sometimes tough calls become more manageable when the customer service representative uses a **script.** Two advantages of using scripts are that they help CSRs deliver consistent responses to common customer problems and they assist CSRs in developing their own problem-solving responses. Often, when the right combination of words is coupled with sensitivity to the customer's position, the result is notable in its impact. When a script is not used well, a customer can often tell that a CSR is reading from it, and this can be annoying. The response not only sounds programmed, but the customer feels like the CSR doesn't care about his or her particular circumstances.

When implemented well, appropriate scripts include four key elements:

1. *Empathy.* CSRs should begin their responses by focusing on feelings. This means understanding the situation and feelings from the customer's point of view.

◉ remember this ...

What to Say When Customers Complain

Problem	What to Say	Why This Works
• Your customer is very upset because a company error has resulted in additional charges to her account.	"I can understand how upset you are that these additional charges have shown up because of our error. I'd be upset about it too. Here's what I can do about it...."	When a customer is upset, acknowledge and restate her concern. This shows you have been listening, you understand, and you are personally interested in getting the problem resolved.
• The customer seems unsatisfied after you have told him the options to resolving his problem.	"I understand that you are disappointed, and you have every right to be. I'm disappointed too that we cannot resolve this. What do you suggest we do next?"	When you have suggested everything you can think of, ask the customer what the ideal solution would be from his point of view. He might say, "All I really want is an apology." That you can do.
• Although you have worked very hard to resolve your customer's complaint, she accuses you of sounding hostile by saying, "You are really being testy today, aren't you?"	"I'm sorry that you have this impression of me. What can I do to change your perception?"	Demonstrating a sincere interest in learning what has upset the customer can give you the information you need to turn her attitude around.

FIGURE 5.1 Source: B. Johnston, "Tough Customer Complaints Require Quick, Focused Responses," *Dartnell's Customers First*, 4 (2000, June 12).

2. *Acknowledgment.* This involves recognizing the validity of the customer's complaint, a key step in the process of reaching a solution to any problem.

3. *Reassurance.* At this point, CSRs need to restore the customer's confidence in the company.

4. *Action.* Empathizing, acknowledging, and reassuring are not enough. Action is what counts.

Figure 5.2 provides an example of a script that demonstrates the four elements in action.

◉ remember this ...

A Sample Customer Service Script

1. "Heather, you sound pretty upset with the information I've just told you." *(empathy)*

2. "Before we dismiss your request for...." *(acknowledgment)*

3. "Let me make sure there's not something I'm unaware of that has changed." *(reassurance)*

4. "I would like to have Mr. Snyder in on this conversation to listen to his ideas about alternatives. I'd be interested in hearing them myself. Is that okay with you?" *(action)*

FIGURE 5.2

People who are really good at solving problems go about it systematically. They have a way of placing the problem in context. They don't jump to conclusions. They evaluate alternatives. A good way to become a systematic problem solver is to adopt the following five-step **problem-solving process:**

1. *Identify the problem.* This is critical: You must try to solve the right problem. Identify the problem by asking the right questions and observing the situation, if possible. What is leading the customer to feel there is a problem? Is it something specific or is it an intuitive sense on the customer's part that things aren't as they should be? Can the customer define the problem?

2. *Analyze the problem.* How often does the problem occur? How severe is it? What might be the causes of the problem? How long has it been going on? Has it gotten worse?

3. *Identify decision criteria.* How will you and the customer make decisions when the time comes? How will you weigh the criteria?

4. *Develop multiple solutions.* Don't stop at the first solution you identify. It may be good, but a much better solution might exist. Evaluate alternative scenarios and as objectively as possible assess the pros and cons of each one.

5. *Choose the optimal solution.* Develop a base of support that will ensure you can implement the solution. Prepare for contingencies.

When problems are solved systematically, you save time, achieve better solutions, and increase your credibility with the customer and the value of what you've done.

Dealing with Unruly Customers

Occasionally, every business will encounter an unruly customer. No matter how carefully you explain your position, this customer will misunderstand and take great offense. Although these situations are never pleasant, understanding a customer's emotions and identifying what actions and words trigger extreme anger can help a service provider work better under these adverse conditions.

E-commerce automatically creates a distance between the customer and the CSR because it eliminates the opportunity for an interpersonal, face-to-face exchange. Dealing with a customer on the phone or online denies you the ability to read nonverbal signals when a customer is upset, because you can't see them. It is a big challenge for CSRs to determine customer emotions when they are not standing face to face.

Why Customers Get Angry

Dale Carnegie said, "The only way to get the best of an argument is to avoid it." Although customers become dissatisfied, they generally have one thing in common: The perceived value of a product or service is less than the customer expected. Here are four shortcomings that can cause a customer to view your product or service negatively:

1. *The customer didn't get what was promised or what was expected.* To overcome this, you must raise the quality of the product or, in some cases, work to make the customer's expectations more realistic.

2. *Someone was rude to the customer.* Whether the employee realized it or not, this was the customer's perception. Remember that a perception is the customer's reality.

3. *Someone was indifferent to the customer.* An employee projected a "can't-do" attitude and left it at that—with the customer feeling frustrated.

4. *No one listened to the customer.* Of all four reasons, this is the most troubling. Failing to listen to a customer is a tragic waste of an opportunity for feedback. This feedback is important in helping improve processes, products, and services.

Although customers' anger or emotions may not be directed at you personally, you are the one who receives them. To help defuse anger, CSRs must understand *why* customers get emotional, upset, and angry. Although the following five reasons do not constitute a complete list, they are among the most important reasons that angry customers behave the way they do:

1. They have had prior bad experiences.
2. They felt as if they would get the runaround.
3. They resented potential loss of money.
4. They disliked being inconvenienced and having wasted more of their time.
5. They felt a loss of control.

Customer Emotions

When customers are dissatisfied, they can become difficult, frustrated, and quick to anger. What CSRs must realize is that an angry customer might not respond to logic. In fact, the more logical you are, the angrier the customer may become. At such times, no matter what you say or how you phrase it, you simply will not be able to penetrate the customer's emotional barrier. Before you can work on the customer's problem, you must be able to deal with the customer's emotions.

Customers have certain expectations in mind. When those expectations are not met, the customer feels betrayed. This can make the encounter emotional. To regain the customer's confidence, you need to communicate in a way that renews his or her faith in the relationship. Such communication usually begins with a genuine apology.

Make sure you listen to *more* than what is being said, because when people are upset, they don't always convey what they mean. Ask questions to gather more information, and use softening techniques. **Softening techniques** include, for example, an open posture (no crossed arms), kindhearted eye contact (no rolling of eyes), and perhaps moving the customer to a quieter area to sit down and talk.

The first step in calming an angry person is to stay calm yourself. Try to keep your voice relaxed. If you hear

focus on   Best Practices

A group of area residents took a local grocer on and now say the supermarket's new corporate owner has been receptive to their complaints. "They've been listening," said Dorothy Parker, who organized the informal group. What began as a casual conversation about spoiled produce among Parker and other women at her health club has grown into an alliance of people aiming to improve a supermarket they say lost its quality when it came under the ownership of a larger corporation.

The group met twice with grocery officials and held a series of monthly focus group meetings with the store's new director. Among the complaints of Parker and others: Products were stocked too high on the shelves; the store wasn't always clean; some of the produce was rotten; employees were treating customers as an imposition; and aisles were cluttered and difficult to navigate. Corporate officials felt the opportunity was perfect for meeting with the group and learning how to provide the best shopping experience possible.

The result? The store hired a more experienced produce manager and instilled a manager-on-duty policy. In addition, customer service training was provided for all employees, as well as retraining on stocking store shelves and working in the checkout lanes. So far the group is satisfied with the efforts. The produce is fresher, the store is cleaner, and the staff is friendlier.

Source: Milwaukee Journal Sentinel (March 9, 2006).

remember this ...
Trigger and Calming Phrases

Avoid Trigger Phrases	Use Calming Phrases
"It's our policy."	"Here's what we can do.... Here's how we can handle this...." (Quote the policy, don't call it "policy.")
"I can't; we don't."	"I can; we do."
"What seems to be the problem?"	"How can I help?"
"I don't know."	"I can find out."
"You should have...."	"Let's do this." (Move to the future, not the past.)
"Why didn't you...."	"I can see why...."
"The only thing we can do...."	"The best option, I think, is...."
"I don't handle that; it's not my job."	"Let's find the right person to handle your concern."

FIGURE 5.3

Selecting the Right Approach

A customer who feels betrayed will be looking for some gesture of atonement or compensation. This is called **service recovery.** To be effective, service recovery should be specific to the situation so it doesn't appear like you're doing something just to get rid of an angry customer. Typically, when a service failure occurs, a customer can be compensated for the inconvenience in the form of any combination of cash refunds, credits, discounts, or apologies.

customer service T I P

When working with customers, always focus on determining "how can we?" and not on "why we can't."

your voice sounding rushed or panicked, take a few deep breaths to help you regain your composure. If you notice your jaw clenching, relax your facial muscles. Once *your* emotions are under control, turn your attention to calming the customer. Use calming phrases to describe what you can do for the customer to help solve the problem. Examples of trigger and calming phrases are listed in Figure 5.3.

If a customer is verbally abusive, go into an office or another enclosure that offers privacy, where the customer can vent without disturbing others. Once the customer is calm, then decide what can be done about the problem. Keep in mind that in a confrontational interchange, it doesn't hurt to agree a little. When you ease a complainant by saying, "I understand" or "What can I do to help?" you

In customer service, CSRs cannot avoid dealing with angry people but should always do so with empathy and tact.

are not necessarily agreeing with the customer's position, only with his or her right to be angry.

The behaviors of angry customers manifest in various ways. The following are some behaviors you can expect to see when an angry person lashes out. When customers are angry, they

- blame others.
- are loud and demanding.
- try to make you angry too.
- have little regard for the rights of others.
- take charge of the conversation by insisting they be heard.
- tend to interrupt the other person who is talking.
- refuse to do what you ask.
- threaten to go to your manager or supervisor.

Even the most experienced CSR has dealt with a customer who would only be satisfied by talking to a supervisor. When this occurs, first collect all the information relevant to the problem at hand and present it to the manager. He or she will then have some prior knowledge of the situation and will be able to handle the customer more effectively.

customer service T I P

Customer complaints are like medicine. Nobody likes them, but they can make us better.

Dealing with demanding customers gets even tougher for CSRs when managers try to treat all customer complaints *equally*. Some complaints are justified, but some simply are not. If, for example, CSRs are reprimanded for

unjustified complaints by customers who are truly being unreasonable, the CSRs may start to become resentful because they did nothing wrong.

One solution that companies use is to provide CSRs a forum to vent their frustrations. This solution is easy to set up. Each week a meeting is scheduled at which service employees can choose to talk openly about their most difficult customer interaction that week. The advantages are many. First, it shows support for and understanding of the stress level of CSRs. Second, it provides a forum for new and seasoned CSRs to learn from each other alternative ways to deal with specific or routine customer problems.

BUSINESS in action

SOUTHWEST AIRLINES

According to Colleen Barrett, president and corporate secretary for Southwest Airlines, the number one complaint over the last 35 years, across the Dallas-based carrier's system, is that there is no assigned seating. In an effort to analyze the widespread customer criticism, Southwest experimented in San Diego with a six-week test of assigning seats to passengers on their flights. The airline was trying to see whether assigned seating might speed up the boarding process and make it less chaotic. In addition, the practice of no assigned seating had given Southwest a "cattle car" image to some in the industry, and Southwest wanted to determine whether a change might be in order.

The results of the assigned seating test drew piles of mail that surprised the airline and Ms. Barrett. Passengers wrote her to say they absolutely did not want the low-fare carrier to change its unconventional practice of open seating. Southwest CEO Gary Kelly says the airline is still in the data-gathering stage and that whether the airline will be changing its seating practices is unclear. Their goal is to improve customer service *and* airline efficiency.

Source: http://dallas.bizjournals.com.

Another strategy that is popular in organizations is to give a short, unscheduled break to the employee who has just handled a particularly tough customer. The employee may need a brief time out to recoup prior to returning to other customers.

Concluding Message for CSRs

The job of a CSR is not designed to be adversarial with the customer. In fact, quite the opposite is true. When you look for common ground, you will find solutions that work for all parties involved.

Every business occasionally performs below customer expectations. Organizations can still be perceived as reputable if they stand behind their guarantees and promises and handle criticism diplomatically. Managing complaints in an exemplary fashion is an integral part of delivering superb customer service.

When customers conduct business with companies, they expect two outcomes: (1) a personal interaction with someone who is courteous and has decision-making authority and (2) products and services that are reliable and readily available. By focusing on these two goals, resolving customer problems becomes easier and complaints can be minimized.

Summary

- Proactive problem solving means anticipating and solving problems before they occur.
- A systematic problem solver uses a five-step method to effectively handle customer complaints. Those steps are to identify the problem, analyze the problem, identify the decision criteria, develop multiple solutions, and choose the optimal solution.
- Understanding and recognizing customer emotions as well as handling their complaints fairly can help bring the conflict to a satisfactory resolution for both sides.

KEY TERMS

conflict

customer relations policy

customer self-service (CSS)

first-call resolutions (FCR)

knowledge base

ping-ponging

proactive problem solving

problem-solving process

script

service recovery

softening techniques

CRITICAL THINKING

1. In what ways is it more productive for CSRs to use proactive problem solving when dealing with customers?

2. Given the list of 12 reasons that customers change providers, prioritize and explain the top three, according to your experiences.

3. In your opinion, are the steps necessary to resolve a customer complaint applicable to nearly all incidents? Explain.

4. What approach would you use to handle a customer who is very angry and verbally attacks you personally?

5. Think of a time when you observed an angry customer at a grocery store, retail outlet, or bank. Describe the behaviors of the person you observed. How, in your opinion, could this anger have been avoided? How, once it occurred, should it have been handed by a service professional?

ONLINE RESEARCH ACTIVITIES

Project 5.1 First-Call Resolution

Assume you are doing a report on the effects of first-call resolution on business profits. As a result of your search on the Internet, list three current items you might use in your report. Include the URLs where you found the information.

Project 5.2 **Product Return Policy**

In tracking customer complaints over the past year, President Collin MacGibson has decided to review the 10-year-old product return policy at On-Time Technology Products. As a result, he needs to know what the return policies of other technology companies are in order to use them as a guideline in developing a new one.

Use your favorite search engine to find various technology product websites (for example, IBM, Dell, Apple), and locate three examples of product return policies. Record your findings for Mr. MacGibson in the table below.

Company	Strengths of Product Return Policy (One or Two Sentences)
1.	
2.	
3.	

COMMUNICATION SKILLS AT WORK

Project 5.3 **Handling Emotions**

Form a group of 3–4 people and pool your ideas to respond to the following three customer situations. Describe how your group might handle each situation and why the approach you suggest for each is the right one to take. Role-play each situation in a more customer-oriented manner.

1. A customer throws a product on the counter and says, "I want my money back now!"

    _____

    _____

    _____

    _____

2. A customer attacks your personal integrity and you can feel your anger ready to erupt.

    _____

    _____

    _____

    _____

3.   A customer says, "I'll never do business with you again!"

_____

_____

_____

_____

DECISION MAKING AT WORK

Project 5.4 "Take Whatever the Customer Doles Out"

Cliff, a fellow CSR, is noticeably upset at work this morning. Yesterday, work was incredibly difficult for him because it seemed he had to deal with *the worst of the worst* customer complaints. Today, Cliff has confided in you that, after talking with his wife last night, he is thinking about quitting. According to Cliff, he doesn't think "employees should be expected to take whatever the customer doles out." You are aware that Cliff has other things going on in his life—most notably, his aging mother, who has the beginning stages of Alzheimer's disease and has recently moved in with Cliff, his wife, and their two teenage children.

1.   If you were having a private conversation with Cliff, what would you say to support his decision?

_____

_____

_____

_____

2.   What would you say to try and keep him from quitting?

_____

_____

_____

_____

3.   What do you think is really behind Cliff's wanting to quit his job at this point in time?

_____

_____

_____

_____

CASE STUDIES

Project 5.5 Relocating the Office

During a recent office relocation, the facilities manager of a local community college consulted with a technical expert on a variety of tools to help communicate among three remote campuses.

The tools that the consultant recommended were exactly what were needed, and several of those items were purchased. A few weeks later, the college received a bill from the technical company for time spent consulting on the tools that were purchased. To the community college's buyer, this seemed unfair because the company had already received a commission on the items purchased.

Form groups of four people each and assume your group is the advisory committee to the facilities manager. With your collective ideas, how might you respond to the following questions?

1. Is there a problem in this scenario? If so, what caused it?

_____

_____

_____

_____

2. What steps would you recommend the technical company follow to resolve the conflict and preserve the customer relationship?

_____

_____

_____

_____

Project 5.6 CSR Forums—Reacting to Customer Complaints

On-Time Technology Products has recently instituted a roundtable discussion for CSRs every other Friday at noon, for which lunch is provided. The purpose is to allow CSRs to vent and share information about customer issues that might be helpful to one another when reacting to typical customer complaints. Today, you are discussing six CSR reactions.

Using the table on the following page, rank the severity of the reactions (1 = worst; 5 = best) in column 2, and describe a more positive approach in column 3. Finally, create an appropriate scenario for each situation and role-play the better approach.

Action Taken	Rank in Severity	A More Positive Approach
Apathy: CSR's attitude of indifference		
Passing the buck: giving the customer the runaround		
Being talked down to: treating customers as if they don't understand basic information		
The brush-off: trying to get rid of or ignoring a customer because the CSR has other things to do		
Rudeness: treating customers in a disrespectful manner		
Unresponsiveness: not following up on a commitment		

Recovering From and Winning Back the Angry Customer

Objectives

1. Describe five types of customers who defect and why they do so.

2. Describe the various types of feedback survey instruments.

3. Identify ways to recover from an angry customer.

4. Identify the key points of a win-back message.

If you are patient in one moment of anger, you will escape a hundred days of sorrow.

—CHINESE PROVERB

Everyone makes mistakes. Processes and procedures fail from time to time. Customers don't expect companies to be perfect, but they do expect companies to care. Companies that care are customer-oriented and make handling customer complaints a priority. Further, they care immensely why customers leave.

Understanding Why Customers Leave

In the book *Customer Winback: How to Recapture Lost Customers—And Keep Them Loyal*, authors Jill Griffin and Michael Lowenstein sort customers who defect into five categories:

1. *Unintentionally pushed-away:* customers whom you want to keep, but who leave because the company's performance, products, or services do not meet their expectations.

2. *Intentionally pushed-away:* customers who are poor credit risks or for whom the service costs are greater than the profits they create for the company.

3. *Pulled-away:* customers who find a competitor who offers a better value or who provides more personable and reliable service. The new provider may be more expensive

remember this ...

Indications That a Customer Is Defecting

Indication	Approach Recommended
1. The squeaky wheel	Companies should track complaints all the way through and make sure that customers emerge from the process happier than when they entered. A customer complaint is a "customer defection alert."
2. The product return	Finding out the reason for returning any product is critical. Is it because the product is defective, the customer doesn't like the product, or it just wasn't the right size? A string of defective product returns is serious and should be considered a red alert.
3. The quiet customer	Beware of the customers who don't complain, because the risk is that they will just leave and never air their grievances. Chances are, however, they will discuss them with family or friends, other would-be customers.
4. A slow pay	There may be negative issues with your products or services that cause customers to put a company at the bottom of their bill pay list. Find out what those issues are.
5. Falling revenue and reduced sales volume	When customer spending decreases, it's an opportune time to talk to customers. It could be that they've either made lifestyle changes or found an alternative product or service.

FIGURE 6.1

and less convenient, but the pulled-away customer's perception is that the overall value is stronger.

4. *Bought-away:* customers for whom price is all that matters. Many competitors make low-ball, introductory pricing offers to get these customers to shop with them. These customers are open to shopping around and typically do not feel a sense of loyalty to any one company.

5. *Moved-away:* customers whose needs change due to age, a life-cycle event, or job relocation. With the help of the Internet, many consumers can still find the products they prefer online, regardless of the distance to a storefront.[1]

The unintentionally pushed-away customers are the most critical to understand. The need for earning back a customer's business and recovering a lost customer has more often than not been attributed to this situation. Unintentionally pushed-away customers no longer buy from a service or product provider for four main reasons:

1. *Unhappiness with product delivery, installation, service, or price.* One incident is unlikely to lose a customer, but several incidents of poor service, late delivery, or inaccurate shipment may cause a customer to look elsewhere.

2. *Improper handling of a complaint.* Customers who feel a complaint hasn't been taken seriously or are displeased with a resolution may search out another competitive product or service.

3. *Disapproval of unanticipated changes.* Whenever companies make changes in the ordering process, price structure, product availability, or sales staff, there is always a risk of offending customers if they were not alerted to these actions in advance.

4. *Feelings of being taken for granted.* New orders and even orders from established customers should not be taken for granted. Every customer should be resold on the quality of the business, product, or service in every transaction and thanked for their business each time a purchase is made.

Today's customers interact with a company using multiple channels and, when they get the same consistent service whether visiting a store, logging onto a website, or calling a service center, often exhibit deeper loyalty than single-channel customers. To gain this loyalty, a firm must internally coordinate sales and service across multiple channels so that customer preferences are accessible no matter how the customer chooses to interact.

Although customers defect for a number of reasons, Figure 6.1 describes five of the most obvious signs that indicate customers may be thinking about shopping elsewhere.

---

[1] Jill Griffin and Michael W. Lowenstein, *Customer Winback: How to Recapture Lost Customers—And Keep Them Loyal* (San Francisco, CA: Jossey-Bass, 2001).

Getting Feedback from Customers

From cost control and customer retention to employee productivity and competitive intelligence, every business has its own unique set of objectives. But one thing remains consistent: gaining insight into a customer's needs and expectations is paramount to reaching those objectives. With customer acquisition costs high and getting higher, customer defection is a burden to a company's bottom line.

Many companies believe that, after years of working closely with customers, they know what their customers want. Not until some of these companies face a customer service obstacle do they think about spending the necessary money to solicit customer feedback. This is a tragic "too little, too late" approach to customer service.

The most important reason for developing quality standards in many industries is a desire for consistency. Customer feedback—formal and informal—is one of the major forces in developing quality standards that helps prevent customer defection. The resulting data from surveys should serve as a compass to guide the development of products and customization of service offerings to meet identified customer needs.

One type of survey strategy employed by savvy companies is an internal survey. Internal surveys are conducted as a way of "walking in the customer's shoes." Managers and staff complete the same questionnaire as the clientele and answer the questions the way they predict customers will answer them. Customers are asked how they would rate the company's performance rather than how satisfied they are with the company. They then measure the gaps and share the results with managers and staff.

Feedback Tools

Companies solicit customer opinions through a variety of ways—web-based surveys, mailed surveys, telephone interviews, comment cards, focus groups, and feedback forms enclosed with finished jobs. The obvious goal of most customer feedback is to evaluate how happy customers are with service, product quality, delivery, and overall experience.

Customer satisfaction is defined as the state of mind that customers have about a company and its products or services when their expectations have been met or exceeded. Most of the time customer satisfaction leads

focus on Best Practices

When the California Chamber of Commerce was logging from 300 to 900 calls each day from people looking for answers on topics ranging from customer service to tourism, they knew they had an escalating problem. The staff was adequately managing the call load, but the process lacked efficiency for both callers and staff. One of the biggest bottlenecks was that the Chamber had no means in place to effectively track questions (many were similar in nature) and route issues to the various departments.

After considering their options, the Chamber decided to establish an answer center on its website. The answer center's purpose was to address frequently asked questions and provide an e-mail link for customers who need assistance beyond the FAQs. Callers were directed to the online answer center by the Chamber's after-hours and on-hold phone system messages.

The result was that messages on the after-hours phone system dropped by 50 percent. In addition, an incident summary is now run once a week, reporting the most common FAQs and giving the Chamber an insight to the information that is most important to its callers.

to customer loyalty and product repurchase. Satisfaction measurement questions typically include items like these:

1. Overall, how satisfied are you with (brand name)?
2. Would you recommend (brand name)?
3. Do you intend to repurchase (brand name)?

People who create survey instruments struggle with the issue of how to measure service quality. Perhaps the most widely used set of measurements is based on five dimensions that are most important regardless of the service industry. These dimensions are

1. Tangibles: the appearance of physical facilities, equipment, personnel, and communication materials.

2. Reliability: the ability to perform the promised service dependably and accurately.

3. Responsiveness: the willingness to help customers and provide prompt service.

4. Assurance: the knowledge and courtesy of employees and their ability to convey trust and confidence.

5. Empathy: the caring, individualized attention the firm provides its customers.

customer service TIP

Surveys should not be designed to tell you what you want to hear but rather what you need to hear.

The benefits of developing a meaningful survey and using an "ask the customer" approach are to

- *Identify unhappy customers before they leave.* The information gathered could signal customer relationships that are in jeopardy. This is important because, unfortunately, most dissatisfied clients walk away and never tell companies why.

- *Pinpoint the products and services that customers actually want and need.* Surveying customers is a great way to identify new business opportunities and to assess what customers *think* you offer. In other words, customers may not be fully aware of all the products and services you offer.

- *Solidify customer relationships.* The act of asking customers their opinions shows that they matter. For example, customers may love your product but be annoyed by such minor incidents as how long they are placed on hold on the phone, how they are treated by the receptionist, or how a finished product is packaged. Companies may not be aware of these issues, but once brought to the surface, they can be addressed and possibly corrected.

When developing customer-satisfaction feedback tools, consider measuring the right issues from the numerous customer-satisfaction attributes listed in Figure 6.2. Remember to refrain from using the word *survey*. Few people want to participate in a survey; however, many are willing to give *feedback*.

remember this ...
Measuring Customer Satisfaction

- Ability to meet deadlines and on-time delivery
- Accurate invoice amounts
- Clear and helpful invoices
- Clear and helpful quotes, estimates, and proposals
- Communication of changes in delivery or back-order situations
- Enthusiasm about a customer's business
- Follow-through on commitments
- Overall value and range of products and services
- Presence of competent people and helpful customer service representatives
- Price
- Problem-resolution approach
- Prompt problem solving
- Prompt shipments
- Quality of product or service
- Readily accessible people and information
- Shipments that match orders and specifications
- Understanding of the customer's needs

FIGURE 6.2

Feedback Sources

There should be few activities as important as finding out what your customers want for products and services and what they think of your current offerings. Fortunately, businesses can use a variety of practical and available resources to get customer feedback.

- *Employees.* An organization's frontline employees are usually the people who interact the most with customers. On a regular basis, ask employees and customer service representatives about products and services that customers are asking for and what issues they complain about the most.

- *Comment cards.* One of the best ways to find out what customers want is to ask them. Provide brief comment cards on which customers can answer simple questions such as "Were you satisfied with our services?" and "Are there any services you would like to see that don't exist?"

- *Competition.* Ask people who shop at your competitors the simple question, "What is the competition offering that we could offer to serve your needs better?"

- *Documentation and records.* Using inventory records and sales receipts, companies can take note of what customers are buying and not buying. If the data are captured on a computer spreadsheet or database file, they can be charted and studied to determine buying trends.

- *Mail surveys.* Many people are willing to fill out and return feedback forms, especially if they get something of value in return. For example, offer survey respondents a coupon if they mail the completed form back by a certain date.

- *Telephone surveys.* Hire summer students or part-time workers for a few days every six months or so to conduct random telephone surveys.

Ethics / Choices

What would you say to a colleague who wanted to put up in your department a cartoon customers could see that says, "The complaint department is in the basement"?

Customers can help businesses improve their service by providing feedback.

The Mystery Shopper

Although many companies spend significant amounts of money on training their employees, few businesses reinforce the training with a monitoring program. One way that companies can improve the level of customer service is through mystery-shopping programs. A **mystery shopper** is a third-party person who anonymously and objectively evaluates a business for the purpose of analyzing customer service, product quality, store presentation, and other elements of the customer experience. Known as "undercover customers," these shoppers visit every type of business from restaurants to retail stores, movie theatres, hair salons, banks, and hotels.

Companies use mystery-shopping services for an assortment of reasons. Some managers believe it is a way to resolve potential problem situations *before* they reach higher-level executives. Other companies establish corporate monitoring programs to observe routine operations that ensure consistency. In still other instances, absentee owners monitor the actions of staff members who play an integral part in the success or failure of the business.

These evaluators follow specific instructions during their visits, complete written reports after leaving the store, and work with management to identify the strengths and weaknesses of the business. Usually, the mystery shopper prepares a final onsite visit report that outlines his or her shopping experience.

Mystery shoppers are the eyes and ears of the business owner. They perform a variety of activities such as unannounced visits, random phone calls to a business, and evaluations of websites and e-mail responses. They may be asked to verify that cashiers are properly handling cash or that salespersons are knowledgeable about the merchandise they sell. Mystery shoppers are commonly asked to shop a client's competitor so the client can compare its operation to others'.

The use of mystery shoppers provides managers and employees with an unbiased evaluation of their operation's quality, service, cleanliness, and value. The general goal of using a mystery shopper is to help in improving productivity, efficiency, and profitability for the company. Specifically, however, smart businesses use the information to reward good employees, identify training deficiencies, and make store improvements.

Which person is the mystery shopper?

Interpreting Customer Feedback

When customers stop buying from a business, it is important to ask why. Certain responses to this question can help you deal effectively with these issues:

- The quality of merchandise
- The quality of service
- An employee's lack of courtesy
- A mishandled complaint
- An invoice or billing problem

These concerns are problematic and compel companies to take action immediately. Further, when customers expand their responses by saying that they informed the company about the problem *before* they stopped purchasing, immediate action is even more important.

Following are four additional issues companies must be aware of prior to interpreting and acting on customer feedback:

1. *Use thorough data-gathering and analysis techniques before acting on complaints.* Often, a company will make a change based on feedback from only one or two customers. That type of limited feedback is called anecdotal information and does not necessarily constitute a trend.
2. *Do not spend lots of time, energy, and money gathering complaint data and then do nothing with it.* This is perhaps the biggest error organizations can make when handling customer feedback.
3. *Don't take feedback results personally.* The fact is, surveys *invite* customers to criticize. Customers who complain the most and the loudest are really your best customers.

4. *Inform customers about the impact their feedback has had on the way issues will be addressed.* When companies that gather customer data research fail to provide this feedback, they lose credibility with clients. Clients who provide feedback appreciate the same in return.

Many service-oriented businesses use customer feedback in a different way. In these companies, the object is to uncover everything that is going right. Managers are always on the lookout for "hero stories"—examples of employees going the extra mile to deliver delight and *wow* experiences. Such feedback becomes the basis for ongoing recognition and celebration. Employees see themselves as winners because someone is always being recognized as a result of customer feedback.

> **customer service TIP**
>
> *When you are trying to understand a customer's situation, the problem is the enemy, not you.*

Recovering from the Angry Customer

Most of the time, service mistakes result from situations that are completely out of the control of a CSR. Regardless of whether a coworker has experienced a computer glitch or made a mistake, remember that placing blame will not fix a customer's problem. Instead, focus on how you can help your company recover from the mistake. Without top-notch service recovery, customers will be lost who were so hard to acquire.

In the long run, business profits are tied to a company's ability to satisfy and retain its customers. With this in mind, these findings from a summary of several studies conducted by Technical Assistance Research Programs, Inc. (TARP), a company devoted to helping businesses measure and manage the customer experience, should be sobering to any customer service professional.

- About 50 percent of the time, customers who have a problem with a product or service are not likely to tell a company about it.
- Between 50 and 90 percent of these "silent critics" will probably take their future business to a competitor.

- Even when a customer does complain, one out of every two will not be thoroughly satisfied with the company's efforts to solve the problem.
- Dissatisfied customers typically tell eight or more people when they have had an unsatisfactory experience with a company.
- Negative statements have twice the impact as positive information when customers finalize a purchasing decision.
- Word-of-mouth advertising is one of the most important factors influencing a customer's decision to buy from a company.
- It costs between 2 and 20 times as much to win a new customer as it does to retain an existing customer who has a product or service complaint.

Some people would be surprised to learn that customers whose problems are politely and quickly resolved rate companies higher than those who experience no problems at all. Companies provide excellent customer care by never making any customer jump through hoops to obtain a remedy to a problem or complaint. This is easily accomplished by taking the following measures:

- Make the response to a customer complaint personal and take ownership of the situation. Stress what you *can* do, not what you cannot do.
- Make complaint resolution a one-on-one transaction.
- Contact the customer immediately and resolve the issue quickly. Speed is critical in retaining customers and building loyalty.

The steps for recovering encompass many of the complaint-handling steps already covered in a previous chapter; however, the list in Figure 6.3 goes into greater detail.

customer service T I P

Angry customers need to vent. Telling them to calm down often only makes matters worse.

remember this ...

Steps in Recovering Lost Customers

1.	Listen and empathize	This is not the time to tell a customer she is wrong or that if she had followed instructions, this would never have happened. Instead, acknowledge that this should not have happened, that there is no excuse for this kind of situation, and that this episode is highly unusual.
2.	Apologize	Resolving a problem is more important than pointing out who is to blame. Apologies are simple, and sometimes an apology is all the customer wants to hear.
3.	Fix the problem quickly and fairly	The faster the problem is solved in a fair manner, the better it is for everyone.
4.	Keep your promises	This is critical. Remember that you have already been unsuccessful once; you cannot afford to fall short again.
5.	Make realistic and achievable promises	Don't promise something that is impossible to deliver because you think it will make the customer happy. Two disappointments will make the customer more unhappy and could result in lost sales and questionable credibility.
6.	Thank the customer	Sincerely tell the customer that you are glad this problem was brought to your attention so you can take steps to ensure this will not happen again.
7.	Offer some form of compensation	Find out ahead of time what the limits of compensation your company allows you to offer are.
8.	Follow up	If you are not the one who will ultimately correct the problem, check back in a few days to make sure everything was done to recover the customer's trust and confidence.

FIGURE 6.3

Creating an Effective Win-Back Plan

The key to success in recovering lost customers is having a well-conceived win-back plan. In most businesses, once customers make a decision to terminate the relationship, they do not communicate their intent to the company. A few reasons that most customers would rather walk than complain are listed here:

- They often don't know whom to speak to about the problem. Customers think the available sales associates don't have the authority to resolve big problems.
- They think that the complaint will never be acted on so don't want to bother with it. Customers perceive that dealing with complaints is a low priority for the company.
- They think that the company really doesn't care about the problem, especially when they hear the phrase "It's company policy."

The task of determining why companies lose clients is made easier because many organizations collect electronic and print data pertaining to customers and their buying habits. For example, you can review the customer account history by looking for clues in letters, call reports, replacement orders, and the like. By looking at the pattern of past orders and comparing it with the date of the customer incident, answers might become clear. Whenever possible, follow up with the most important recovery question, "If we fix that, will you try us again?"

When you are reapproaching any lost customer, your win-back message should include these four points:

1. Acknowledge the customer's past patronage.
2. Point out improvements and changes made since the customer's decision to stop buying.

3. Emphasize the ease with which the customer can re-engage and place another order.
4. Provide a financial incentive, if possible.

Customer service representatives are a company's frontline of communication, and the quality of their communication greatly affects retention and win-back success with customers. People buy from people, not a company. Upset customers want to be taken seriously. They don't want to hear "You're kidding" or "No way" or "Whatever." They want the CSR to behave professionally and treat them with courtesy and respect.

The secret to successful retention, marketing, and customer fulfillment is to get inside the heads and under the skin of your customers. In other words, think as they think, feel what they feel, and literally become your own customer. In that mindset, most things become clear. Always under promise and over deliver. Then, when the product is received and used, ideally it should be better than what the customer expected.

BUSINESS *in action*

IBM

At IBM Rochester, the Customer Partnership Call Process is a tool for thanking customers for purchasing an IBM system. A call is made 90 days after a shipment is sent, and the customer is asked about likes and dislikes of the system and suggestions for improvement. The comments are then compiled into a database to be analyzed and distributed regularly among engineering, programming, marketing, manufacturing, and service teams. The information helps guide them in their work toward customer satisfaction.

Concluding Message for CSRs

Customer-centered companies make dissatisfied customers feel as if they have been true agents of change, spurring the company to make improvements, not merely treat symptoms. You can create loyal customers by admitting a mistake, expressing appreciation for help in improving service, and exceeding your customers' expectations by providing something extra.

Two recovery steps that customer service representatives should follow are crucial:

1. *Acknowledge the receipt of every complaint immediately.* This shows that you are sufficiently concerned about the problem to contact the customer and that the customer service team is on the job to resolve any issue that concerns customers.

2. *Explain in writing exactly how you will remedy the problem.* Tell your customer *what* will be done to fix the problem and *when* he or she can expect full resolution.

Summary

- Five categories of customers who defect are those who are unintentionally pushed away, intentionally pushed away, pulled away, bought away, or who have moved away.
- The goal of most customer feedback is to evaluate customer satisfaction with service, product quality, delivery, and overall experience.
- The key to success in recovering lost customers is to have a well-conceived win-back plan.
- The secret to thriving retention, marketing, and customer fulfillment is to think as customers think, feel what they feel, and, in essence, become your own customer.

KEY TERMS

customer satisfaction

mystery shopper

CRITICAL THINKING

1. Of the five types of customers who defect, which is the most serious from a win-back point of view? Explain.

2. If you were designing the best feedback survey for the following businesses, which type would you create and why? For a car repair shop? For a four-star hotel? For a hair and nail salon?

3. Why might it be unwise to always accept any and all customer feedback?

4. Think of a time when you or someone you know walked away from a business rather than staying to complain about its service or products. Explain why the situation was handled this way.

5. Write a simple win-back message to a customer who received a product (in other words, food item, electronic gadget, and so on) that was of poor quality.

ONLINE RESEARCH ACTIVITIES

Project 6.1 Creating a Customer Survey

Create a 10- to 15-question customer service feedback survey for an industry or a company of your choice. Research several websites and locate sample customer service survey questions you might use as guides in completing this assignment.

Project 6.2 The Feasibility of Using a Mystery Shopper

Sam Brown, vice president of sales at On-Time Technology Products, is interested in researching the impact of using mystery shoppers in technology companies. He feels that using an unannounced third party to visit, phone, or check OTTP's website and e-mail responses could provide meaningful data in evaluating the effectiveness of the company's marketing and customer service areas.

Using your favorite search engine, type the keywords *Mystery Shopper* and locate three articles that will help Mr. Brown with his research and subsequent analysis. Write a brief summary of your findings, including the URLs and key points you learned about mystery shoppers.

URL	Summary
1.	
2.	
3.	

COMMUNICATION SKILLS AT WORK

Project 6.3 Handling Customer Complaints

Respond to the following three statements an angry customer might make to a customer service representative. Provide an appropriate response to each statement in column 2 that is customer-friendly and will help retain the customer. Finally, role-play each situation with a fellow student, as directed by your instructor.

Statement	Appropriate Response
1. "I have waited on the phone for 20 minutes. What takes you people so long?"	•
2. "Your service has been totally unsatisfactory. You promised to deliver my computer three weeks ago, and I haven't heard from anyone since I placed the order. I want my computer delivered—today!"	•
3. "You have done this completely wrong. You are incompetent. I want to see your supervisor immediately so I can have you fired."	•

DECISION MAKING AT WORK

Project 6.4 "Bad Product Shipped—Increase in Customer Complaints"

Layla is the senior CSR at On-Time Technology Products and the person to whom other CSRs refer most major customer problems. She never fails to service customers in a calm and collected manner and is always kind and courteous to others—coworkers and customers alike. Over the past few weeks, the company has experienced a bad shipment of product. Consequently, customer complaints are on the rise. As a result, Layla simply cannot handle the majority of these complaints herself, although the other five CSRs continue to transfer all of the bad-product calls to her.

1. How could OTTP have avoided putting its Customer Service Department in the current situation?

_____

_____

_____

_____

2. Given the bad-product situation, what should the other CSRs do now to respond to these increased complaints?

_____

_____

_____

_____

3. What steps should OTTP take to avoid customer service situations like this one in the future?

_____

_____

_____

_____

CASE STUDIES

Project 6.5 When the News Isn't Good...

During a session at a recent customer service seminar, Tom was asked what to say and do when CSRs have to turn down a customer's request or deliver other bad news. Tom shared the following three scenarios with his colleagues to find out how they might react. How would you respond to each of the following scenarios? Break into groups and write a script for each situation.

1. You are unable to provide information on an ex-wife's account balance because it is illegal.

    _____

    _____

    _____

    _____

2. You are unable to wire flowers to a customer's sister in Phoenix without first receiving payment.

    _____

    _____

    _____

    _____

3. You are unable to sell weight-loss products to a customer without first having her evaluated by the company dieticians.

    _____

    _____

    _____

    _____

Project 6.6 Action Plan: Survey and a Win-Back Strategy

On-Time Technology Products has no formal win-back plan because, until recently, it has not experienced any significant loss in its customer base of about 400. The sales manager has noticed a drop in sales and has recognized that major customers appear to be ordering fewer products at one time.

As a result, OTTP wants to contact at least 50 customers over the next few months. Assist in the design of this action plan by suggesting several attributes that measure customer satisfaction, and prepare a brief script, using key components of a successful win-back plan that CSRs might use.

1. Using Figure 6.2 on page 86 as a reference, select what you believe are the top five attributes that OTTP should use to measure customer satisfaction.

    1. _____

    2. _____

    3. _____

    4. _____

    5. _____

2. Work in groups of three or four to write a brief script that CSRs could use when contacting these customers. Use the following steps as a guide to writing the narrative script:
    a. Acknowledge the customer's past business.
    b. Point out improvements to service and products.
    c. Emphasize the ease with which the customer can place another order.
    d. Provide a financial incentive.

    _____

    _____

    _____

    _____

    _____

    _____

Problem Solving, Time and Stress Management Skills

chapter 7

Objectives

1. Describe the steps involved in solving customer problems.

2. Identify techniques to better manage time.

3. Discuss the importance of stress management.

4. Understand the difference between positive and negative stress.

People forget how fast you did a job—but they remember how well you did it.

—HOWARD W. NEWTON, AUTHOR

H ow well we solve problems and deal with time- and stress-related issues is a reflection of our attitudes, beliefs, behaviors, and organizational skills. At times, we all struggle to maintain a healthy balance between our professional and personal lives. Setting priorities and keeping them straight is a challenge in this fast-paced world. Too many conflicts and demands on our time can lead to feelings of stress and loss of control. Learning to manage our time and stress levels can increase productivity and improve overall attitude and well-being.

Practicing Problem-Solving Skills

In situations that require handling customer problems on a daily basis, effective problem solving by customer service representatives is a highly regarded ability. CSRs who are considered especially good problem solvers are systematic, analytical, and have first-rate interpersonal skills. They not only solve problems but simultaneously handle customers' feelings. Statistics show that 70 percent of complaining customers will return if a problem is resolved in their favor.

remember this ...
Problem-Solving Skills Quiz

Yes	No	Questions
☐	☐	1. When faced with a new problem, do you start by trying to determine its major cause?
☐	☐	2. Do you compare the problem with other dilemmas you have solved previously to see whether a pattern emerges?
☐	☐	3. Can you set aside trivial details while getting a grasp on the problem's major facets?
☐	☐	4. Can you look at a problem from several different perspectives?
☐	☐	5. Do you feel comfortable asking for input from your supervisor?
☐	☐	6. If a person helps you solve a problem, do you give proper credit to him or her?
☐	☐	7. When you are making limited progress on your own, do you brainstorm with coworkers?
☐	☐	8. Do you know when to stop gathering facts so you can make a decision in a timely fashion?
☐	☐	9. When decisions turn out differently than expected, do you still consider alternatives?
☐	☐	10. When you are still confused despite all your best efforts, do you set the problem aside for a short time to get a fresh perspective?

A total of eight or more "yes" answers suggests that you have excellent problem-solving abilities and the interpersonal skills to make things work for customers and coworkers. Five to seven "yes" answers indicate that you can solve problems but could probably do so more effectively with help from your peers. If you scored lower, reevaluate the process you follow when you are confronted with problems, and use these questions to guide you toward better problem-solving solutions.

FIGURE 7.1

That number grows to 95 percent if the problem is resolved on the spot.[1] How good a problem solver are you? Take the quiz in Figure 7.1 to find out.

Many failures in customer service initially seem like successes to us. Based on our perception of the facts, we come up with a solution to solve the problem that makes sense to us. The problem is, we didn't get the customer's perception of the facts, so our solution may not be sensible to him or her.

Effective listening skills are essential to "read a situation" correctly. The ability to solve problems, resolve differences, and capture opportunities involves actively listening and carefully analyzing a situation. Further, asking the right questions to clarify problems, needs, and opportunities is required to gain a full understanding.

Service-oriented employees deal with complaints on the spot. The benefit of handling complaints immediately is greater customer satisfaction, which ultimately results in lower customer service costs. Problem solving with customers is a process that involves these four steps:

1. *Determine whether the situation is a disagreement or a true conflict of interest.* Ask the customer to state the problem from his or her point of view, and then state the problem from your own perspective. This can help determine where the problem lies.

2. *Analyze your interests and the customer's interests.* Determine ahead of time what concessions management will empower you to make on the customer's behalf and what limitations you have.

3. *Brainstorm solutions and generate ideas together.* If the issue is complicated, start with the easy issues and then proceed to the more difficult ones. Always attempt to establish points of agreement early in the process.

4. *If step 3 doesn't resolve the situation, make some mutual low-priority concessions.* Be patient. You may have to go through steps 3 and 4 more than once.

---

[1]"Reduce Cost of Poor Service with Effective Problem-Solving Techniques," *The Dartnell Corporation* (July 2001): 9.

1. Keep your composure.
   - Focus on the real issues.
   - Be flexible in your solutions.
   - Know your hot buttons and keep them in check.
   - Break the link between your emotions and the action that needs to occur.

2. Play it "side by side."
   - Put yourself in your customer's shoes by showing respect, not hostility.
   - Express concern for the relationship.
   - Make reasonable requests.
   - Ask questions and invite specific criticism.
   - Use humor, when appropriate.

3. Be firm, but agreeable, to further negotiation.
   - Respond to reason, but not to force or personal attacks.
   - Take sarcasm at face value.

4. Sidestep personal disagreements and keep talking about the problem.
   - Warn, don't threaten. There's a fine line between the two actions. A threat sounds like, "Here's what I'll do to you." A warning sounds like, "Here's what the situation will be."

5. Look to the future.
   - Say, "How do we make sure this never happens again?" or "What do you think will happen if we don't resolve this conflict?"
   - Suggest a third-party mediator, if all else fails.

FIGURE 7.2

Figure 7.2 offers five additional suggestions for ways service professionals can work together with customers.

When complaints are passed on to the next level of the organization, the price of service goes up. Successful problem solving early in the process is critical to a company's financial success. Accessibility, ownership, explanation of policies, and follow-through promote effective problem solving in the most efficient manner:

1. *Accessibility.* When customers call your business, they need to know that they will be getting an answer quickly from an employee who is not only willing to help but also very knowledgeable.

2. *Ownership.* When a customer makes a complaint, a CSR should accept responsibility for the situation (even if it's not his or her fault) and apologize without assigning blame.

3. *Explanation of policies.* When problems occur because of a company policy, a CSR should provide a clear explanation of *what* happened and *why* the company has this policy.

4. *Follow-through.* When commitments are made to customers, CSRs need to be sure they can deliver as quickly as possible on all promises they make.

Improving Time Management Skills

Webster's Dictionary defines time as "the period between two events or during which something exists, happens, or acts; measured or measurable interval." We have the ability and power to use time in constructive ways. Rather than time controlling us, we can control it. **Time management** is not about squeezing more activities into an already overloaded schedule, but about using the time you have in the most effective way possible. One result of proper time management is a reduced level of stress.

For many people, it seems that time controls us. This doesn't have to be the case. Time management is self-management. To manage ourselves, we need to gain a better ability to examine our work habits, our environments, and ourselves. The key to improving skills in this area is increasing awareness of our attitudes, thinking, and behaviors regarding how we manage our time and organize our workload. Do we manage it or does it manage us?

Effective time managers find that the key to controlling how they use time is to write everything down rather than keep everything in their heads. Using an electronic device such as a **personal digital assistant (PDA)** can help organize a busy schedule. Questions to ask while organizing your time include:

- What do I want or need to do that I am currently not doing?
- What do I want or need to complete that has not yet been completed?
- What do I want or need to start that has not yet been started?
- What do I want or need to say that I am not saying?

After completing the list, determine the highest priorities using the following system:

- A = Highest priority; must be completed

Good time management is one of the most important skills
for customer service reps to master.

- B = Important to be completed; not absolutely essential for today
- C = Nice to do; spare time project

Time Management Tips

Productivity will increase a great deal when a few time management techniques are followed.

KNOW YOUR PURPOSE What do you want to achieve? The first step in time management is to know *why* you are doing something. To change your behavior without a good reason is an uphill, and usually unsuccessful, battle. Write down the goals you want to achieve and look at them frequently to remind yourself why you are spending your time as you are.

KEEP YOUR TIME IN PERSPECTIVE If you kept a record of your time over the course of several weeks, you would probably discover the following:

- Everything takes longer than you expect. In fact, most of us underestimate the amount of time an activity will take to complete by 50 percent. Learn to build extra time into your plans.
- You waste more time than you think. Watching TV and surfing the web aren't necessarily bad activities unless they are cutting into the time you should use to fulfill your goals. Think twice before turning on the TV or computer.
- A lot of legitimate activity is pure maintenance. For example, the laundry still has to get done, whether it's a goal or not.

PLAN AHEAD Research shows that an hour spent planning is worth three or four hours of just "doing." To avoid interruptions, try to do your planning at night so the priorities for the day are fresh in your mind. When you wake up, you will have the day's direction already carved out for you.

SET YOUR PRIORITIES When everything on your to-do list seems important, determine your true priorities by asking,

- Will doing this task help me reach a larger goal?
- Does the task have a deadline?
- Is it a task from a superior (such as a boss or an instructor)?

BREAK A PROJECT INTO SMALLER PIECES To manage a project effectively, use the "VPIC" process.

- *Visualize* What will the project look like when done?
- *Plan* Break the project into pieces; decide who will do what, when, where, and how.
- *Implement* Monitor your progress to stay on schedule. Adjust activities when necessary.
- *Close* Celebrate and wrap up the project.

PACE YOURSELF Know when your peaks of energy are. By honoring your personal time clock, you will have a more balanced life. For example, if you are a morning person, schedule important decisions and activities early in the day while you are at your prime. If you are a night person, do those important activities in the afternoon or early evening. If you must work past your peak time, give yourself a break by going on a walk, stretching, or phoning someone who cheers you up.

remember this ...
Time Management Quiz

Yes	No	Questions
☐	☐	1. Do you carry scraps of paper with to-do items listed on them?
☐	☐	2. Do you have trouble focusing on the task you are doing because you are thinking of other things that need to be done?
☐	☐	3. Are you often behind schedule and routinely in a catch-up mode?
☐	☐	4. Have you started many projects that you cannot seem to complete?
☐	☐	5. Do interruptions on the job destroy your momentum?
☐	☐	6. Do you feel overwhelmed when you walk into work and look at your desk and work space?
☐	☐	7. Do you have so many small items on your mind that you get easily distracted from your important work activities?
☐	☐	8. Are you often remembering other priorities left undone at home while you are at work and vice versa?
☐	☐	9. Do you arrive home feeling unfulfilled in your job, so tired that you want to escape?
☐	☐	10. Do you feel that you cannot take time for physical fitness, recreation, or just plain fun?
☐	☐	11. Do you find that during and after your workday, your stress level is so high that you find it hard to relax?

If you answered "yes" to more than two or three of these questions, you may be showing symptoms of poor time management. The question is then, Do you control your time or does time control you?

FIGURE 7.3

Time Wasters

Poor time management can interfere with everything you do. To eliminate time wasters, be honest with yourself. How effective a time manager are you? See for yourself by taking the short quiz in Figure 7.3.

From time to time, people get themselves into time management trouble without intending to.

- *They can't say "no."* Be honest about your commitments. Use your schedule to explain why you can't comply with all requests for your attention. Keep in mind that you should probably say "no" to someone if the request is a last-minute one that requires an immediate response, skills that you do not have, or more time than you can reasonably provide.
- *They are buried in paperwork.* Schedule a specific time for doing paperwork and stick to it. Try not to look at the same piece of paper twice; deal with it the first time.
- *They procrastinate.* It's said that the hardest part of doing anything is getting started. Once you have started, however, you gain momentum, which makes it easier to keep going. **Procrastination,** the act of putting

something off, comes in many forms, as described in Figure 7.4. If you suffer from this tendency, admit it, analyze it, and make a commitment to conquer it. The enormity of the task could be causing you to stall. Attack the task by taking "baby steps" at first, and you'll be on your way to more effective time management.

customer service TIP

Enjoy what you're doing while you're doing it. The results will show on your face and in your attitude with customers, coworkers, family, and friends.

Organizational Skills

It seems as though many people are looking for a more enjoyable, balanced life. Because we cannot control how many hours are in a day, we must try to control how we spend the hours we do have. Developing effective organizational skills is one tool that can help add a sense of balance to our lives.

remember this ...
Procrastination

Form of Procrastination	Justification	Cure
Not wanting to do the task	Because procrastination usually involves something we don't want to do, we fill our available time with smaller, easier, and more comfortable projects. We avoid tasks, issues, and problems that are uncomfortable to us.	Tackle your biggest project first instead of getting the little ones out of the way. The little ones will be easy to take care of in your spare time.
Interrupting yourself	You may be interrupting yourself by getting another cup of coffee, stopping to talk with someone, making a quick phone call, or answering e-mail messages.	Set a time frame for the task you are by doing and seat belt yourself to the chair.
Making the project too big	It is easy to procrastinate when the job seems too big to even get started.	Divide your project into smaller parts; then set realistic goals to accomplish each one.
Convincing yourself of defeat	Why bother trying when you are doomed to fail? Negative self-talk, such as, "I wouldn't be able to do that job anyway," is at work here.	When you start to think of a negative message, replace it immediately with a positive thought.
Rationalizing it away	Telling yourself a job wasn't that important anyway or that it was too much work.	Look back at your original goal list and remember why you put this particular goal on the list in the first place.
Feeding poor self-esteem	The final outcome for "letting it slide" is a loss of self-esteem. As our esteem decreases, so does our motivation and energy. This in turn feeds future procrastination and begins a negative cycle.	Honestly commit to accomplishing a task. Evaluate your own process of getting off track when tackling your goals and work toward rectifying the problem areas.

FIGURE 7.4

Organizational skills help you cope better with the world. These skills provide structure and reduce daily stress levels. The organizational skills you apply toward planning each day provide a framework for productivity. More important, they direct the demands on your attention and give you a sense of control.

People who manage their time well often are also those who tend to be organized and on top of things. What makes some people appear organized and not others? Organized people tend to do most of the following activities as a matter of *routine:*

- *Prepare a monthly schedule.* At the end of every month, make a schedule of events and deadlines for the next month. Use the schedule to highlight or mark off duties as they are accomplished.

- *Prepare a file folder for each item on your schedule.* Make notes on a particular project and immediately file them in the proper folder to save time by not having to search for them later.

- *Rely on technology.* Use your computer or PDA as an electronic assistant. There are several good personal information-management software packages, such as Microsoft Outlook, which allow you to track and schedule your activities, take notes, manage meetings, and so on.

Use technology as much as possible to stay organized.

© GETTY IMAGES/PHOTODISC

- *Organize your work area.* Arrange your desk and paperwork flow in a logical sequence. Disorganized personal space is a very big time waster.
- *Manage your communications.* If you need to focus on a special project and not be interrupted, let your voicemail become your secretary. Return calls every two or three hours, and keep a log of messages and their disposition.

A good sense of organization will make you more efficient; and if one of your main sources of stress is the sheer number of things that need to be done, getting organized should help you feel more at peace and in control.

Understanding Stress

We live in an interesting age. People have never before experienced the amount of change and number of choices we encounter every day. Each of us has stress, regardless

of age, gender, position in life, and income, and so we are ultimately responsible for our own stress management and personal well-being.

Compare stress levels to blood pressure. High blood pressure or low blood pressure can be problematic, but blood pressure cannot disappear completely. The same is true with stress. When unregulated, uncontrolled, or ignored, stress can be harmful to your health and well-being. Conversely, too little stress can lead to apathy, fatigue, and illness. A major step toward successful stress management is to find and maintain a personal equilibrium, a balance that works for you at each stage of your life.

What triggers your stress response? Except for major catastrophes, few events are stressful in themselves. Stress arises when you perceive a situation as demanding. For example, your morning commute may make you anxious and tense because you worry that traffic will make you late. Others may find the trip relaxing because it allows more time to enjoy music or quiet time while they drive.

Stress is a basic component of most customer service jobs. Primarily, stress arises from four main causes: lack of control, leadership issues, interruption or incompletion of tasks, and lack of confidence or self-esteem. Figure 7.5 explains each one in more detail.

remember this ...
Causes of Stress

- Lack of control
  Not being able to get things done, get others to cooperate, satisfy customers' needs, and assimilate and organize the workflow manifests in a feeling of lack of control.

- Leadership issues
  Managers often unknowingly contribute to CSRs' stress level through poor communications, unwillingness to delegate, failure to respond to inquiries and requests, changing priorities at the last minute, and perceived disrespect.

- Interruption or incompletion
  When job priorities are changed and others redesign workflow processes, workers find it difficult to complete a task in progress, and this builds stress.

- Lack of confidence or self-esteem
  Training and various kinds of empowerment including participative management provide tools to deal with lack of confidence and self-esteem.

FIGURE 7.5

customer service T I P

Working with positive stress and getting rid of negative stress can be considered a "facelift for the mind."

Positive versus Negative Stress

Not all stress is bad. There is such a thing as **positive stress,** which is needed every so often. If you believe that you do your best work under pressure, you are creating your own stress. You could be right—you may do your best work under pressure. This is an example of when stress is good. By viewing positive stress as a force that motivates and energizes you rather than makes you anxious and frustrated, you can channel its energy into productive results. So, how do we get rid of unwanted stress?

- *Don't worry.* **Negative stress** comes from worrying about things you have no power to change. By recognizing that sometimes you worry about things you can do nothing about, it's easier to channel your worry into something productive. For example, you cannot prevent freezing rain, but you can put salt on the driveway to prevent slipping.
- *Set goals.* Focus your energy in a positive direction instead of feeling defeated by negative self-talk. For example, stop getting stressed if you are unhappy in your job, and take action to change it.
- *Finish unfinished business.* Make plans to complete an unfinished task or decide to drop it altogether, and stop causing yourself stress over it.
- *Resolve conflicts.* Apologize to a friend, family member, classmate, or coworker that you've disagreed with. This is the kind of negative stress that can keep you up at night.

The Effects of Stress

According to the American Institute of Stress, more companies are helping employees deal with stress because it is affecting their bottom line by $300 billion annually. An estimated 1 million U.S. employees are absent from work each day due to stress-related complaints. Stressed-out workers result in diminished productivity, employee turnover, and increased medical, legal, and insurance fees.

Primary care physicians report that stress is responsible for more than 75 percent of all office visits. Stress leads to high blood pressure and can manifest itself in infections, which over time can affect the immune system.[2]

On a philosophical level, managing stress means learning how to be flexible and how to adapt to new events. Observations show that *how* people deal with change and other situations is what makes some people feel out of control and stressed. Among the effects of stress are fatigue and lowered response time, loss of focus and attention, tight and tense muscles, and a conscious choice to take shortcuts or bypass procedures.

Studies further show that people who see new situations as threatening feel alienated, out of control, and have a 50 percent greater chance of getting sick. On the other hand, people who embrace change and get involved with life events and other people feel in control and tend to stay in better health.[3]

Behavioral patterns that can indicate stress are a decline in job performance, sloppy work habits, poor housekeeping, irritable and quarrelsome behavior, alcohol or drug use, an uncooperative attitude, and general negativity. In many organizations, stress results in worker burnout and negative office chatter.

BURNOUT Worker **burnout** is one of the most common reasons why employees quit their service-industry jobs; psychological exhaustion and decreased efficiency result from overwork and prolonged exposure to stress. Ironically, the more you enjoy your work and the more seriously you take the task of serving customers well, the more vulnerable you may be to the effects of burnout.

Burnout produces feelings of hopelessness, powerlessness, cynicism, resentment, and failure, as well as stagnation and reduced productivity. These reactions can result in levels of depression or unhappiness that eventually threaten your job, relationships, and health.

Burnout is associated with situations in which a person feels

- overworked.
- underappreciated.
- confused about expectations and priorities.

[2]Karen Connelly, "Easy Does It," *Inside Business* (April 2001): 47.
[3]Michael Topf, "Managing Change," *Occupational Hazards* (July 2000): 63.

- concerned about job security.
- overcommitted with responsibilities.
- resentful about duties that are not commensurate with pay.

To guard against burnout, try these four tips:

1. *Don't take work too personally.* Keep in mind that when customers lash out, their frustration is over the difference between what they want and what they are getting; it is not about you personally.

2. *Don't take problems home.* Give complete attention to your job while you are at work, but leave concerns at work when you go home.

3. *Get help from others.* Remember that your coworkers are going through stressful situations also. It helps to talk over these situations together.

4. *Focus on the good news.* When customers approach you with problems, remember that most of them will become satisfied once you've handled their complaints to the best of your ability.

NEGATIVE OFFICE CHATTER Negative office chatter is a time waster and stress inducer. Time spent complaining about work, the boss, coworkers, and customers affects your attitude and that of others. People tend to absorb negativity through constant repetition. Staying positive can lessen stress and can be accomplished by agreeing

Negative office chatter can be a stress inducer during times that we need to show a positive frame of mind.

not to talk about work at lunch and refraining from excessive complaining.

Managing Stress

Part of managing stress is setting attainable goals and not taking on too many commitments at one time. People need to enjoy the process of living, not just be directed by the goal of getting through each day. Most people who are stressed out have very unbalanced lifestyles because they cannot accomplish everything they want to do. Exercise and staying physically fit rejuvenate us and help to counteract the loss of concentration that is caused by stress. CSRs who manage stress well make time for relaxation activities and humor each day. In addition, they have developed their own stress management plans from some of the tips described below.

STRESS MANAGEMENT TIPS Devising a stress management plan that incorporates the following suggestions is a good idea.

- *Pay attention to yourself.* Identify the factors that cause stress in your life so you can change or manage them. Make a list of the situations, relationships, and events that are stressful for you. Once you have a stress awareness checklist, you can begin to make decisions about which ones need immediate attention.

- *Don't try to control everything.* Focus on the situations that you can control and let go of those you cannot. For example, you can control your reaction to an angry customer, but you cannot control whether the customer is angry.

- *Alter your lifestyle.* Know when to say "no." Avoid rush-hour traffic. Do not procrastinate. Prioritize tasks. Avoid perfectionism. Use time-saving tools and technology to your advantage.

- *Change your thinking.* Substitute positive thoughts for negative ones. "I don't know how to do this, but I can learn" is better than "I can't." Drive away anxiety-producing thoughts. Give yourself a pep talk by focusing on your good qualities.

- *Create an outlet.* Exercise or practice yoga, aromatherapy, or meditation. Know how to relax, plan, play, and get silly by taking physical and mental breaks. Nurture and develop your spiritual life by not neglecting matters of the soul. For many people, it brings a sense of inner peace and helps counteract the effects of stress.

RELAXATION A fundamental part of any stress management program is relaxation. It is a much needed activity for overstimulated bodies and minds. Stress causes tense muscles, shallow breathing, increased heart rates, and elevated blood pressure. Relaxation reverses those effects.

The word *relaxation* refers to a state of being, is self-initiated, and causes physiological and psychological changes. People relax differently, but doing what works for you is the key to making this technique successful.

HUMOR Did you know that a child laughs an average of 300 times a day, whereas an adult's count is just 6 to 8 times? A well-balanced life requires laughter and fun. One of the best ways to deal with stress is through humor. Exposing yourself to humor and determining the nature of your own sense of humor is the initial step in using humor to cope with stress.

Laughter helps reduce muscle tension, release anger, deal with the unexpected, and increase your sense of control, well-being, and joy. What can be done to promote the spirit of a more amusing workplace? Here are some ideas that companies are promoting to lessen stress through humor:

1. *Sponsor weird apparel days.* Wear silly hats, funny T-shirts, outrageous ties, and so on.
2. *Celebrate holidays.* Dress up for Halloween or coordinate a holiday meal.
3. *Hold "match the baby picture" contests.* Display childhood pictures of employees and see how many coworkers can correctly match babies with adults.
4. *Organize lunch-hour board game tournaments.* Whether it's chess, Scrabble®, or Monopoly®, a midday diversion of a fun activity can help us cope better.
5. *Participate on an intramural sports team.* Compete against other departments in regular golf, volleyball, or other no-contact events.

Competing for fun promotes unity among coworkers.

© GETTY IMAGES/PHOTODISC

BUSINESS *in action*

GOOGLE

For a company that has roughly doubled its workforce each year since 2002, Google doesn't act like the big company it has become. One of the ways it has preserved its tech startup philosophy is decidedly low-tech: dozens of whiteboards placed in common areas and corridors throughout the headquarter offices. Some are businesslike, used by product teams to exchange ideas. But the two largest ones, about 30 feet long, are devoted to the equivalent of corporate graffiti. One is packed with cartoons and jokes that workers have scrawled under the slogan "Google's Plan for World Domination." "It's collaborative art," says David Krane, Google's director of communications, speaking about one of its earliest whiteboard posters. "We're in a growth period, and when new hires see the boards, they get a quick, comprehensive snapshot of our company's personality."

Source: http://www.money.cnn.com.

Concluding Message for CSRs

Being successful involves staying on top of your workload, delivering on your promises, and excelling at your job. These actions can ultimately lessen stress levels. The process takes diligence and a strong commitment to developing practical skills in problem solving and time and stress management to work smarter and stay healthy, both on and off the job.

No one is immune to stress. Although we can't avoid it, experts agree that we can learn to manage it. Start with the basics: get plenty of sleep, eat a balanced diet, and exercise regularly. The key to maintaining a healthy, safe, and stress-reduced lifestyle is successful time management.

Summary

- CSRs who are considered especially good problem solvers are systematic and analytical and have first-rate interpersonal skills.
- Time management is not about squeezing more activities into an already overloaded schedule, but rather about getting important tasks completed in a less stressful way.
- Applying organizational skills results in improved structure to our activities and reduces daily stress levels.
- Positive stress can motivate and energize a person, whereas negative stress often makes a person anxious and frustrated.

KEY TERMS

burnout	positive stress	relaxation
negative stress	procrastination	time management
personal digital assistant (PDA)		

CRITICAL THINKING

1. Assume you work in a shoe store, and a customer has a complaint about the quality of a pair of shoes she bought last week. What steps would you take in addressing the issue?

2. List two techniques that you use when managing your time. What are two techniques you are not currently using that could improve your time management skills?

3. Describe the behavior of a person who procrastinates doing a job or handing in a class assignment on time.

4. Why are organizational skills important? Can you usually identify a person who exhibits these skills? What observable characteristics does the person possess?

5. Cite a situation when you experienced positive stress that served you in a beneficial way. Explain.

6. What are some methods a person can use to overcome negative stressors?

7. If you were asked to devise a plan that manages your personal stress level, what five actions would you include?

ONLINE RESEARCH ACTIVITIES

Project 7.1 Time Management Seminars

Research a number of websites and locate several time management consultants who provide onsite time management seminars. Write a short paper that compares the content offerings of any three of these seminars.

Project 7.2 Stress- and Work-Related Illnesses

James Woo, vice president of human resources and customer relations, has been charting the incidence of absences at On-Time Technology Products. It appears that each month, absences have been increasing. As a result, he is curious to learn the extent to which stress-related illnesses affect workers today. He has asked Mary Graeff to assist him in this research.

Go to various health-related websites (for example, Mayo Clinic, WebMD, medical training schools, or local hospitals) and locate seven factors or issues related to mounting stress-related health problems in the workplace. Show your findings, informing Mr. Woo where you got your information and what factors or issues you were able to uncover. If instructed, participate in a class panel discussion describing your research.

Websites	Factors/Issues Related to Health Risks of Stress
1.	
2.	
3.	
4.	
5.	
6.	
7.	

COMMUNICATION SKILLS AT WORK

Project 7.3 Time Management Suggestions

Respond to the following items with a personal example of either how you have implemented or how you would implement each suggestion. After you have completed the form, share your suggestions with three other students in class.

Time Management Suggestion	A Personal Example
1. Start with the most worrisome task.	
2. Complete deadline work early.	
3. Know your capacity for stress.	
4. Stay organized.	
5. Get physical.	
6. Have fun.	

DECISION MAKING AT WORK

Project 7.4 Positive Customer Responses

Someone made a copy of an article from a customer service newsletter that Mary Graeff receives each month and has shared it with all the CSRs at On-Time Technology Products. The article deals with solving customer problems. Specifically, the article presents several customer scenarios, gives a negative response to each scenario, and asks the readers to provide a more positive problem-solving response.

Working with another student, provide a positive problem-solving response to each customer scenario.

1. **Customer:** "I would like to be on the preferred customer mailing list." **Staff:** "You need to have spent $1,000 or more." (Sounds negative) **Your positive response:**

   _____

   _____

2. **Customer:** "Why haven't I received my refund?" **Staff:** "Because you filled out the form all wrong." (Sounds negative) **Your positive response:**

   _____

   _____

3. **Customer:** "Are there any more of these forms?" **Staff:** "I don't think so." (Sounds negative) **Your positive response:**

    _____

    _____

4. **Customer:** "How do I get to the exercise room?" **Staff:** "There's a map over there." (Sounds negative) **Your positive response:**

    _____

    _____

CASE STUDIES

Project 7.5 "If I Knew How to Solve My Own Problem, I Wouldn't Need You!"

Melissa Devlin, the manager of Baby's Little Store, overheard an angry customer say rather loudly, "If I knew how to solve my own problem, I wouldn't need you!" It was obvious that Keanna, her new sales associate, was in a tight spot with a customer.

As the situation revealed itself, this new mother had recently bought a baby mattress for her newborn and was very dissatisfied with the quality of the product after using it only a short time. She felt the mattress was made with unsafe materials and was concerned for her baby's health and safety. When the customer said she wanted her money back, Keanna said nicely, "I'll have to check with the store manager to see whether or not we can take this mattress back for a full refund." At that point, the customer lost her temper and said, "If I knew how to fix my own problem, I wouldn't need you!"

1. Evaluate the manner in which Keanna handled the situation. What did she do well and what are some errors she inadvertently made?

    _____

    _____

2. What suggestions could you make concerning this problem-solving approach so that future dilemmas of this type have more customer-oriented and positive solutions?

    _____

    _____

    _____

Project 7.6 Time Management

You planned to get to work early to finish the project that's due today, but your car won't start. You know the mechanic's name is written down somewhere but can't remember where you put it. Frantically you search through your notes piled on the kitchen counter, but you can't find it anywhere. There's no way you are going to have time to finish your project (which you've had for more than two weeks). You start to panic, and the clock keeps ticking.

Brainstorm with three other students and indicate three time management–related problems in this situation. In column 2, respond with a suggestion that could either eliminate the time management problem or reduce its effects in the future.

Time Management Problem	Ways to Reduce or Eliminate the Problem
1.	
2.	
3.	

Action Plan

Based on your study of Part 2, think about the essential customer service and personal skills that a service professional should possess in order to serve customers in an exemplary fashion, and then complete the following activities.

Activity 1

Divide a sheet of paper into four columns and create the following list in column 1: Customer-Oriented Attitude, Proactive Problem Solving, Time Management Skills, Organizational Skills, and Stress Management Skills. Label column 2 *Strength*, column 3 *Needs Improvement*, and column 4 *Method of Improvement*.

Give some thought as to how you would rate yourself on each item in column 1. How do you measure up? If there is a skill that you are especially strong in, put an X in column 2 next to that item, showing it as a strength of yours. If it is a skill that you may need to work on in some way, place an X in column 3. Finally, in column 4, indicate how you might improve those skills you've identified in column 3.

Activity 2

As a class, assign a person to write on the whiteboard or chalkboard. Break the writing space into three areas: Time Management Skills, Organizational Skills, and Stress Management Skills. Devote some class time to brainstorming about each of the three areas on the board. When class members respond, they should use the sentence stem, "Remember to...."

Finally, each student should select from each group two reminders that the student feels have the most relevance to him or her and place those items on note cards to be posted in a workspace or at home.

P A R T

3

Communication Skills for Customer Service

chapters

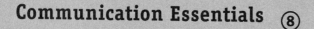

PHOTO © THERESA ALVARADO

profile

Government Profile

by Theresa Alvarado,
Human Resources Director,
City of Flagstaff, AZ

In your experience, how has serving customers well changed recently?

In the past, this city has always promoted customer service, and we had no reason to think serving customers any differently was necessary. However, with the election of a new city mayor with a background in retail management, customer service became the number one priority for all 1,000 city employees. As Human Resources Director, I was asked by the mayor to establish a new customer service committee. The mayor's statement was, "When walking through City Hall, I can't tell who is a customer and who is a city worker. Don't you think we need to fix that?"

It wasn't easy, but six months later, every day, employees are wearing nametags that they helped design. Employees in city offices are now asking citizens, "Are you lost?" and "How can I help you?" Saying, "It's not my job" or "I don't know" to any person in City Hall is prohibited.

What important customer service skills should a person working in a government administrative center possess?

The skill set needed to work in any level of government goes beyond the rote smile and basic

problem-solving abilities to this higher level of service:

- Listening skills that show sincere empathy for a citizen's concern.
- Problem solving that goes beyond a worker's own job parameters. An employee should recognize when it is time to move the customer to another level to solve a problem. Employees must feel comfortable taking that risk and follow through to make sure a citizen's problem is solved.

Our mantra in the city of Flagstaff is, "Community first, team second, and ourselves last." When facing any work dilemma, applying this mantra helps clarify the issue. I truly believe that to be successful in a career of government service, customer needs must come first, because customers pay our salaries. We are truly their servants, and as such, we are here to do *whatever it takes* to make sure citizens' needs are met through great service.

••••••• # Industry: Government

Government Activities

1. Think about your total experience the last time you communicated with any government agency (for example, reporting a crime to police, paying a city water bill, getting tax information from the IRS, talking with a military recruiter), and respond "yes" or "no" to the following questions:

   _____ Did you feel that the fundamentals of communication were followed well?

   _____ Was the nonverbal communication appropriate and complementary to the total message?

   _____ Did you feel the person who served you was dressed appropriately and that he or she demonstrated good manners?

   _____ Did you feel your situation was understood and the employee used effective listening skills?

   _____ If you had occasion to telephone or receive a telephone call from the government agency, were good techniques as well as voicemail used effectively?

   _____ Were any written documents you received (letters, notices, or e-mail messages) from the government agency appropriately written and presented with a professional image in mind?

   How would you rank the customer service provided by this government agency (1 = poor; 5 = superior)? _____

2. At the completion of your study of the material in Part 3, briefly explain why you evaluated the government agency as you did.

   _____

   _____

   _____

3. Assume you are the mayor of your city and want to create a customer service policy that promotes effective communication with the citizens. What are three essential communication skills that should be emphasized in this policy and why?

   _____

   _____

   _____

   _____

Communication
Essentials

chapter 8

1. Explain each of the elements in the communication process.

2. Identify the behaviors of people who communicate using different communication styles.

3. Compose examples of open, probing, closed, alternative choice, leading, and direct questions.

4. Understand the fundamentals of business writing.

We are what we repeatedly do. Excellence is not an act but a habit.

—ARISTOTLE, GREEK PHILOSOPHER, 384–322 BCE

Communication is important to business. Most people spend about 80 percent of their workday communicating—one-half is spent listening, the other half is spent reading, writing, and speaking. In every point of contact with customers, customer service representatives communicate something. As more contact is made with an organization, customers combine their perceptions into an overall impression of the company's customer service. The three basic purposes of business communication are to inform, persuade, and build goodwill. Any CSR who achieves these objectives is comfortable with the communication process.

The Basics of Communication

The truth is, great service requires great communication skills. Think of a time you experienced poor customer service. What made the service poor? Did a failure to communicate contribute to the problem?

- If you didn't get what you wanted, did you say so?
- If your expectations were not met, did you communicate that to the service provider?
- If you perceived that you were being treated rudely, did you discuss the service provider's behavior toward you?

As a working definition, we'll consider that **communication** has been successful if there is shared understanding between two or more persons. So what is the result of shared understanding? Put another way, what are the implications of a lack of shared understanding? To answer these questions, we must first have an understanding of communication fundamentals.

The Communication Process

Understanding the communication process can help CSRs become better communicators. The process shows that each communication event is unique—that one mind is different from another mind. Unless the words or other signals used to send a message have the same meaning or frame of reference, communication suffers in some way in the minds of the sender and receiver.

The human communication process follows this pattern: first, a message arrives from a sender, and the senses pick up the message through signals and relay it to the receiver's brain. This is called the **encoding process**. Next, the receiver's brain filters the message and gives it a unique meaning. The meaning triggers a response, and the receiver returns (by voice, writing, or gestures) the shared understanding of this message to the sender. This is the **decoding process**. Finally, a message transmitted back to the original sender is called **feedback**. This cycle may continue as long as the people involved want to communicate.

There are seven elements in the communication model: the sender, the receiver, a message, signals, the brain, shared understanding, and feedback.

1. *The sender.* The sender has an idea to share with another person. That idea is in the sender's mind and the goal is to get it into the receiver's mind.

2. *The receiver.* The receiver is the person or persons with whom the sender is trying to communicate. The receiver has the responsibility of hearing, listening, and providing feedback to the sender.

3. *A message.* The message is not just some words. The message is a combination of thoughts, feelings, words, and meanings.

4. *Signals.* Signals are the means by which the sender encodes a message and broadcasts it to the intended receivers. Signals include more than the sounds of words; they encompass feelings, attitudes, facial and body gestures, and the sender's unique personality traits.

5. *The brain.* All communication is filtered in the sender's and receiver's brains through personality, background, upbringing, culture, and current state of being. When a person is tired, stressed, or in an unpleasant circumstance, communication is that much harder.

6. *Shared understanding.* The degree to which a receiver understands what a sender is trying to communicate depends on many factors. How much alike are they? Do they share any background experiences? Are their language skills, attitudes, and beliefs similar? What assumptions have they made about each other based on stereotypes and previous perceptions?

7. *Feedback.* Feedback is the receiver's reaction sent back to the sender. Each of us has experienced from time to time the feeling, "He doesn't have a clue what I'm talking about." In most cases, we reach this conclusion by interpreting the verbal or nonverbal feedback the receiver is generating.

Communication theory attempts to explain what happens when we communicate successfully. Here is an example of when communication with a customer goes wrong: A company offers a high-quality product at a competitive price. Customer service policies and systems are flexible and user-friendly. Everyone in the organization knows the value of the customer, and all accept the philosophy that the "customer is king"—yet the customer, based on his or her perception, may still not be satisfied. Often, the problem is mixed messages.

Mixed Messages

A **mixed message** is a single communication that contains two meanings. One part of the message—usually the verbal part—is positive, while the other part of the message—usually the nonverbal component—contradicts the verbal portion and is negative. For example, a salesperson says, "Thank you" to a customer as she rings up the purchase, but does so in a hurried tone and with no eye contact. When the verbal portion and the nonverbal portion of a message contradict one another, the nonverbal portion is almost always believed. This is because nonverbal communication is perceived as less conscious, more honest, and harder for people to fake.

Mixed messages cloud the communication process.

7. An ability to anticipate the client's needs

8. A calm and pleasant tone of voice

9. Honest communication with good eye contact

10. Ease with admitting fault and a sincere desire to set right any misunderstanding

> ## customer service T I P
>
> *Seek to treat each customer fairly, demonstrate sound business practices, and resolve disputes using effective communication techniques.*

Organizations unintentionally send hundreds of mixed messages to customers every day. One example is company policies that claim to be intended for the convenience and protection of the customer, that some customers feel are actually designed to make life easier for managers and their employees. Procedures that require customers to move from one workstation to another to get "taken care of" may provide assembly-line efficiency for the company, but what they communicate to the customer is quite different. When one person sees to our needs, it feels warm and caring. When we interact with many different people, we don't feel nurtured and "taken care of"; instead, we feel processed.

Service-Oriented Communication

What does service-oriented communication look and sound like? Think of a time when you felt you were the only customer the vendor had or when someone went the extra mile for you. In every story you can recall, think about the positive effect communication had when it was factored into the overall buying experience. Service-oriented communication takes on the following ten dimensions:

1. Listening skills that make the other person feel heard

2. Questions framed in a respectful manner

3. A willingness to perform the work needed to reach the desired goal

4. An ability to remain calm and centered, despite chaos or challenge

5. Flawless follow-up by taking full responsibility for bringing communication full-circle

6. A demonstrated understanding of the other person's perspective

focus on Best Practices

The American Management Association® recognizes how hard it is to manage conflict in business so that it doesn't end up managing you. This professional organization offers communication training seminars around the country to improve a person's success in business.

A three-day seminar entitled "Responding to Conflict: Strategies for Improved Communication" is one such opportunity for business professionals who want to better their business communication skills. This seminar teaches participants to understand their own emotions and behaviors when addressing conflict and to find productive ways for managing it. When service professionals become aware of their emotional triggers to prevent explosive situations, they improve their communication performance and ultimately increase the success of customer interactions.

Source: www.amanet.org.

Communication Styles

Good communication skills—both verbal and written—require a high level of self-awareness. By becoming more aware of how others perceive you, you can adapt more readily to their different styles of communicating. This means that you can make another person more comfortable with you by selecting and emphasizing certain behaviors that fit your personality. The selection you make should help you respond naturally to another person's communication style. In business and in our personal lives, we encounter and practice three basic communication styles: aggressive, passive, and assertive.

Aggressive Communication

A person who has an **aggressive communication style** is closed-minded, listens poorly, has difficulty seeing another person's point of view, interrupts other people while they are talking, and tends to monopolize the conversation. Typically, an aggressive communicator feels he or she must win arguments and usually operates from a win or lose position.

Unfortunately, this communication style fosters resistance, defiance, and retaliation. It exacts a high price in personal and business relationships, especially when it comes to satisfying customers. Aggressive communicators express their thoughts and feelings in ways that violate or disregard the rights of others. They tend to

- humiliate and dominate others.
- make choices for others.
- show a lack of respect for others' rights.
- use sarcasm, insult others, and make unfair demands.

Passive Communication

People who communicate using a **passive communication style** tend to be indirect and hesitant to say what is really on their minds. By avoiding or ignoring problems, passive communicators are likely to agree externally, while disagreeing internally. They often feel powerless in confrontational situations because they don't like to make waves or upset anyone.

Passive communicators fail to express their feelings, thoughts, and beliefs, and so, typically give in to others. As a result, they allow others to make choices for them. In general, passive communicators

- believe that other people are more important or more correct than they are.
- are concerned that they will anger someone if they express their true feelings.

In this room, which participants are using aggressive, passive, or assertive communication styles?

- beat around the bush when trying to make a point.
- say nothing is wrong and then become resentful about the situation later.

Assertive Communication

A person who practices an **assertive communication style** tends to be an effective, active listener who states limits and expectations and does not label or judge people or events. By confronting problems at the time they happen, assertive communicators leave themselves open to negotiating, bargaining, and compromising in such a way that everyone involved wins.

The greatest advantage assertive communicators have is the ability to exercise their rights without denying the rights of others. Moreover, they express feelings honestly and directly, while practicing mutual respect for others. Assertive communicators state their message without being blunt or rude and consciously practice good eye contact, while using appropriate hand gestures and other suitable body language.

The assertive communication style is the one to strive for when serving customers. However, the reality is, very few people use only one communication style. In fact, the aggressive style is only essential when

- a decision has to be made quickly or during an emergency.
- you know you are right and that fact is crucial to the outcome for both parties.

The passive style also has its critical applications, such as when

remember this ...

Communication Styles

Style	Behaviors	Nonverbal Cues	Verbal Cues
Aggressive	• Puts others down • Has a know-it-all attitude • Doesn't show appreciation • Is bossy	• Frowns • Squints eyes critically • Glares and stares • Is critical • Uses a loud tone of voice • Has rigid posture	• "You must (should, ought, or better)..." • "Don't ask why. Just do it."
Passive	• Sighs a lot • Clams up when feeling badly treated • Asks permission unnecessarily • Complains instead of taking action	• Fidgets • Smiles and nods in agreement • Has slumped posture • Speaks in a low volume • Is meek	• "You have more experience than I do." • "I don't think I can..." • "This is probably wrong, but..." • "I'll try."
Assertive	• Operates from choice • Is action-oriented • Is realistic in expectations • Behaves in a fair, consistent manner • Is firm	• Has open, natural gestures • Uses direct eye contact • Has a confident, relaxed posture • Uses a varied rate of speech	• "I choose to..." • "What are my options?" • "What alternatives do we have?"

FIGURE 8.1

• an issue arises that is much more important to the customer's happiness than to the business's. In this case, passive communication on the CSR's part may be the best option to keep the customer happy.

• emotions are running high, and it makes sense to take a break to calm down and regain perspective about the situation.

Refer to Figure 8.1 for more information about behavior and nonverbal and verbal cues of each communication style.

Communicating with Customers in Person

Telecommunications, computerization, and self-service have reduced person-to-person communication to minutes and sometimes seconds. For CSRs to provide superior customer service in this fast-paced, competitive business world, they must be able to gather information appropriately by asking and answering questions. When working with customers, *how* CSRs pose a question is often as important as *what* they ask.

Asking Questions

Time and again, customers call with questions. To answer customers' questions and address their needs, you should ask questions also. Typically, questioning others continues a discussion or pinpoints and clarifies issues when gathering pertinent information.

Asking a question skillfully increases the likelihood of quickly getting a good understanding of the issues. The person doing the questioning is usually in control of the discussion. Therefore, all questions should be asked in a positive way. A **positive question** is one that the customer is not afraid to answer. By rewording a "you" statement into an "I" statement, you can steer clear of questions that use sarcastic language or a threatening tone.

For example, avoid, "What exactly are *you* getting at?" or "Could *you* get to the point a little quicker?" and say instead "*I* don't understand what you are trying to tell me" or "Could you please try to explain it in a different way so *I* can understand better?"

Relative to questioning techniques, avoid bombarding the customer with questions or using a multiple-question approach when serving customers.

- *Bombardment approach.* Asks too many questions in a short period of time and puts customers on the defensive. This tactic controls the conversation but may limit the information gained. "Why" questions, if improperly asked, often cause individuals to become defensive.
- *Multiple-question approach.* Asks many questions wrapped up as one. When a question actually contains several questions, clients may get confused about which one to answer. In addition, individuals from non-Western cultures do not receive rapid-fire questions favorably, and this creates distrust.

To get the response you want, you need to know how to choose the appropriate type of question to ask. During the course of a normal conversation, you will be using all types of questions to gather a lot of data into information you can use. Depending on the situation, use an assortment of open, probing, closed, alternative choice, leading, and direct questions.

1. An **open question** requests information in a way that requires a fuller answer than a simple "yes" or "no." Open questions encourage an individual to talk and elicit maximum information to identify causes so you can work more quickly and effectively toward solutions. Open questions usually begin with action verbs or "How," "What," or "Why." As a result of asking open questions, CSRs are able to gain more information, which makes offering solutions or suggestions to customer problems much easier. Examples are, "Describe the kind of engine noise you are hearing," "How can I assist you?" and "What information were you given when you spoke with the CSR yesterday?"

2. A **probing question** uses information already established to clarify points and ask for more details. Often, these questions promptly follow up a previous question and response, for example, "Whom did you speak with yesterday?" "When did you purchase the product?" "Can you always be reached at this telephone number?" and "Tell me more about how you are feeling."

3. **Closed questions** usually elicit a "yes" or "no" answer. Closed questions can be useful in the concluding minutes of a customer conversation to confirm small details and to make sure that you have

covered all the topics concerning the customer's query. These questions elicit specific information and usually begin with "Where," "Are," or "Do." Examples are, "Do you want these items delivered?" and "Are there other questions you have for me at this time?"

4. **Alternative choice questions** provide alternatives for the customer to choose from. These questions can be particularly useful when dealing with difficult customers. The approach is to ask customers what they would like you to do for them, but to limit their responses by providing them with two or three alternatives that also suit you. Examples are, "I could find this information for you and call you with an answer by the end of the morning, or would you prefer me to fax the information later in the day?" and "Would you like me to get our supervisor, or would you like to give me an opportunity to try to help first?"

5. **Leading questions** help speed up interactions with people who find it difficult to make a final decision, and they help the customer confirm information in an easy way. Some examples are, "You would like to receive the catalog updates on a monthly basis, then?" and "So, you would agree on a delivery this coming Thursday, if I can get you a discount?"

6. **Direct questions** can be open or closed; however, all direct questions have two characteristics in common: the name of the other person is always used, and the question is posed as an instruction. Examples are, "Tell me, Mr. Harkins, . . . ," "Explain to me, Mr. Siskowski, . . . ," and "Describe to me, Ms. Chada, . . ." Using the other person's name puts you in a better position to get his or her immediate attention. In phrasing the question as an instruction ("Tell me, . . ."), you are giving a subconscious order.

customer service TIP

Don't answer your twentieth question of the day as if it were your twentieth question of the day. Instead, answer your twentieth question as if it were your first question. It may be the twentieth time you hear the same question, but keep in mind, it's probably the first time the customer has asked it.

Answering Questions

Answering customer questions effectively is equally important as asking the right questions. Here are several tips to consider before answering customer questions:

- *Understand the question.* Pay attention to every word the customer uses when asking a question. Once you understand the question, then respond.

- *Decide whether you know the answer.* If you are not sure that your response is accurate, do not answer. Although quick responses are preferred, providing correct information is always the first priority.

- *Remember, you are an expert.* As a CSR, you know your job better than anyone else. If you are certain you are right and you can back up your answer with facts, politely claim the truth of what you say. Again, do not promise something you cannot deliver.

- *Take enough time.* If a customer needs assistance, don't refuse to help because you are too busy. Also, do not pass the client from person to person.

- *Smile.* If you've got a cranky customer or one who insists you are not right, bend over backwards to make him or her happy. Be pleasant at all times when answering the customer's questions.

- *Never answer a question with a question.* Questions should be asked only to clarify the original question; beyond that—answer, don't ask.

- *Be careful with your power.* Never belittle a customer or criticize a question you receive. Don't say, "Can't you see the sign over the door that says . . . ?" or "You mean you don't know?"

- *When you don't know, admit it.* If you are sure you don't know the answer to a question, say so. Admit you don't know, but make an effort to find someone who does.

Using Positive Language

Language is an exceedingly powerful tool. Whatever the method of communication, verbal or written, the way you express yourself affects whether the message is received positively or negatively. The impact of unpleasant news can be softened by the use of positive language. **Positive language** projects a helpful, encouraging feeling rather than a destructive, negative one.

No doubt you are familiar with "the cynic," the person who often criticizes ideas or provides reasons why something won't work. If you've ever worked or associated with such a person, you know that this kind of negative communication is very arduous. Additionally, the cynic's constant challenging creates a negative environment and increased confrontational situations.

People who are cynical don't always have negative attitudes. In many cases, they simply use language that gives the impression of negativity. They have not learned to phrase their comments in more constructive, positive ways. **Negative language** conveys a poor image to customers and may cause conflict and confrontation where none is necessary or desired. Its use should be avoided. Falling into the negative language pattern, however, is very easy, and many of us do so without being aware of it. Read the following dialogue that could take place at a business service counter:

> "We regret to inform you that we cannot process your application to register your business name because you have neglected to provide sufficient information. Please complete *all* sections of the attached form and return it to us promptly."

Note the high incidence of negative words—*cannot* and *neglected*. The message has a tone that suggests that the recipient is to blame for the problem. Contrast this example with the following rewritten, more positive approach:

> "Congratulations on your new business. To register your business name, we need some additional information. Please return the attached form, completing the highlighted areas, so we can send your business registration certificate within one week. We wish you success in your new endeavor."

Notice that the negative example tells the person what he or she has done wrong but doesn't stress the positive things that can be done to remedy the problem. The information is all there, but it sounds bureaucratic, cold, and negative. The positive example sounds completely

remember this ...
Common Negative Language

Expressions that suggest carelessness	• "You neglected to specify..." • "You failed to include..." • "You overlooked enclosing..."
Phrases that suggest the person is lying	• "You claim that..." • "You say that..." • "You state that..."
Expressions that imply that the recipient is not too bright	• "We cannot see how you..." • "We fail to understand..." • "We are at a loss to know..."
Demanding phrases that imply coercion and pressure	• "You should..." • "We must ask you to..." • "We must insist that you..."
Phrases that might be interpreted as sarcastic or patronizing	• "No doubt..." • "We will thank you to..." • "You understand, of course, ..."

FIGURE 8.2

different; although it contains a lot of the same information, it has a more upbeat and helpful tone. Negative language often has these characteristics:

- It tells the recipient what cannot be done.
- It has a subtle tone of blame.
- It includes words such as *can't*, *won't*, and *unable to*, which tell the recipient what the sender cannot do.
- It does not stress positive actions that would be appropriate.

Positive language displays these qualities:

- It tells the recipient what can be done.
- It suggests alternatives and choices available to the recipient.
- It sounds helpful and encouraging rather than bureaucratic.
- It stresses positive actions and consequences that can be anticipated.

The first task in moving toward more positive communication is to identify and eliminate common negative

remember this ...
Examples of Positive Phrasing

- "If you can send us your bill of sale, we will be happy to complete the process for you."

- "The information we have suggests that you have a different viewpoint on this issue. Let me explain our perspective."

- "Might we suggest that you ... [suggestion]."

- "One option open to you is ... [option]."

FIGURE 8.3

phrasing. Figure 8.2 lists some familiar expressions that should be avoided whenever possible in communicating with customers. Figure 8.3 offers some examples of conveying the same information with positive phrasing.

Handling Customer Requests

When handling customer requests, special service skills are sometimes required. The best response to a request is "yes," but sometimes "I'm not sure" cannot be avoided, or "no" is even required. Here's how to handle each circumstance:

SAYING "YES" Use a friendly voice tone, combined with positive, cheerful words. Clearly tell the customer what you can do for him or her.

SAYING "NO" Empathize with the customer and help if you can. Explain why you cannot complete the request. Choose words that are calming and soothing. When customers are distracted or emotionally upset, they may not hear what you intended to say, so make every effort to use positive, clear, effective phrases.

SAYING "I'M NOT SURE" Use this phrase when you are not sure if the request can be completed or what options you can offer, or if you don't have the authority to address the request.

customer service T I P

Use creative ways to say "no" to a customer. If you must use the word policy, do so only for matters of legal compliance, ethics, or absolute performance standards, such as employee or customer safety.

Sensitive Issues

In the rush of doing our jobs, we sometimes forget that we are not merely serving customers; we are in the business of serving people who have real lives and experiences. When individuals approach us for assistance, we see only a snippet of their existence. We have no way of knowing what challenges or crises they are quietly coping with as they approach us. Providing rude or apathetic service is always bad business, but to provide it to a person who is suffering mental or physical pain is simply bad human behavior.

When serving others, it is safe to assume that some of the customers you encounter on most days are undergoing personal distress. Who these people are or what crises they face will likely never be revealed, but rest assured, your actions will make a positive or negative impact on their outlook for the day. The following are some sobering statistics about various crises people (customers) in America face every day. For each situation, reflect and then ask yourself how you will treat these people when they come to you for service.

- *Death of a loved one.* Each day in America, more than 6,500 people die, and many customers walking around today are dealing with shocking news about the death of a loved one.
- *Suicide.* Today, more than 90 people will take their own lives, and another 1,350 will attempt suicide. This means that sometime today, many CSRs unknowingly have the opportunity to convince these people they are valuable human beings.
- *Divorce.* Today, 3,440 spouses will be served with papers for divorce. For many of them, this will be a surprise causing absolute devastation.
- *Missing children.* Today, more than 2,000 children will be listed as missing. How will you treat their parents when they come to you for service?
- *Death of pet.* Today, more than 16,000 faithful house pets—dogs and cats with an average age of ten years—will die. Losing a loving pet saddens us greatly.
- *Loss of job.* Today, more than 7,000 people will be laid off, fired, or otherwise removed from their jobs. How will you treat these people when they come to you for service?[1]

---

[1]Mike Johnson, "You Never Know What Crisis Your Customer Is Facing," *A Supervisor's Guide to Improved Customer Service and Retention* (December 2000): 6.

Ethics **/ Choices**

How would you react if a customer began talking to you about a faulty product, and suddenly her eyes filled with tears and she was unable to continue?

Fundamentals of Business Writing

From simple e-mails to formal customer letters, CSRs will need to compose documents that educate, persuade, inform, or enlighten the customer. Writing is an essential element of business communication. The ability to write effectively is a skill you learn; it comes naturally to only a few gifted individuals.

Business writing experts say that the most important strategy behind good written communication is to be clear. Striving for clarity is important, even if the subject is difficult. It is much better to be as honest as you can be, within whatever limits are set by your work, rather than to write around the problem. Second to clarity is the skillful and professional presentation of the written communication. Presentation reflects your company's professionalism, quality, and reputation. The costs of sloppy and poorly written documents with spelling or grammatical errors can be staggering to organizations.

customer service **T I P**

When writing to customers, some important books to have on hand are a good dictionary, a thesaurus, and one or two office handbooks. These reference books are also available in electronic form, either online or as part of a complete word-processing software package, such as Microsoft® Word.

Identify the Audience

Clear writing is essential if you want your message to be understood by the recipient; what makes writing clear will vary and is ultimately dependent on your target audience. Before you write, it is critical to understand whom you are addressing.

When conveying information, put yourself in your audience's shoes. What is important to them? How can you make sure that what you have to say becomes important to the reader? Answering these questions takes an awareness of your audience and an understanding of how people best receive messages. The vocabulary you use and the organizational structure you give the piece of writing depend on whom you are addressing and what your message is.

Write Clearly with a Purpose in Mind

Before writing the first sentence, decide what the message should be. Are you conveying information to an upset customer? Are you following up with a customer to clarify issues from a recent phone conversation? Do you want your reader to *do* something when he or she finishes reading your message? If you aren't sure what your purpose is, your reader won't be either. If you want your reader to take some type of action, clearly state the benefits *he or she* will receive by doing what you ask in terms that are meaningful to this person.

Because most people today spend little time reading, they want the whole picture in concise, easy-to-understand, and grammatically correct language. At the heart of effective writing is the ability to organize a series of thoughts. Once you've identified your true objective, take the time to list and prioritize the key points you want to make supporting that purpose. For some, an outline works best, because it allows writers to visualize their thought processes on paper and in some detail. For others, the best ideas come from using the creative approach of simply jotting down ideas as they brainstorm the major elements of the message they want to convey.

Get to the point by presenting your primary message or call to action as quickly as possible. Few busy people today have the time or patience to wade through long introductory paragraphs before coming to the point of a document. Provide just enough information to capture readers' attention and let them know what is being asked of them.

Use the Proper Tone

Tone is present in all communication activities. The overall tone of a written message affects the reader, just as one's tone of voice in oral exchanges affects the listener. **Tone** refers to the writer's attitude toward the reader and the subject of the message.

BE CONFIDENT Careful preparation and knowledge about the ideas you wish to express instill confidence.

BE COURTEOUS AND SINCERE A writer builds goodwill by using a tone that is polite and sincere. Be respectful and honest, and readers will be more willing to accept your message, even if it is negative.

USE NONDISCRIMINATORY LANGUAGE Nondiscriminatory language addresses all people equally and expresses respect for all individuals. It does not use any discriminatory words, remarks, or ideas.

STRESS THE BENEFITS FOR THE READER A reader will want to know, "What's in it for me?" Your job is to write from the reader's perspective, or with a "you" attitude. It's better to say, "Your order will be available in two weeks" than "I am processing your order tomorrow."

BUSINESS *in action*

TEXT ALERTS

On the edge of a new kind of communication, some innovative companies are providing a text-messaging service to their customers. For example, customers can sign up to receive up-to-date information about their auto insurance policies or banking transactions through text messages sent directly to their cell phones. If they would like, customers can also sign up to receive payment reminders, payment confirmations, and other account information. The beauty of this communication method is that customers get the information instantly, without having to be connected to their e-mail.

Concluding Message for CSRs

How important is practicing good communication skills with customers? More customers leave one company for another because of poor customer service than dissatisfaction with a product. A lost customer is never just one lost sale, or even just one lost customer, but a chain of events that has an impact on a large scale.

One unhappy customer talks to someone who may have been a satisfied customer, but now is not so sure, and so on. Keep in mind that it doesn't matter whether customers are right or wrong; what matters is how they *feel* when they leave an interaction or a conversation with you, the representative for a company. Before ending an interaction with a customer, always ask, "Is there anything else I can do for you? If you need me, you can reach me by...."

Summary

- The seven elements in the communication process are the sender, the receiver, a message, signals, the brain, shared understanding, and feedback.
- Communication styles vary and include aggressive, passive, and assertive.
- When clarifying issues with customers, consider the information you want to get and choose from among the six types of questions: open, probing, closed, alternative choice, leading, or direct.
- In written communication, understand whom you are addressing, what you want your message to accomplish, and how to incorporate the right tone for the message.

KEY TERMS

aggressive communication style

alternative choice questions

assertive communication style

closed questions

communication

decoding process

direct questions

encoding process

feedback

leading questions

mixed message

negative language

open question

passive communication style

positive language

positive question

probing question

tone

CRITICAL THINKING

1. Recount two situations you participated in or observed this past week in which mixed messages were sent.

2. Describe the behaviors of a person you know who predominately uses a passive communication style; an aggressive communication style; an assertive communication style.

3. Assume that a customer returns an article of clothing or a household item for a refund or credit. Develop six queries a CSR might use in this situation that make use of each type of question: open, probing, closed, alternative choice, leading, and direct.

4. Describe your reaction to a personal or business letter you've received recently that you perceived as having an inappropriate tone. How did it make you feel?

ONLINE RESEARCH ACTIVITIES

Project 8.1 Communication Styles

Research a number of websites and locate several articles on communication styles in a working environment. As a result of your research, prepare a short oral presentation (ten minutes or less) entitled "The Impact of Communication Styles on Customer Service," as directed by your instructor.

Project 8.2 Popular Word-Processing Features

On-Time Technology Products is in the process of revising its correspondence manual in the Customer Service Department. Mary Graeff has decided to incorporate the use of many of the electronic writing tools in word-processing software packages in revising the current manual.

Go to the websites of Microsoft and Corel® that sell the popular word-processing packages, Microsoft Word and Corel WordPerfect®. In the table below, compare the features listed for each package. If possible, also locate online a consumer report comparing the two packages feature by feature.

Feature	Microsoft Word	Corel WordPerfect
Templates and wizards		
AutoCorrect		
AutoFormat		
Spelling and grammar check		
Research tool		
Mail merge		
Thesaurus		

 COMMUNICATION SKILLS AT WORK

Project 8.3 Language That Makes a Difference

Brainstorm with other students to provide more appropriate responses to each of the negative language statements shown here. *Hint:* Use "I" statements rather than "you" statements.

1. "You didn't do this right."

_____

_____

_____

2. "You are wrong."

_____

_____

_____

3. "Wait here."

_____

_____

_____

4. "It's not my job."

_____

_____

_____

5. "What's your problem?"

_____

_____

_____

6. "You aren't making any sense."

_____

_____

_____

7. "Why are you so upset?"

_____

_____

_____

DECISION MAKING AT WORK

Project 8.4 The New CSR—Temporary Hire

A temporary, six-month CSR position has just been filled at On-Time Technology Products. The new hire is Abhey Patel, a very nice and bright person, who everyone agrees works extremely hard. Abhey has recently established citizenship in America from his homeland, India. Realizing the need to write to customers using proper English and grammar, the other CSRs have been covering for Abhey, doing his letter writing and e-mail messaging for him. He is trying very hard to learn English, but he hasn't mastered all the fine points yet.

Respond to these questions regarding Abhey's situation:

1. Can you think of ways to help Abhey complete his duties on his own more easily?

_____

_____

_____

2. Do you feel that the supervisor should be informed that Abhey has not yet developed his business writing skills and that others are doing his work for him? Is this practice of covering for Abhey hurting anyone or OTTP?

_____

_____

_____

CASE STUDIES

Project 8.5 "I'll Take That Customer!"

Neal Erwin has a reputation he has always been proud of in the Haskin's Bookstore customer service department. He takes calls from customers that others don't want to deal with. Sometimes when he is on the phone with a customer, he asks coworkers to come near his desk to hear his side of the argument. In the past, he has gotten loud and belligerent with customers and later has even boasted of "winning." Things have changed, however, and Neal is now in trouble with management because of a recent incident.

A loyal 20-year customer, who spoke to Neal last week, has just left the store and expressed in no uncertain terms that she was taking her business elsewhere.

1. In your opinion, should Neal have been allowed to get away with his behavior to customers? Explain.

_____

_____

_____

2. As a coworker of Neal's, would you have any responsibility to report his aggressive communication style to his supervisor?

_____

_____

_____

Project 8.6 "I Understand How You Might Feel That Way"

Doug went into work this morning at On-Time Technology Products and casually mentioned to his fellow CSRs that his wife had just been to a communications in-service training for her company, where she learned the "feel, felt, found" technique for responding to customer questions and concerns. Doug wasn't sure how using this technique would work at OTTP, but he thought it was worth discussing with his coworkers.

According to what Doug's wife told him, the technique works this way: when a customer expresses a concern, the CSR should respond by saying, "I understand how you might *feel* that way. Others have *felt* that that way too. Then they *found,* after an explanation, that this policy protects them, so it made sense."

1. What is your first reaction to communicating with customers using the "feel, felt, found" approach?

_____

_____

_____

2. How extensively do you think it could be applied to most customer problems and concerns?

_____

_____

_____

3. Identify and discuss with fellow students situations when it would not be advisable to use this approach with customers.

_____

_____

_____

Customer-Focused Listening Skills

Nature has given to man one tongue, but two ears that we may hear from others twice as much as we speak.

—EPICTETUS, GREEK PHILOSOPHER, C. 55–135 CE

Customers have needs beyond completing a simple business transaction; they have emotional needs as well. They need to feel welcome, important, valued, and understood. There is no better way to show customers respect, concern, and understanding than by listening to them. Successful customer service representatives understand the benefits of customer-focused listening, and they continually fine-tune their listening skills.

Three Levels of Listening

People listen at different levels of efficiency throughout the day, depending on the circumstances, their attitudes about the speaker, and their past experiences. Most people have difficulty listening effectively when dealing with conflict or emotionally charged people, when criticism is being directed at them, or when they're feeling anxious, fearful, or angry.

A conscious awareness of your listening behavior will go a long way toward helping you become an effective listener. By dividing listening into three levels, it is easier to characterize certain behaviors that affect listening efficiency. These levels are not sharply distinct but, rather, are general categories into which people fall. They may and often do overlap, depending on the situation.

As a person moves from the least effective level to the most effective level, the potential for understanding and retaining what is said increases. The following descriptions of the three levels will help you understand the distinctions in how each level is expressed by listeners.

Level 1 Listening

A person listening at level 1 demonstrates the characteristics of a good listener. These listeners look for an area of interest in the speaker's message; they view listening as an opportunity to gather new and useful information. Effective listeners are aware of their personal biases. They are better able to avoid making automatic judgments about the speaker and avoid being influenced by emotionally charged words.

Good listeners suspend judgment, are empathetic to the other person's feelings, and can see issues from the other person's point of view. Level 1 listeners take extra time to mentally summarize the stated message, question or evaluate what was said, and consciously notice nonverbal cues. Their overall focus is on listening with a high degree of understanding and respect.

customer service T I P

Former President Lyndon Johnson had a plaque on the wall of his office that said, "You ain't learning nothing when you are talking."

Level 2 Listening

At level 2, a person is listening mainly to words and the content of what is being said, but the listener does not fully understand what the words mean. Although there are thousands of words in the English vocabulary, the average adult in the United States uses only 500 of them. Given that each one of these words has between 20 and 25 meanings, this signifies that on a regular basis, we are using approximately 500 words with the possibility of 12,500 different meanings. Adding to the confusion is the large amount of slang in everyday language. The important factor here is that words themselves don't communicate; the meaning and understanding of words make communication work.

In application, level 2 listeners focus on words, but many times they miss the intent—what is being expressed nonverbally through tone of voice, body posture, gestures,

facial expression, and eye movement. As a result, level 2 listeners hear what the speaker says but make little effort to understand the speaker's intent. This can often lead to misunderstandings, incorrect actions, and loss of time. Because the listener *appears* to be listening by nodding his or her head in agreement and not asking clarifying questions, the speaker may be lulled into a false sense of feeling understood when that may not be the case.

Level 3 Listening

A level 3 listener may be daydreaming, forming a premature reply, or faking attention while thinking about unrelated matters. In general, this type of listener is more interested in talking than in listening. When level 3 listening occurs, it can cause relationship breakdowns, conflicts, and poor decision making. These listeners find fault and judge what is being said by responding defensively or becoming overly emotional. This reaction can result in either the speaker or the listener moving away from the conversation.

About 20 percent of the working population spends most of their time at level 1, with the other 80 percent fluctuating between levels 2 and 3, only occasionally reaching level 1.[1] There are many benefits for customer service representatives who listen effectively to the customers they serve. When customers know they are talking to an active level 1 listener, there is an open communication to problem solving rather than placing blame on others.

Active Listening

Listening is not a passive activity. Fully understanding the meaning of what someone says requires energy and discipline, both of which contribute to what is known as active listening. **Active listening** is listening with your whole mind and body—not just your ears. It requires putting one's own feelings aside while trying to understand what the other person is saying. Failing to listen actively results in not fully understanding the customer's needs. Don't assume you know what a customer wants after he or she speaks the first few sentences.

Two things happen when you practice active listening: the customer senses you care, and you gain a more comprehensive picture of the service situation. Greater

---

[1] Madelyn Burley-Allen, "Listen Up: Listening Is a Learned Skill," *HR Magazine* (November 2001): 10.

understanding allows you to respond more effectively and to meet a customer's biggest need—to be heard.

Listed below are five strategies that will help improve your active listening skills:

1. *Be ready to listen.* Do this with your eyes, head, and heart as well as your ears. Have paper and a pencil handy, or clear your computer screen and be ready for the next customer contact. Eliminate all distractions that are not conducive to an effective listening environment. Be aware of any internal, physical distractions that you feel, such as hunger, fatigue, headache, or emotional stress. These can affect your ability to listen carefully.

2. *Be ready to take notes.* If you are speaking to the customer on the phone, let him or her know you are taking notes. Say, "I'm concerned about this, so I'm writing it down." When customers know you are taking notes, they are less likely to repeat themselves. This may also help them organize their thoughts so they state their messages more clearly.

3. *Demonstrate that you are listening.* While the speaker is talking, nod in agreement or ask questions if something is unclear. Use your body language, stance, posture, and eye contact to show attentive silence. When talking on the phone, use caring words, such as "okay" and "I understand," to provide verbal reinforcement. This lets the customer know you are actively listening.

4. *Ask questions.* The goal is to get the customer talking. Ask appropriate and thoughtful questions in order to clarify the speaker's words and determine the true nature of the problem.

5. *Restate the customer's points.* Don't just repeat what the customer said, but put the message in your own words and emphasize the main points as you understand them to be. This way, you will know when you are on the right course, because the customer can correct you, if necessary.

Take the quiz in Figure 9.1 to determine how your listening skills rate.

Effective Listening

Customer service representatives who are skilled listeners communicate more effectively and make better decisions. As human beings, we tend to filter the information we hear. All too often, what we think we hear is not the correct understanding of what was said. **Filtering** is the process of

remember this ...
Listening Skills Quiz

True	False	
☐	☐	1. During a conversation, I ask questions to clarify details.
☐	☐	2. I don't let distractions pull my attention from the conversation.
☐	☐	3. I don't use expressions such as "really" and "uh-huh" to mask my inattentiveness.
☐	☐	4. I don't allow myself to think about other topics while listening to others.
☐	☐	5. I maintain eye contact while talking to others.
☐	☐	6. I don't fidget or do other tasks while another person is speaking.
☐	☐	7. When someone asks me for advice, I make sure my facts are correct.
☐	☐	8. If I can't ignore a distraction, such as a ringing telephone, I make plans to continue the conversation at a later time.
☐	☐	9. I don't rush the other person to make his or her point in a conversation.
☐	☐	10. I follow up with the person from time to time to see what progress has been made since our initial conversation.

How did you do? Each "True" response puts you one step closer to giving customers the great service and attention they deserve. Consider "False" responses as opportunities for improvement.

FIGURE 9.1

interpreting messages through our own biases. Using our personal filters can result in our deflecting or stopping the listening process.

Listening requires participation and involvement. Customer-focused listening is based on looking for the underlying feelings in each message. Feelings are often more important than the words themselves. Here are some winning strategies for developing effective listening skills:

- *Realize that listening is hard work.* To listen well, prepare yourself mentally. Don't allow yourself to do other things as you listen, such as answering the phone, doing paperwork, playing on the computer, or checking your e-mail.
- *Make good use of the thought–speech ratio.* People can think roughly four times faster than a speaker can talk. As a result, it is difficult to concentrate on what another person is saying because we let our minds wander or start thinking ahead to fill in the gap.
- *Seek to listen in more than one way.* Listen with your eyes as well as your ears. Look for nonverbal clues to see whether they reinforce or contradict what the person is saying.

- *Give the speaker space.* Avoid invading another person's personal space. In a customer service situation, 4 to 6 feet is the optimum distance for helping another person feel at ease while talking with you.
- *Don't begin speaking the moment the person stops talking.* Pause a moment before responding to demonstrate that you are not rushing through the conversation and are trying to understand what was said. As a result, the speaker will feel comfortable in sharing more information with you.
- *Develop an open posture that encourages the other person to talk.* Lean toward the speaker while maintaining a comfortable distance, gesture toward the person as you listen and respond, and use the speaker's name in the conversation.

Effective listening involves more than just *hearing* (the physical act of processing sounds) what the other person is saying. It requires finding the real meaning of the words as well as the unspoken message behind those words. Refer to Figure 9.2 for additional listening techniques.

remember this ...
Listening Techniques

1.	Pay attention	Concentrate on what is being said. This means putting aside whatever you are doing for a few minutes—including your thoughts, worries, and preoccupations—and listening to the speaker.
2.	Be courteous	Listen respectfully to everything that is being said, even if you do not agree. Don't interrupt or cut the person off in mid-sentence.
3.	Nod your head	This nodding gesture indicates that you hear and understand—but do not necessarily agree with—what is being said.
4.	Repeat the statement	For clarification, repeat the ideas as you understand them. This lets the speaker know whether further explanation is needed. You could say, "What you are saying is..." or "If I heard you correctly, ..."
5.	Don't be judgmental	Allow the other person to state his or her case in full. Listen to the whole idea and think about its merits without passing judgment. Set aside your own prejudices, frames of reference, and desires so that you can experience—as much as possible—what is happening in the other person's world.
6.	Ask follow-up questions	Demonstrate that you've been attentive by asking an intelligent question. Changing the subject immediately after a person makes a statement sends the message that you are not interested in what the person has just said.
7.	Listen with your entire body	Sit up straight, lean forward slightly, and look at the person's face as he or she is speaking. Listen for the words between the words. Listen for feeling. Listen for meaning. Give your undivided attention as you weigh each word, phrase, and sentence being spoken.
8.	Respect the other person	Use an inclusive, friendly, and sharing tone of voice rather than an exclusionary, hostile, or condescending tone.

FIGURE 9.2

Feedback

Feedback is the final link in the chain of the communication process. After receiving a message, the receiver responds in some way and signals that response to the sender. The signal may take the form of a spoken comment, a long sigh, a written message, a smile, or some other action. Even a lack of response is, in a sense, a form of response. Without feedback, the sender cannot confirm that the receiver has interpreted the message correctly, if at all.

Feedback plays an important role by indicating significant communication barriers: differences in background, interpretations of words, and emotional reactions. It not only regulates the listening process but also reinforces and stimulates it. To better understand what speakers are really saying and show understanding of the message, a listener can draw on three types of feedback: reflective, responsive, and reactive. **Reflective feedback** mirrors content and intent: "If I understand you correctly, what you are saying is..." or "So, you feel that... because...." **Responsive feedback** characterizes the listener's feelings: "When you [action], I feel [reaction]." **Reactive feedback** affirms the speaker's message: "I had a similar experience. It was...." (Be careful not to use this technique to achieve one-upmanship over the speaker.)

Passive Listening

While effective listening is an active process, **passive listening** is characterized by hearing without sending any feedback. Because passive listening takes very little energy, most information is lost. Examples include forgetting a person's name when introduced, not hearing a customer's true needs, and forgetting critical commitments you've made to a customer over the phone. Passive listening offers no indication of acceptance or rejection of the message, no evidence of evaluation or support, and no empathy with or sympathy for the speaker.

Some reasons why people fall victim to passive listening when serving customers follow:

- It's human nature to have an agenda when it comes to communication. We get preoccupied with what we are going to say next and fail to pay attention to the present situation.
- Preexisting conditions are issues that have gotten into our minds prior to a conversation. This takes our attention away from the current conversation and puts us in a passive listening mode.

focus on Management

According to a recent study of more than 1,400 leaders and managers by The Ken Blanchard Companies®, a global consultancy group, the biggest mistake business leaders make is not communicating with or listening to their workforce. Four listening-related questions from the study revealed this information:

1. Forty-one percent of the workforce felt inappropriate use of communication or listening was the biggest mistake leaders made when working with others.

2. Forty-three percent felt the most critical skills a leader could possess were communicating and listening, followed by effective management skills, emotional intelligence and empathy, values and integrity, and vision and empowerment.

3. Eighty-two percent indicated that the one action managers failed to do most often when working with others was to provide appropriate feedback.

4. Eighty-one percent felt that failing to listen or involve others in the process was nearly as big a failing as not providing appropriate feedback.

Source: http://www.management-issues.com.

The best way to eliminate or minimize passive listening is to be aware of it and make a conscious effort to avoid it.

Selective Listening

Most people have the ability to be good listeners if their minds aren't cluttered, if they agree with what is being said, or if they like the person they are conversing with. However, when any of these conditions are not met, it is difficult to listen accurately. Although unintentional, it still happens.

A speaker may be an excellent communicator, but if the listener is distracted by outside interference, selective listening may occur. **Selective listening** is hearing only what you want to hear—filtering out what's not important or of no interest to you. A selective listener finds concentration difficult, has a cluttered mind, or may be tense with emotion. Effective listening under these circumstances is difficult, at best.

Reasons for selective listening abound. One may be as simple as the kind of day you are having and how you are reacting to it. It's important to recognize that when you feel anger, joy, excitement, or boredom, each of these conditions affects your listening habits. Another reason might be that you tune out someone who strikes you the wrong way due to appearance, ethnic background, or manner. When this happens, notice how little you hear of what this person says.

When people say things we don't want to hear or express opposing viewpoints, many of us slip into a selective-listening mode. We either tune these speakers out or we become so busy planning our responses to their ideas that we don't hear what they are saying. Instead, we should hear them out. It is through attentive listening, not selective listening, that we discover important information that may alter our opinions and subsequent actions during customer service exchanges.

Empathetic Listening

When customer concerns have emotional overtones, empathize before giving an answer or advice. **Empathy** is seeking to understand the other person's position without getting emotionally involved yourself. Putting yourself in the customer's place can help you analyze the message from his or her perspective.

Empathy not only bolsters understanding but also is a powerful tool for customer loyalty. As an effective listener, you set in motion a positive, mutually rewarding process by demonstrating interest in the customer and what he or she is saying. Empathetic listening encourages honesty, mutual respect, understanding, and a feeling of security in the customer. When we listen empathetically, we seek to understand the beliefs, emotions, and goals of other people.

Here are some guiding principles to follow when listening thoughtfully:

- *Be attentive.* When you are alert, attentive, and relaxed, the speaker feels important and more secure.
- *Be interested in the speaker's needs.* Show you are listening with understanding and mutual respect.

- *Listen with a caring attitude.* Be a sounding board by allowing the speaker to bounce ideas and feelings off of you while you assume a nonjudgmental, noncritical manner. Be careful not to ask a lot of questions right away, so as not to put off the speaker.
- *Act as a mirror.* Reflect what you think the other person is feeling. Summarize by restating what the person has said, to make sure you understand.
- *Don't get personally involved.* Getting personally involved in a problem usually results in anger and hurt feelings, which can result in jumping to conclusions and becoming judgmental.
- *Use verbal cues.* Acknowledge the person's statement using brief expressions, such as "Hmmm," "I see," "Right," or "Interesting." Encourage the speaker to reveal more by saying, "Tell me about it," or "I'm interested in what you have to say."

> ### customer service **T I P**
> *Be aware that people listen, process, and react to messages in a variety of ways, depending on their behavior, cultural background, and relationship to the speaker.*

Roadblocks to Communicating and Listening

While listening, you transmit and receive. As a CSR, you have a great deal that is of value to share with your customers. Unintentional listening errors can result in misunderstandings and wasted time and money as well as missed business opportunities. The messages delivered by truly great communicators are clear, consistent, direct, human, and personal.

However, even the best communicators occasionally encounter obstacles when responding to another person. The good news is that you can remove these communication roadblocks by becoming better at listening. Being aware of the following six communication roadblocks is an important step to becoming a better listener.

1. *Judging or criticizing.* Although we are often taught that criticism helps people improve, it is not always the best response when trying to help a person with a problem. Even if the intention is to be supportive, by

judging and criticizing, we may inadvertently demean a person who is already struggling.

2. *Naming or labeling.* Responding to a person in this way makes him or her feel inadequate by attaching a stigma to the person, a problem, or a behavior.

3. *Commanding or ordering.* Sometimes we think we have the best, most obvious solution to a person's problem, but responding with a command or an order about what someone should do implies that the person is not competent to judge or act independently.

4. *Moralizing.* When a listener responds by telling someone what to do and then backs up the solution with a moral or theological authority, it is known as moralizing. Moralizing implies that the speaker lacks the moral compass to come up with a responsible solution on his or her own.

5. *Diverting.* Diverting happens when listeners attempt to throw aside a speaker's problems by switching to a more comfortable topic. By doing this, the listener loses the opportunity to truly understand the speaker's concerns and therefore loses the chance to strengthen the relationship.

6. *Advising.* Advising is premature problem solving that tells the other person how to solve a problem. We tend to do this when we see our solution as the only one. It implies, though, that the speaker is not able to see a solution to the problem.

Figure 9.3 provides examples of each of these roadblocks, as well as an alternative that describes an improved approach to listening.

Ethics / Choices

Suppose you work with a person who, after serving certain ethnic customers, makes racial slurs or comments about how slow to understand he feels certain ethnic groups are. Would this bother you enough to let your coworker know how you feel about his service attitude?

Effective Communication with Non-Native Speakers

Many workplaces require interaction with speakers whose first language is not English. Interacting with customers who are foreign-born or who retain a strong ethnic identity has created difficulty in customer service departments across America. Serving a "world of customers" is here, and knowing how to provide sensitive service that effectively communicates with all customers is vital for successful customer relations.

remember this ...
Communication Roadblocks

Roadblock	What It Sounds Like	An Alternative
Judging or Criticizing	"You're wrong," "I disagree," "You're not thinking clearly."	Step back from your own situation and try to see the problem from the perspective of the speaker.
Naming or Labeling	"That's a silly idea," "You are just being shy," "Why are you so careless?"	Try to see through your immediate responses and truly listen to the speaker.
Commanding or Ordering	"You must ...," "You have to...."	Try to work together to develop a solution.
Moralizing	"It's the right thing to do," "You should know that what you are doing is wrong."	Recognize that everyone has a personal choice and set of values and that the speaker does not necessarily share yours.
Diverting	"Just forget about it," "Something similar happened to me; let me tell you about it."	Try to put the speaker's issues ahead of your own. Before you move on, ask the speaker whether he or she has finished speaking.
Advising	"Why don't you ...," "It would seem to me that you should...."	Try to let the speaker talk through a problem. Often the solution will emerge with little more than a few nods or words of encouragement from you.

FIGURE 9.3

Workforce diversity is one of the most widely discussed management and communication topics. Demographic differences result in a workforce of customer service representatives and consumers who hold different values and working assumptions. Combined, these can produce misunderstandings and disagreements because each culture dictates its own behavioral norms. The concept of diversity is complex. In terms of customer service, it describes differences two people experience as a result of gender, race, age, disability, nationality, sexual orientation, or other issues.

As immigration increases and local businesses spread into global markets, the chances are great that you will be listening to speakers for whom English is a second language. Although many **ESL** (English as a second language) customers have studied English and generally comprehend it, they may have difficulty speaking it, for several reasons. Vowels and consonants may be pronounced differently. Learning the inflection and sentence patterns of the English language is hard when those patterns conflict with those of the speaker's native tongue. Also, there are numerous idioms and homonyms that make learning the English language extremely difficult. What can native speakers do to become better listeners while non-native customers are speaking?

- *Avoid making judgments about incorrectly accented speech.* Many multi-lingual speakers use an insightful but complex variety of English. Although their speech may retain remnants of their native languages, don't assume that their struggle with pronunciation means that they are unintelligent.

- *Be a patient listener.* Strive to overcome the urge to hurry the conversation along. Give non-native speakers time to express their thoughts fully.

- *Don't finish the speaker's sentences.* Allow non-native speakers to choose their words and complete their sentences without volunteering your help. You may find that customers end up saying something quite different from what you had expected.

- *Don't correct grammar and pronunciation errors.* Although you might be trying to help, it is better to focus on what's being expressed and to refrain from teaching English.

- *Don't pretend to understand.* It's all right to tell a non-native speaker that you are having difficulty understanding him or her and ask the person to please repeat the thought.

BUSINESS in action

AFLAC

According to AFLAC CEO Dan Amos, "The engine of a company is its people." The American Family Life Assurance Co., now known as AFLAC, remains today a family-run operation that values fun. The people there work hard but have a lot of fun doing it. As Amos says, "Who else would have a duck as a mascot?"

Because the Georgia-based supplemental health and life insurance company is a service company, they have always put their strongest people in the human resources department. When Audrey Boone Tillman was chosen to head AFLAC's Human Resources operations in 2001, the reason was clear. Top management knew there was no one better in the entire organization, because she is a master at understanding people and, "She's got a listening ear."

With 4,400 U.S. employees and 65,000 U.S. agents working as independent contractors, the company operates on a lean head-count model. Employees are urged to "work smarter, not harder." The focus is on getting the job done by using great communication skills, not by working long hours.

AFLAC regularly shows up on lists of great places to work. Some of its recognitions include being named in *Fortune* magazine's list of "The 100 Best Companies to Work For in America" for seven years in a row; making *Fortune's* list of "America's Most Admired Companies" for five consecutive years; and being featured in *Working Mother* magazine's list of the "100 Best Companies for Working Mothers" for the past four years.

Source: Ann Pomeroy, "Keeping Her Balance: Audrey Boone Tillman Makes Sure That HR at AFLAC Runs Like a Business—But That Family Still Comes First," *HR Magazine* (November 2005).

© DIGITAL VISION

When helping non-native customers, special care and understanding are sometimes required to serve their needs.

Concluding Message for CSRs

Effective listening has many benefits. It saves time and money. People who listen well make fewer mistakes and create fewer interpersonal misunderstandings. Good listening skills result in happier customers and less employee turnover.

When companies listen to their employees, employees feel more valued and display higher morale; moreover, innovation flourishes, and company performance improves. Good listeners at work see tangible rewards in the form of promotions and selection for prestigious positions, and they are frequently better informed than are poor listeners.

Focused listening earns respect because good listeners are perceived by others to be patient, open-minded, sincere, and considerate. Good listeners stand out in a crowd. Employers, teachers, and friends cherish them because they assist speakers in making their points and conveying meaning efficiently. Improving listening skills is never a waste of time; the benefits are vital to success and self-worth—certainly in the world of customer service.

Summary

- The levels of efficiency at which people listen throughout the day are influenced by circumstances, people's attitudes, and their past experiences.
- Active listening means listening with your whole mind and body—not just your ears.
- To understand better what speakers are saying, listeners can use feedback that is reflective, responsive, or reactive.
- Six roadblocks to communicating and listening are judging or criticizing, naming or labeling, commanding or ordering, moralizing, diverting, and advising.
- Interacting with non-native customers requires service professionals to be patient, nonjudgmental listeners.

KEY TERMS

active listening	filtering	reflective feedback
empathy	passive listening	responsive feedback
ESL	reactive feedback	selective listening

CRITICAL THINKING

1. Relative to the three levels of listening, which level is most commonly in use as you interact with others at work and school? Explain.

2. Describe three communication incidents you've had recently in which (a) active listening, (b) passive listening, and (c) empathetic listening took place. Compare the outcome for each occasion.

3. Of the six communication and listening roadblocks, which two do you think CSRs should most avoid using? Explain.

4. List two approaches you might use to become a better listener to non-native speakers.

ONLINE RESEARCH ACTIVITIES

Project 9.1 Planning a Listening Workshop

Research a number of training websites and locate several national or statewide companies that conduct listening seminars or workshops. As a result of your research, write a one-page lesson plan describing the topics you would include in a customer-focused listening workshop for service professionals.

Project 9.2 Non-Native Speaking Customers

Research the latest issues surrounding serving ESL customers. Use keywords such as *non-native speakers, communicating with international customers, non-native communication techniques*, and others you may think of as you study this topic. Prepare a one-page report on your findings, either to present in class or to hand in as a written assignment, as directed by your instructor.

 COMMUNICATION SKILLS AT WORK

Project 9.3 Words That Smile

Note your reactions as you hear a classmate recite the statements in the following table. For the speaker: frown while making the statement the first time, and then repeat the same message with a smile. Assume that you are speaking with a real customer. How different are the messages communicated to the customer when you frown compared to when you smile?

For the listener: in columns 2 and 3, describe your reactions when you heard the statements.

Statement	Frown Reaction	Smile Reaction
"Our commitment is to top-quality service."		
"I'm glad you chose to do business with us today."		
"What can I do to help you?"		

DECISION MAKING AT WORK

Project 9.4 The International Traveler

Assume you are working in the hotel industry, and an international traveler is asking directions to a local landmark or popular restaurant in the area. Although you have repeated the instructions several times, the traveler just doesn't seem to understand your directions. You are wondering what you should do next.

What are two creative steps you might suggest that you or your hotel can take to prevent this situation from happening in the future?

1. _____

_____

_____

2. _____

_____

_____

CASE STUDIES

Project 9.5 "I Know You Believe..."

Everyone in the administrative offices at the On-Time Technology Products was laughing so hard that many of the employees were near tears, as each person cited a real-case scenario that fit with the meaning of a well-known quote. The anonymous quote that caused the laughter and subsequent discussion was, "I know you believe you understand what you think I just said, but I'm not sure you realize that what you heard is not what I meant."

1. How does this statement relate to the topics covered in this chapter?

_____

_____

_____

2. To what extent do you think this statement is true and applicable to service encounters?

_____

_____

_____

3. Relate a personal situation you've experienced recently when the outcome was illustrative of this quote, and share it with your class members.

_____

_____

_____

Project 9.6 Active Listening

Robin, a long-time CSR, was looking forward to her annual review at work and believed she was going to get high marks and a raise in salary. Unfortunately, the review didn't go as expected and Robin was terribly disappointed. Her boss expressed serious concerns with her ability to listen actively. His examples included these:

- You can't talk and listen at the same time, so try to limit your talking during conversations with customers.
- Avoid interrupting a customer when he is speaking. Remember, a pause, even a long one, doesn't always mean that the sender has finished what he or she wants to say.
- So that you won't forget important points you hear, it's advisable to take brief notes during an encounter with a customer.

Outline some ways Robin can become a better listener. Research active listening in various texts or on the Internet. With a partner, summarize your research and your answers in a two-page report to the instructor. Be prepared to discuss your findings in a team discussion.

_____

_____

_____

_____

_____

10 chapter

Nonverbal Communication, Dress, and Manners

1. Understand the elements and interpretations of body language.

2. Recognize the importance of having a dress code in the workplace.

3. Cite examples of business etiquette and manners.

Your words tell me a story, but your body tells me the whole story.

—ANONYMOUS

"Stop slouching and sit up straight. Stand with your back flat, your shoulders back, your head held high, and your feet planted firmly on the floor." How many times have you heard this from someone—most likely your mother—over the years? Showcasing our intelligence and professional abilities is as much about presentation, including body language, dress, and manners, as about verbal communication.

Sensing people's needs through nonverbal communication is important, because valuable information can be gained about your customer's state of mind by paying attention to what you see and hear. Customers are also able to read your responses to them by observing your nonverbal signals. Understanding body language in the workplace isn't trivial—it's a career necessity.

Customer-Friendly Body Language

When we communicate, we send nonverbal messages, called **body language,** that include tone of voice, eye movement, posture, hand gestures, facial expressions, and more. Body language is the oldest and most genuine means of communication in the world. Learning to interpret it will give you a big advantage in all communications. To really understand the full meaning of a message, pay special attention to a person's body language, because nonverbal cues are more immediate, instinctive, and uncontrolled than verbal expressions. They bring attitudes and feelings out into the open.

Clues about a person's character come through in the quality of that person's voice and the expression on his or her face, as well as through posture and hand gestures. However, even though these behaviors are important, they can be interpreted differently from culture to culture.

The Importance of Body Language

Customer service often comes down to one person doing something for another person. One study concluded that when companies lose customers to their competition, 67 percent of the time, it happens because of one incident with one employee. Every contact contributes to customers' impressions of a company. Therefore, each employee's communication skills contribute significantly to those impressions.

Without realizing it, we frequently send messages to customers with posture, facial expression, tone of voice, gestures, and eye contact. Body language communicates our attitudes to customers, and it can either reinforce or contradict our words. Understanding body language can help us strengthen our own verbal messages as well as understand our customers' messages better.

Nonverbal signals constitute a silent language that has about four and a half times the effect of spoken words. Linguists who study the nonverbal elements of a conversation have concluded that these silent elements make up 55 percent of a message, and tone of voice contributes another 38 percent, leaving 7 percent for the words we use.[1] The net result, therefore, is that up to 93 percent of every conversation is interpreted through body language. We react more to what we *think* someone meant than to the words he or she actually said. For example, you may tell a customer that you are happy to help her, but if you frown, slump, or refuse to make eye contact, the customer, in most cases, will not believe you. This is because people are more likely to believe nonverbal signals, such as a frown, than words.

Because body language is a crucial communication tool for delivering great customer service, Figure 10.1 describes several body language signs and their possible meanings.

remember this ...
Body Language

Nonverbal Behavior	Interpretation
Brisk, erect walk	Confidence
Standing with hands on hips	Readiness, aggression
Arms crossed over chest	Defensiveness
Walking with hands in pockets, shoulders hunched	Dejection
Putting hand to cheek	Evaluation, thinking
Touching, slightly rubbing nose	Rejection, doubt, lying
Rubbing the eye	Doubt, disbelief
Clasping hands behind back	Anger, frustration, apprehension
Resting head in hand, eyes downcast	Boredom
Rubbing hands	Anticipation
Gesturing with open palm	Sincerity, openness, innocence
Pinching bridge of nose, eyes closed	Negative evaluation
Tapping or drumming fingers	Impatience
Steepling fingers	Authoritative
Tilting head	Interest
Stroking chin	Trying to make a decision
Looking down, face turned away	Disbelief
Biting nails	Insecurity, nervousness
Pulling or tugging at ear	Indecision

FIGURE 10.1   *Source:* http://www.deltabravo.net/custody/body.php.

Ethics / Choices

A manager says he is very interested in receiving suggestions from you; however, while you try to outline an idea for reducing copier costs, he reads his mail and accepts incoming phone calls. How would you handle this situation? How would this exchange make you feel?

[1] Carol Smith, "Face to Face with Customers," *Professional Builder* (June 2001): 20.

Interpreting Body Signs

Besides communicating an attitude of caring and cooperation, body language conveys professional stature and self-confidence. Listeners consider those who speak with conviction in a calm voice to be competent and trustworthy. The major elements of body language include eye contact, tone of voice, smiling, posture, and gestures.

EYE CONTACT The eyes communicate more than any other part of the human anatomy. For example, staring or gazing at others can create pressure and tension. Rolling your eyes sends the message that you aren't taking the other person's ideas seriously. Shifty eyes and too much blinking can suggest deception, whereas people with eye movements that show they are relaxed and comfortable, yet attentive to the person they are conversing with, are seen as more sincere and honest. Because of increasing diversity in the marketplace, you may encounter customers from other cultures in which direct eye contact is considered offensive. Be sensitive and take your cue from the customer.

TONE OF VOICE You may have noticed that you can "hear" a smile on the phone. The muscles that form your smile also cause your vocal cords to produce a warmer sound. Your tone of voice can sound either interested and caring, or aggressive. Interested and caring works best for most customer situations. Notice the tone of voice others use and the feelings created in you in response. Tone of voice is especially important on the phone, when visual cues are missing from the conversation.

SMILING Show customers you enjoy helping them by smiling at appropriate times. If you smile even when you are not feeling your best, your own brain does not distinguish the difference and sends signals that you are happy. The result can be that you cheer up yourself—and the customer.

POSTURE Slouching and leaning postures send the message, "I'm tired, bored, or uninterested in your concerns." A military stance is unnecessary, but an alert posture reinforces the customer's feeling that you are interested in helping.

GESTURES Gesturing, especially during tense conversations, can mean the difference between sending a message of trust and cooperation and one of suspicion. Placing your hands on your hips typically conveys annoyance. Crossing your arms over your chest suggests distrust. Slamming something down abruptly indicates you are angry.

By paying careful attention to body language and noticing when someone makes a sudden transition from one attitude to another, you'll have a good idea of what the other person is *thinking*—whether or not that is what he or she is *saying*. When serving customers, remember these four typical interpretations of noteworthy body language cues:

1. *Openness and warmth:* open-lipped smiling, open hands with palms visible

2. *Confidence:* leaning forward in the chair, keeping the chin up, putting the tips of the fingers of one hand against the tips of the fingers of the other hand in a "praying," or "steepling," position

3. *Nervousness:* smoking, whistling, fidgeting, jiggling pocket contents, clearing the throat, running fingers through the hair, wringing hands, biting on pens or other objects, twiddling thumbs

4. *Untrustworthiness or defensiveness:* frowning, squinting, tight-lipped grinning, crossing arms in front of the chest, darting eyes, looking down when speaking, clenching hands, pointing with the fingers, rubbing the back of the neck

Understanding other people's body language is not enough—controlling your own nonverbal signals can improve your image and increase your success. If you want to appear confident, open, and in control, then practice the following moves in front of a mirror until they become second nature:

- Walk with a brisk, easy stride and with eyes looking forward.

- Stand evenly on both feet. Keep your arms relaxed and casual. For example, keep one hand in your pocket and use the other one for gesturing as you speak.

- Move slightly closer to others if you want to warm up the relationship. Avoid hostile postures, such as hands on your hips or clasped behind your head. Also avoid defensive gestures, such as turning your body away from the listener or keeping your arms folded over your chest.

- Look at others straight on. Meet their eyes and then occasionally let your gaze drift elsewhere to keep from staring.

- Keep your gestures loose, yet controlled. If those around you seem reserved or nervous, avoid excessively exuberant or frantic movements.

Dressing to Make a Good Impression

Most of us have heard the expressions, "There's never a second chance to make a first impression," and "First impressions are lasting ones." Whether interacting with fellow employees on the job or meeting with customers, your attire, behavior, and attitude say a lot about you. Those who wish to move ahead in their careers must think carefully about what they wear. Clothing choices can help or hinder those goals.

Workers today don't dress as formally as they once did, yet the concept of dressing for success is just as relevant given the competitiveness of today's workplace. Knowledge and skills are instrumental, but image and appearance still continue to be key factors in moving into better jobs. To achieve success, you must look successful by presenting an image of competency, self-confidence, and professionalism.

focus on (Best Practices

Many corporations and industries around the country are passing employee dress codes that ban formfitting, revealing, or ripped and faded clothing. In addition, no body-piercing jewelry, other than on the ears, can be visible at work, and displaying tattoos is prohibited. Employees who don't follow the dress code are being sent home and are not paid for time away from work.

Many workers feel these policies are too strict; however, the majority of people who work full time in an office setting have a dress code, according to a BizRate Research study, with only 26 percent allowed to wear casual work attire. The majority—64 percent—work under a business casual dress requirement.

Dress Code

Whereas employees have to deal with the decision of what to wear to work every day, employers must decide what parameters to put on that decision and how to enforce those guidelines. A generation ago, most professional workers were expected to dress up for work, wearing business suits that demonstrated their conformity with corporate America. Today, most workplaces allow business casual dress, a more relaxed look. This allows workers to express their individuality—and therein lies the problem. What happens when a worker's choices do not conform to the image that the employer wants to project?

Ideally, each company has developed a written description of the types of clothing that are acceptable. Some companies seek legal counsel to ensure that their policies do not discriminate against men or women and that the wording is explicit. By using common sense and exercising good judgment, dressing to make a good impression is easy. Following is a list of suggested dress-for-success guidelines in business today:

- *Hair.* Your hairstyle should be neat, and your hair color should be natural looking and complementary to your complexion.
- *Nails.* Long, elaborately decorated nails may be frowned upon in many companies. Short, clean nails in a French manicure or one-tone polish (light pink or earth tones) are always stylish. For men and women, clean and cared-for nails send a positive message to customers.
- *Makeup.* Your makeup should be subtle and paired to your overall look. Choose shades that are natural and flattering to your complexion.
- *Dress.* Your clothes should not be too short, too formfitting, or too revealing in the office—that could send a message that you are not serious about your job.
- *Footwear.* Shoes should be polished and not run-down. Stockings and socks should be traditional and in shades that are compatible to your outfit or your skin tone.
- *Jewelry and accessories.* Jewelry should always be kept to a minimum in the office. Avoid facial jewelry. Nose jewelry, lip jewelry, or studs in the tongue or eyebrows are generally inappropriate in most businesses. Invest in fun accessories that showcase your

individuality. Colorful silk scarves, pins, and bracelets can add a touch of individuality and interest to your wardrobe. Men can select vibrant ties, if the occasion calls for one.

• *Perfume and cologne.* Use discretion and taste in choosing office scents. Fragrances can linger in a closed office and seem stronger to others than you believe they are. Some people are chemically sensitive to perfume and cologne, and more and more places of business are discouraging their use.

Ethics / Choices

Bonnie, a 19-year-old new hire and community college student, stormed out of the customer service manager's office and belligerently said for all to hear, "She can't tell me what to wear! This is America and I'll wear what I want to work!" In your opinion, is this type of thinking by workers unique to Bonnie, or is this attitude becoming the routine in today's workplace? Discuss.

The Business Attire Issue

It is important to get a clear idea about what is acceptable apparel from your employer. Your choice of work clothes sends a strong nonverbal message about you and can affect the way you work. That's why many employers have mixed feelings about the current trend toward casual business attire.

If CSRs deal extensively with the public, it is fitting for organizations to require certain standards of appearance. If, on the other hand, CSRs have no contact with the public, as in a telemarketing environment, then wearing more casual clothes seems more acceptable. When deciding whether a dress code is appropriate and what it should be, most organizations take into consideration the following three factors:

1. The business's public image
2. The nature of the work performed by the employees affected by the dress code
3. Safety standards

Some employers oppose casual dress because, in their opinion, too many workers push the boundaries of what is acceptable. They contend that absenteeism, tardiness, and flirtatious behavior have increased since dress-down policies began to be adopted. Moreover, and perhaps more important, they feel that casually attired employees turn off some customers.

Regardless of what critics say, employees generally love casual-dress policies. Supporters argue that comfortable clothes and a more relaxed working environment lift employee morale, increase employee creativity, and improve internal communication. Employees also appreciate reduced clothing-related expenses.

The popularity of casual days is increasing in corporate America. Still, among those companies that allow casual dress, there is a need to have some type of appearance standards, as covered earlier. In most companies, employees should go to work well groomed and dressed for a professional work environment. Clothing such as casual shorts, sandals, T-shirts, jeans, and sneakers is not appropriate.

Your industry, age, geographical location, position in the corporate hierarchy, and personality will contribute

If first impressions count, which CSR would you prefer assist you?

to determining what is appropriate dress. Regardless of how informal the outfit, clothes should always be clean and pressed, stain- and odor-free, and not ripped, torn, or frayed.

customer service **T I P**

Respect is at the heart of good manners. All good manners are based on thoughtfulness for others and respect for them as individuals of equal value.

Practicing Business Etiquette and Manners

In the United States, we live in a business casual world, but many people forget the first word is still *business*. As such, we have to mind our manners. Having good manners will help you regardless of the business you are in. Any time you make contact with a customer, you are making a mini-presentation of yourself, ultimately representing your company, service, and products.

Proper business etiquette goes beyond using the right fork at a lunch meeting, to include developing effective people skills. By definition, **business etiquette** dictates the rules of acceptable behavior that identify the application of correct or polite manners in a general business situation. Considering the welfare of others is all part of having good business manners—a practice that many experts say is missing in the American workforce.

The rules of etiquette can be compared to a common language that all successful professionals must learn to speak. People make choices in the business arena, and they choose to do business with people they like and respect. Etiquette skills can help establish productive relationships with colleagues and clients. Successful relationships begin when you exhibit courtesy, respect, and concern for the comfort of others. Better relationships mean better business.

Practicing good manners makes life more enjoyable for everyone because of the courtesy and respect shown to one another. In today's stress-filled world, coupled with the ups and downs inherent in everyday life,

experiencing day-to-day pleasantries is very nice. Good manners are said to be two-thirds common sense and one-third kindness. Experiencing a moment of pleasant kindness can be uplifting. Respecting others is truly empowering as well.

No matter how tired you might be or how abrasive a customer might become, service professionals must practice good manners. An environment in which people treat each other with kindness and consideration is certainly one in which a client enjoys doing business. Learning the rules of business etiquette is not hard to do or costly, and it is the best professional development tool business persons can use to increase their chances of success.

Employers value well-mannered employees because they are a reflection of the company itself. Do people really notice good manners? Even though lifestyles are more informal and relaxed in today's society, good manners are appreciated. Using polite language, turning off cell phones, holding the door, sending a thank you note, offering a smile—these are just a few favors people appreciate. Saying "please" and "thank you," warmly greeting customers and coworkers, and showing patience are essential skills for anyone's success.

A smile seems very simple, but it's amazing how people's moods and words are misjudged because their expressions are often overly serious. A smile shows that you like yourself; you like your current place in the world; and you're happy with the people you're interacting with. A smile says, "I'm approachable and confident."

Some may ask whether **soft skills** like punctuality, positive attitude, and cooperation are more important than knowing how to perform a job. These soft skills, also referred to as people skills, are just as important because they help you become successful. A dependable worker will most likely be given more responsibility, advancements, and pay increases over an undependable coworker. Employees who practice the soft skills of business etiquette and manners will have the ability and confidence to make a better impression. People who display refinement make better impressions, and others want to be around them. Customers do business with people they like; it's that simple.

People with good attitudes usually respect their coworkers, accept responsibility, and accomplish more each day. Your attitude is evident in your body language, the way you complete tasks, your attention to detail, your consideration of those around you, the way you take care of yourself, and your general approach to life. Good

BUSINESS in action

UNIFORMS

Some symbols are world famous, others are less well known. This is also true for the image uniform. When it comes to having a positive corporate identity, employees in distinctive uniforms can be a surprisingly powerful symbol. Companies increasingly understand that public perception of employees is vital to creating and maintaining customer trust. An instantly recognized corporate appearance can result in a competitive edge, so essential in today's marketplace.

There are many advantages to corporate attire. Uniforms project a consistent and unified image for companies that regularly interact with the public, and they allow customers to quickly identify employees for assistance. They permit employers to control the appropriateness and condition of the clothes worn by the employees, who are not required to buy, clean, or repair their own clothing.

An estimated 32 million people in the United States go to work each day wearing a uniform. They are worn by employees in fast-food restaurants, hotels, and major retail stores, such as Target®, Home Depot®, and Wal-Mart®. While uniforms have traditionally been associated with single-color shirts and pants, companies can generally select whatever they choose for their employees. Garments such as aprons or vests promote a more consistent corporate image without requiring each person to be outfitted in the same clothes.

manners, attitude, and self-discipline work together to make good things happen for customer service representatives.

Understanding the use of good manners helps you relax and feel confident and capable in your job. Practicing them allows you to appear comfortable and competent to others and builds self-respect in the process. According to a survey conducted by Eticon, a South Carolina–based consulting firm specializing in business etiquette, lack of proper etiquette can have a major negative impact on business. Fifty-eight percent of respondents say they react to rudeness by taking their business elsewhere.[2]

Concluding Message for CSRs

Customer service representatives should be aware of the impact of their body language on others. To become customer-friendly communicators, CSRs must interpret nonverbal signals from others and become cognizant of their own nonverbal cues. Your total communication—body language, tone of voice, and word choice—helps you deal with each customer situation. As important as your verbal and nonverbal responses to your customers are, don't overlook other important components: dressing appropriately and practicing business etiquette and manners with customers of all types. Behaviors that go against kindness, logic, and efficiency get in the way of good business.

Summary

- Total communication involves sending nonverbal signals, called body language, which include tone of voice, eye movement, posture, hand gestures, and facial expressions. Using appropriate body language is critical when dealing with customers.
- Dressing appropriately and being well groomed make a statement about you and your employer.
- Good manners contribute to a positive first and lasting impression in social and business situations, as well as give you a favorable reputation.

---

[2] Andrea C. Poe, "Mind Their Manners," *HR Magazine* (May 2001): 40.

KEY TERMS

body language   business etiquette   soft skills

CRITICAL THINKING

1. Of all the elements that constitute body language, which three would you describe as the most important when serving customers? Explain.

2. If one customer expressed confidence and another expressed nervousness, what types of body language signals would you look for in each instance?

3. In your opinion, what societal factors make it difficult for organizations to establish a proper dress code in today's workplace?

4. When shopping in a retail store, how important is it for service professionals to practice good business etiquette and manners? Explain.

ONLINE RESEARCH ACTIVITIES

Project 10.1 Writing a Dress Code

Research a number of websites and locate several articles featuring appropriate dress for the workplace. Suggested magazines to research include *Working Woman, Ebony,* and *HR Magazine.* As a result of your research, develop a simple dress code that would be appropriate in the banking and financial industry. Might this dress code be different for a fast-food worker than for a telemarketing CSR? Explain.

Project 10.2 Soft Skills

Research a career exploration website or a number of websites for large corporations, and locate several job descriptions for customer service representatives and other administrative services positions that have been posted within the last 30 days in a major city near you. Pay particular attention to the descriptions that request soft skills, such as punctuality, positive attitude, willingness to learn, and cooperation.

As a result of your research, prepare a simple poster of the printouts of job descriptions you were able to locate, and highlight the soft skills that are mentioned. Present your poster findings to your class, as directed by your instructor.

COMMUNICATION SKILLS AT WORK

Project 10.3 Good Manners Strategies

Manners are being taught less and less. Supporters of this statement believe that knowing and practicing good manners is not a matter of vanity, snobbery, or trying to impress, but simply a matter of being kind and sensitive to the needs of others. The use of good manners creates a considerate, gracious, and respectful atmosphere in which to live and work.

Form a discussion group and discuss some strategies for dealing and communicating with persons who do not use good manners when interacting with others. Report back to your class on the top three strategies your group came up with.

DECISION MAKING AT WORK

Project 10.4 Manners and Business Etiquette

While eating lunch at the food court in the mall, Keanna, a CSR at a retail store within the mall, witnessed a customer service incident in action. A woman approached the counter with a crushed Styrofoam cup and said, "This cup fell off our table and broke. I need another drink and I need someone to come clean up our table and the floor." The tone of her voice suggested that somehow the restaurant was responsible for her broken cup. At that point, Keanna noticed that the staff quickly gave her a new drink. Then the manager appeared with a smile and said, "I would be glad to clean that up for you." The staff who served the woman were exemplary in their manners and etiquette throughout the service exchange. When Keanna went back to work, she relayed her observations to her colleagues.

1. What do you think the likelihood is of this type of customer service practice in most businesses today? Can you name some businesses you are personally aware of that provide exemplary customer service similar to that shown at the restaurant?

_____

_____

_____

2. In your opinion, what do you think contributes most to staff with manners and etiquette—were they hired with these qualities or were they trained in these behaviors by the restaurant?

_____

_____

_____

3. If you had been the person confronted by the woman who complained, what would have been your first reaction or response? Describe.

_____

_____

_____

CASE STUDIES

Project 10.5 Enforcing a Dress Code

Molly Delecki recently went to work for a telecommunications firm in San Francisco as the receptionist and customer service representative. In the first week, several other employees went out of their way to go through the lobby just to see her. She is very attractive, and everyone soon learned she was a former local model.

Molly's image started to create problems within the company. Though Molly was a nice person and didn't appear conceited, her appearance was a distraction to the organization. The office manager discovered that work had slowed down since Molly was hired. For instance, male sales reps were stopping by and spending time chatting with her; female workers were saying catty things behind her back and seemed to be spending more time having negative conversations. Three comments overheard were, "She's too perfect," "She wears heavy makeup," and "She dresses too nice for this place."

Make notes regarding what is happening here. Include the roles in this situation of the receptionist, visitors to the front lobby, other employees, and the office manager. Each person or group is playing a role. Using the questions below as a guide, be prepared to discuss how you would resolve this situation.

1. Do you think the office manager should view this problem as one that will work itself out with time? Why or why not?

   _____

   _____

   _____

   _____

2. What steps should be taken to get work back on track? What should the manager say to the other workers? Is Molly to blame at all in this situation?

   _____

   _____

   _____

   _____

Project 10.6 Casual Dress Debate

Mary Graeff at On-Time Technology Products is becoming increasingly concerned with the way CSRs are dressing. It seems as if the concept and application of casual dress are going from bad to worse, with workers in halter tops, ripped blue jeans, and scuffed and dirty athletic shoes.

Today, Ms. Graeff has called in ten people from various departments to debate the following proposition: business casual dress at On-Time Technology Products will be left up to each employee's interpretation and taste. You are among the ten people on the panel. Brainstorm with others in class to answer the following questions:

1. What are three support statements you could make in favor of this proposition?

   _____

   _____

   _____

2. What are three opposition statements you could make against this proposition?

   _____

   _____

   _____

chapter 11

Effective Telephone Communication

Objectives

1. Detail the essential customer service skills needed when communicating over the phone.

2. Understand the purpose of voicemail and how to leave a customer-friendly message.

3. Learn how to evaluate the quality and delivery of your voice, especially when speaking on the phone.

4. Distinguish between outbound and inbound telemarketing.

Don't speak unless you have something to say.

Don't be tempted to go on after you have said it.

—JOHN BRIGHT, BRITISH POLITICIAN

Despite the increased popularity of using the Internet to conduct business, the tried and true telephone continues to be our culture's most vital link between businesses and customers. Whether a caller is asking a question about office hours or ordering merchandise, the politeness and helpfulness of the person at the other end of the phone are paramount for building relationships, instilling trust, creating a positive experience, and, ultimately, driving repeat business for an organization.

Companies spend good money on their *Yellow Pages*™ listings, websites, stationery, and advertising campaigns, to get people to call. All that money is wasted if the caller's first contact with those businesses is less than favorable. When companies choose employees who will give that first greeting to customers, it is money well spent if they select individuals who sincerely care about the business and can convey that sentiment to customers who call.

customer service TIP

Because only sound is involved when speaking with customers on the phone, make your voice friendly and approachable.

Answering the Telephone

How many times have you called a company at its main number, only to be put on hold immediately by the receptionist, without even getting a chance to say anything? Or gotten trapped in an automated phone system intentionally designed to deprive you of actual contact with a live person?

Telephone greetings are critical because they help form first impressions. From a new customer deciding whether to do business with you, to an irate customer judging your competence, how you answer the phone will make a difference. When developing that all-important opening message, there is power in simplicity. For best results, incorporate three fundamental rules into your first message: be pleasant, brief, and sincere.

The key elements of a telephone greeting are the department or company name, your name, and an offer of assistance. An example from someone in the customer service department might sound like this: "Customer service, this is Melissa. How may I help you?" It may sound simplistic, but practice saying your standard phone greeting until you can hear each word clearly. Keep in mind that even though you have spoken the same greeting all day long, this is the first time your caller has heard it.

A pleasant greeting is essential to a successful call because it sets the stage emotionally. Listeners tend to mirror the emotional state of a speaker. It is typical for people to respond in kind to what they are getting. For example, if you answer the phone gruffly, chances are the caller may become bad-tempered, but if you answer the phone pleasantly, the caller will be more agreeable. We all know which caller is easier to work with.

The Basic Process

Contact between customers and customer service representatives most often takes place on the telephone. Therefore, the manner in which CSRs handle themselves on the phone is critical. The following list offers tips for becoming effective telephone communicators:

- *Stay close to the phone.* Try to answer the phone by the second or third ring. When customers call, they do not want the phone to ring multiple times, nor do they want to leave a message. They want to speak to a live person, conduct business, and move on to their next activity. CSRs need to talk to customers from a quiet workplace, where all the necessary computerized database information, notepaper, and writing materials are available.

- *Be friendly and pleasant.* State your name and ask how you may assist. This greeting tells callers that they have reached the right person and that you want to help.

- *Do not use technical language or abbreviations.* The caller may not understand industry jargon, which prevents sharing effective and clear information.

- *Always remain courteous, even if the caller is not.* CSRs often must firmly state unpleasant truths to customers—but, in doing so, must know the difference between being firm and being impolite. Customers deserve to be treated with respect, no matter what message you are delivering to them.

- *Have paper and pencil handy to take notes.* This will allow you to focus on solving the problem rather than remembering a myriad of significant details.

- *Bring closure to the call.* Tell the caller what action you will take as a result of the call and when the customer can expect the issue to be resolved.

Transferring Calls

To provide the best service for customers, sometimes you will have to transfer callers to another person or department. Unfortunately, this is something customers usually don't like. If you are receiving a large number of transferred calls, perhaps other team members should have information in response to common customer inquiries in advance, so they won't have to transfer calls as often and irritate customers needlessly. When calls must be transferred, keep it simple and positive, transfer with care, and follow these strategies:

1. *State what you can do, not what you cannot do.* Turn a negative into a positive by letting customers know you are acting for their benefit—for example, "I can help you by letting you talk to Jessica in Accounts Receivable. Should we get disconnected, her extension is 279. May I connect you now?"

2. *Avoid using the word "transfer."* Customers don't like this word. Instead, say, "Let me connect you to . . ." or "I'll let you talk with. . . ." Communicate the benefits of your actions clearly to the customer.

remember this ...
Phone Tips

Use welcoming words.	Answering callers' requests with, "I'll be glad to help you" makes customers feel more confident in your ability.
Treat each call as if it is the first call of the day.	From the caller's perspective, it is the most important call.
Use the caller's name often.	A caller's name is the most personal possession he or she has; by recognizing and using it frequently, you make the caller feel better about the service.
Maintain an enthusiastic and personable tone.	Your voice is an all-important delivery system for your words. Speak distinctly and clearly, while matching your talking speed and volume to that of the other party.
Take detailed notes during each call.	Taking notes will help keep names and facts straight during the call and will also serve as a good record afterward. Moreover, it will help you see whether patterns develop that need to be addressed in a more systemic way to avoid similar problems in the future.
Be flexible.	Callers want to know what you can do, not what you cannot do. Always look for any possible solution that stays within company guidelines and yet goes that extra mile for the caller. First-call resolution is the goal.
Keep language simple.	Present the best options to the caller rather than several different ones that could easily be confusing. Refrain from using technical jargon, industry buzzwords, and complicated explanations.
Avoid negative and controlling words.	"Problem," "complaint," "You need to . . . ," and "You should have . . ." are words and phrases that push hot buttons with callers and can illicit negative responses from them. People call customer service departments to resolve a problem, not to reaffirm that they have one.
Give verbal clues to show you are actively listening.	Remember, over the phone people cannot see a nodding head or other visual signs of interest. Phrases such as "I see" and "Please tell me more" are welcome words to the caller.
Use probing skills wisely.	Use open-ended questions to get more information. Use closed questions to focus on one area and pin down specific details, so you can move more quickly to problem resolution.
Promise to call back on unresolved issues and then follow through.	If a call involves some research of the facts, assure the person that you will call back before the end of the day. It may only be a telephone call to say, "I don't have the answer yet, but I'm still researching it."

FIGURE 11.1

3. *Pass along customer information.* When transferring a call to someone else, pass along the customer's name and any facts you have obtained so far. This will make customers feel that they are making progress, because they don't have to repeat their information. You can pass along customer information in two ways:

   • If you have conference call capability, send the caller directly to the desired party while you are still on the line. You will be able to tell the receiving CSR why the customer is calling while the customer is listening.

   • Convey the message to the receiving person while the caller is on hold, so the caller does not have to repeat the information again.

4. *Stay on the line.* Attempt to become familiar with the general responsibilities of each department and person, so you transfer the caller only once. Try not to transfer a call if the next employee is unavailable to work with that customer. Also, before transferring a

customer's call, it's good practice to ask for his or her phone number. If you accidentally disconnect the call, you are prepared to call the customer back.

5. *Don't guess whom to transfer a call to.* Instead, collect as much information as you can from the caller and say that you will get back to him or her. Research the issue, get the solution or information the customer needs, and call back. If another employee returns the call for you, follow up and make sure the problem has been resolved.

6. *Do not transfer the customer, if that is his or her preference.* Customers will likely tell you if they have already spoken to multiple people. A good rule of thumb is not to have the customer talk to more than three different CSRs about one issue. If you are not the correct person to address a particular problem, find out as much as you can about the situation and agree on a time to call the customer back. Do the research yourself and try to resolve the issue without passing the customer off again.

Ethics / Choices

If an employee is not allowed to use a business phone to make personal calls, how can these calls be made? Some personal calls are important and cannot be made after business hours. In your opinion, what should a fair policy state about employees making personal calls while at work?

Placing Callers on Hold

If customers don't like the idea of being transferred, they certainly don't like the idea of being put on hold. Pushing your hold button a little too quickly or a little too often can easily damage consumer relationships. The best alternative is not to put a customer on hold at all, but that option is not always reasonable. Ask the caller whether he or she can be put on hold, and then wait for a response before doing so.

When putting a caller on hold cannot be avoided, follow these basic telephone courtesies:

- *Tell the caller why you would like to put him or her on hold, and ask for permission to do so.* Simply put, this is

the polite thing to do. Also, the caller might not have time to wait and may prefer to call back or that you return the call later.

- *Keep callers on hold no longer than 45 seconds.* Time moves more slowly when you're waiting on the phone; 45 seconds seems like much longer to busy people, and they may become angry and simply hang up.

- *Thank the customer for holding.* Always say, "Thank you for holding" rather than "I'm sorry you had to hold." Emphasize the positive—thanking the customer, not the negative—apologizing.

- *Offer to call the customer back instead of putting him or her on hold.* If you know the process will take a little extra time, offer to call back within a certain time frame, and then do it.

- *Check back frequently.* If resolving the problem is taking longer than you thought it would, return to the caller at least every 45 seconds to explain what's happening and to ask whether he or she can continue to hold.

Most people who call businesses understand that it could be a while before they speak with a customer service representative. That doesn't mean they appreciate waiting in silence. A **messaging on-hold** system plays a pre-recorded program for callers to listen to while they are on hold. Companies can choose to have the system play music, a voice message, or a combination of both. The average length of a program is typically 4–6 minutes.

The advantages of using this phone feature are that it lets callers know they are still on the line and waiting for the next available person to speak with them. It can also let them know where they are in the call order (queue) and the average wait before they will get a live person on the phone. Many customers prefer this feature while on hold, and it often prevents them from hanging up in frustration.

Handling Irate Callers

With telephone technology expanding, customers are more sensitive than ever about the way they are treated on the phone. Customers are tired of being put on hold and getting transferred to voicemail or to the wrong person. They want their needs addressed by competent, caring service professionals within a reasonable time frame. Even if you hear the same question or complaint a dozen times each day, remember that this is the caller's first time saying those words. Show the irritated customer that the issue is important to you by

- expressing empathy as the customer conveys his feelings about the situation.
- resolving the problem with a smile in your voice.
- using listening responses, such as "yes," "okay," and "I see."
- using active listening techniques, such as paraphrasing, summarizing, repeating, and questioning for clarification.
- telling the customer the issue is important to you—for example, by saying, "Thank you for bringing this matter to our attention."
- expressing a sense of urgency and ownership regarding the customer's concern by saying, "I'll take care of this right away."
- apologizing at least twice—once on hearing the problem and again after finding a solution.
- thanking customers sincerely for doing business with your company.

Customer service surveys show that almost 75 percent of people who complain will do business with the same company in the future if the problem is resolved quickly and to the customer's satisfaction.[1] Customers simply want to reach a solution and move on with other things that are important in their lives.

Using Voice Response Units

Any contact with an organization contributes to a customer's perception about that organization, whether it is with an employee in a phone conversation or through voicemail. Voicemail, which functions much as an answering machine does, allows callers to leave a voice message for the called party. How does voicemail work? Unlike answering machines, a voicemail system has a computer that converts the voice message into digital form. Once digitized, the message is stored in a voice mailbox, which is a storage location in a computer's voicemail system.

A voicemail system usually provides individual voice mailboxes for many users, such as each employee within a company. By accessing a voice mailbox, the called party can listen to messages, add comments to a message, and reply or forward a message to another voice mailbox in the voicemail system. At many organizations, voicemail is a primary way employees communicate with each other.

These voice response units give customers an impression of a company. The sound of a caller hanging up before leaving a voicemail message should be viewed as dissatisfaction with a phone system and is similar to a customer closing the door angrily when leaving a business. Research shows that 34 percent of callers will not call back after hanging up, resulting in future lost revenue, which can be considerable.[2]

Although voicemail has grown increasingly popular, do not assume that customers will be satisfied with leaving a message. Instead, understand voicemail from the caller's perspective. Customers want to feel that their telephone calls are important to a company. What drives customers to frustration about some phone systems is not the fact that they are automated, but that they think no one is paying attention to their needs.

A well-designed phone system is fast, easy to use, cost effective, and, most important, caller-friendly. Whether you are planning a simple voicemail system to take messages or a sophisticated voice-processing system that lets people choose from a menu of recorded options, the key is keeping callers in mind and making the process easy for them to use.

Some companies approach voicemail as a way to reduce head count, and that's a good side benefit; however, if designed correctly, the real benefit of using voicemail is for customers. A well-designed system is a responsive tool for productivity and customer service. Some tips on the fine points of designing voicemail systems are shown in Figure 11.2.

> ### customer service T I P
>
> *To improve telephone communication, speak as if you were in a face-to-face dialogue—even smiling and gesturing, if those actions make you sound more natural.*

---

[1] Michael Bordner, "How to Get Unhappy Customers to Buy More," *Inbound Service and Selling* (September 29, 2000): 4.

[2] John Tschohl, "Telephone Technology: Friend or Foe," *Service Quality Institute* (November 2000): 11.

remember this ...
Customer-Friendly Voicemail Systems

Stay on top of it.	Update your voicemail greeting frequently, stating the date, which lets callers know you actually use the system. Inform callers your messages are checked frequently, so they have confidence their call will be heard and returned.
Avoid "voicemail jail."	When callers bounce from message to message and can't reach a live person, they begin to feel uncomfortable, unsatisfied, and locked in to the event. Early on, give callers an easy way to transfer directly at any time to a receptionist by pressing one or two digits on their phones' keypad. If no one is available after business hours, post an alternative greeting suggesting callers leave a message that will be returned early the next day.
Keep greetings and instructions short.	Strive for a 5-second voicemail greeting and 15 seconds for instructions. Callers get impatient; they want action.
Attempt to give instructions the same way every time.	Always state the action first, then the correct key to press—for example, "To transfer to our receptionist, press zero." If you reverse the statement, callers may forget which key to press by the time you've finished telling them the result.
Limit menus and options.	A phone system is not a restaurant—callers can't remember more than three choices at a time.
Encourage two-way dialogue.	Ask callers to leave a detailed message or a complete request for information.
Sound as natural as possible.	When recording your greeting, vary your voice tone and speak more loudly or softly for emphasis. Be careful of background voices or music that are distracting to the listener.
Don't make technology a villain.	Voicemail should not be used to avoid phone calls. People expect that you will regularly answer your own phone. Most successful companies use voicemail as an exception rather than the rule.

FIGURE 11.2

Recording an Outgoing Greeting

It is important that CSRs answer their phones whenever possible. If callers always get voicemail, they might become convinced that the company is trying to dodge them or is too busy to take care of their needs. Sometimes, however, voicemail is a necessary substitute. CSRs cannot always remain at their desks. They do eat lunch and take care of other personal needs. They also talk to and help other customers.

Because voicemail has a strike against it—the caller wants to talk to a live person, not a machine—use the following suggestions to make an outgoing voicemail greeting more efficient:

- State your name and title and give reasons you cannot answer the phone at this time. Indicate how often you check your voicemail. Customer service representatives should return calls at least every two hours.

- Request key information from a caller, including full name, company's name (if applicable) and phone number, when the caller can be reached, and a brief explanation for the call.

- Above all, remember to return calls promptly. Even if you are not ready with all the answers, do not leave callers wondering whether you received their messages. Calling customers with simple updates can spread more goodwill than many companies realize.

Leaving a Voicemail Message

When making a call, savvy communicators know they might have to leave a recorded message, so they plan before dialing a number. Be clear and brief in any voicemail message you leave. To deliver a communiqué effectively, move through it quickly, and be straightforward so the receiver understands what's expected by the end of the message.

Focus on Best Practices

The explosion of the Internet and the global economy has produced a new business opportunity known as the virtual assistant. To be successful, the virtual assistant must have excellent communication, technology, and customer service skills.

A virtual assistant is an independent entrepreneur who provides administrative, creative, or technical services by using advanced technological modes of communication and data delivery. Hired on a contractual basis, a professional virtual assistant provides a specific area of expertise to clients, working from his or her own office space. No formal certification is required, but several organizations offer it along with job placement after successful completion of a certified virtual assistant exam.

Not every company or busy professional can afford to hire an on-site assistant. However, almost everyone will agree that missed phone calls equal missed opportunities. With an estimated 60 percent of all consumers becoming angry or frustrated at using an automated telephone system, a virtual assistant is not only an economical, but a practical, solution for many organizations.

Here's a plan that works well when leaving voicemail messages:

1. State your name, the date and time, your company name, and why you are calling.
2. Say what you would like the receiver to do. This is a statement or a request.
3. Give a reason for the statement or request.
4. Say, "Thank you."
5. Finish with, "Feel free to call me back at the following number"; then state the number slowly and clearly so it can be written down.

Finally, be aware that voicemail is company property. Voicemail messages can easily be forwarded, so don't leave a message unless you're comfortable having it heard by other people.

Evaluating Your Voice Qualities and Delivery

A person's voice can reveal many emotions: happiness, sadness, anger, even ambivalence. When you speak, customers listen to your tone of voice, words, and overall delivery techniques. Are you sincere? Do you sound kind in your approach with others? Do you show empathy and concern for their needs? A positive and caring tone in customer situations says, "I understand how you feel and I'd be frustrated, too, if that happened to me."

Voice Qualities

The following list offers general guidelines for using your voice effectively, especially while on the phone:

1. *Use a steady, moderate rate of speech.* Speaking too fast can suggest to the customer that you are nervous or in a hurry; speaking too slowly can signal that you are bored or lack confidence.
2. *Never allow your voice to become overly loud or shrill.* If a customer is yelling at you, you may be tempted to respond in kind, but don't. Maintaining a moderate volume and rate of speech can help calm an upset customer.
3. *Keep a smile in your voice.* The smile on your face is reflected in the sound of your voice. Keep smiling, even if you are speaking on the phone. Your customers will hear the difference.
4. *Increase the energy in your voice.* The telephone can rob your voice of some of its natural expressiveness and energy, so be sure to compensate adequately with more enthusiasm.

Delivery Techniques

Showing courtesy to others and incorporating good telephone etiquette can help businesses gain a competitive edge for one basic reason—people are more likely to return to a company and to buy more products and services when they are treated well. Customers are impressed when a customer service representative demonstrates friendliness, proficiency, and intelligence.

Customers will have a good impression of you and your organization if you are pleasant, courteous, and helpful.

- *Friendliness.* This shows that you are genuinely interested in helping the caller.
- *Proficiency.* You should be able to handle the caller's request without much delay, through the use of a script or from lessons learned in previous customer transactions.
- *Intelligence.* You need to be familiar enough with the various products and services to converse competently and answer questions about them.

In addition to the tips previously discussed, also remember to

1. *Identify the problem.* Keep the caller talking. The more you learn about what the caller wants, the more opportunities will surface for helping to fulfill his or her needs.
2. *Listen for facts.* Reflect with words of understanding, probe for information, determine potential solutions, and provide options to the caller.
3. *Allow an angry person to vent.* This may calm the caller down and provide you with valuable information to better serve the customer.
4. *Bring the call to a polite close.* Always thank the caller for giving you an opportunity to serve him or her.

Telephone conversations tend to be rather informal in both business and personal situations. Figure 11.3 shows some noteworthy suggestions to keep in mind when speaking on the phone.

remember this ...
Acceptable Telephone Language

Action	Acceptable Statements
Introducing yourself	"This is Ken." "Good morning, Ken speaking."
Asking who is on the telephone	"Excuse me, who is calling, please?" "May I ask who is calling, please?"
Asking for someone	"May I have extension 321?" "May I speak to Jack?" "Is Jack available?"
Connecting someone	"I'll put your call through." "Please hold while I connect you."
Taking a message	"May I take a message?" "May I tell him who is calling?" "Would you like to leave a message?"
Replying when someone is not available	"I'm afraid Susan is not available at the moment." "I'm sorry, but Susan's line is busy." "Susan is out at the moment."

FIGURE 11.3

Call centers perform many types of telemarketing activities and contact hundreds of customers each day.

Understanding Telemarketing Activities

Selling or serving customers over the phone is not as easy as face-to-face transactions. Telemarketing is the use of a telephone to sell directly to consumers. It consists of outbound sales calls, usually unsolicited, and inbound calls, orders through toll-free 800 numbers or fee-based 900 numbers. A **fee-based 900 number** is a premium telephone number whereby individuals or businesses provide information and services that are billed directly to the caller's local telephone bill. No special licensing is required. Any individual or business may use 900 numbers to provide information and services as a means of reaching new markets and communicating with customers. One of the major benefits of 900 numbers is that they generate qualified responses. Although the charge may reduce the total volume of calls, the calls that do come through are from customers who have a true interest in the product, or they wouldn't be paying for the call.

Outbound telemarketing is a direct marketing technique used by many organizations because of rising postage rates and decreasing long-distance phone charges. **Inbound telemarketing** programs are used mainly by companies to take orders, generate leads, and provide customer service. Inbound 800 telemarketing is not new and has successfully supplemented direct-response TV, radio, and print advertising for several years.

The CSR-Telemarketer Perspective

Telemarketers can become so busy following their own scripts that they often don't hear customers' needs or desires. Should you work for an organization that telemarkets, don't forget these reminders when carrying out your work:

- *Display enthusiasm.* Second only to product knowledge, the most important asset telemarketers have is their enthusiasm. If there's any doubt on your part

that your product is not what you claim it is, your prospects will sense it immediately. Insincerity will come across in your voice inflections and tone. The opposite is true as well. When you believe in a product, your prospects will have confidence in you and trust that you know what you're talking about. Once you establish that belief, you are on your way to closing the sale.

- *It's all in the details.* People get calls from vendors all the time, so what makes one telemarketer different from all the rest? More often than not, it is the CSR's attention to detail. That attention might be really listening to what the prospect is saying, or it might even be sending a thank-you note after the call.

- *Anticipate objections to your sales presentations.* Telemarketers have probably heard every sales objection imaginable: "We're not interested." "We're happy with our present vendor." "It's too expensive." "I don't have time." As a CSR-telemarketer, you cannot argue with any of these points because, as soon as you do, you lose. That's when the "feel, felt, found" approach to dealing with customers' objections can be useful.

When you hear an objection, pause and let it sink in. Don't rush to answer. Listen carefully, and then empathize with your prospect by saying, "I understand how you *feel*" or "I can appreciate that." Then build on the success you've had with other customers by saying, "Many of my present customers *felt* the same way, but when they *found* out how much time they saved using our system, they were amazed. I'd like to see whether we can do the same for you." This 3-F method has been used over and over in telemarketing sales and customer service activities, and it works when you know—inside and out—the benefits to your customer of the product or service you are selling.

The Customer's Perspective

At some point, each of us has received calls from telemarketers, and we've responded to them in various ways. Whether a customer's response is interest or annoyance, part of a telemarketer's job is dealing with every range of emotion he or she encounters.

On January 1, 2005, telemarketers and sellers were required to begin searching the National Do Not Call Registry at least once every 31 days and to drop from their call lists the phone numbers of consumers who had

BUSINESS *in action*

KEYNOTE

Founded in 1995, Keynote Systems is a leader in services that improve online business performance and communication technologies. Keynote Systems helps corporate customers and individual subscribers become "the best of the best" online. The business premise supporting Keynote's mission is, "Online businesses can't manage what they don't measure." As an independent and trusted third-party, Keynote performs testing on a website's content and applications prior to its public debut, before any customer or business is affected by it. The company provides competitive analysis and operational metrics *from the customer perspective.* This data measures service levels and customer experience of websites, broadband services, and mobile communications.

Voice over Internet Protocol (VoIP) is one such technology Keynote tests. VoIP is a technology that allows you to make voice calls using a broadband Internet connection instead of a traditional (analog) phone line. A great deal of attention has been paid to VoIP because of the potentially large cost savings to businesses and consumers. Because of service and hardware limitations and issues with call reliability and audio clarity, the adoption of VoIP is yet to be widespread. The benefits of this technology—increasing customer satisfaction and ease of global communication—make it an important factor in the future of customer service.

The Federal Trade Commission, the Federal Communications Commission, and individual states are enforcing the National Do Not Call Registry. Placing your number on the registry will stop most, but not all, telemarketing calls.

Ethics / Choices

Sometimes a boss or another employee is on the telephone when you wish to speak to him or her, so you must wait. What do you typically do in these circumstances? Do you stand far enough away so that you do not hear the conversation? Or, if it is a private office, do you stand outside the office until the call is finished? Explain the best way to handle this situation.

Concluding Message for CSRs

When you think of the times you have had great experiences as a customer, you probably think of the people who made those experiences happen for you. We recognize instantly when we encounter a remarkable CSR, so why is it that some customer service professionals stand out? The simple answer is that great customer service reps make a choice. *Every day,* with *every* customer, on *every* call—they choose to do *all* they can to make their customers' experiences as *positive* as they can be.

Summary

- When answering a customer call, be professional and courteous throughout the entire transaction.
- Treat voicemail systems as an extension of yourself and use them to help serve the customer.
- When speaking with customers over the phone, pay attention to your tone of voice, choice of words, and overall delivery technique.
- Telemarketing is the use of the telephone to sell directly to consumers; it consists of calls that are outbound, inbound, or a combination of both.

registered. The **National Do Not Call Registry** puts consumers in charge of the telemarketing calls they receive at home. The Federal government created the national registry to give consumers the choice of whether to allow telemarketing calls to their homes. Registration for this service is free and can be requested either online or by calling a toll-free number.

KEY TERMS

fee-based 900 number

inbound telemarketing

messaging on-hold

National Do Not Call Registry

outbound telemarketing

CRITICAL THINKING

1. If you were hiring a receptionist or customer service representative, what essential phone service skills would you look for in your top candidates? Explain.

2. Describe a voicemail system you have used that you consider to be customer-friendly. Describe one that you consider not to be user-friendly.

3. Based on the chapter material, evaluate your voice and describe two qualities that you are proud of and two that you would like to improve.

4. If you were employed in a telemarketing environment and had the choice of performing either outbound or inbound telemarketing activities, which would you prefer and why?

ONLINE RESEARCH ACTIVITIES

Project 11.1 Voicemail Update

Research a number of websites and locate several articles about recent developments in the installation and advantages of using voicemail systems. As a result of your research, write a simple paper recommending additional features or upgrades to the voicemail system at your school or at work.

Project 11.2 Evaluate Your Voice

Mary Graeff, customer service supervisor at On-Time Technology Products, has received four complaints within the past six weeks about her CSRs' unhelpful interactions with customers. Specifically, one comment said that although the CSR used the proper words and phrases, she still conveyed the wrong impression over the phone. Ms. Graeff is very protective of her CSRs but realizes how important it is to act on any customer concern as soon as possible. She has asked all of her CSRs to take the following quiz to evaluate their voices.

	Yes	No	
1.	—	—	Does your voice sound high-pitched?
2.	—	—	Do you speak too loudly or too softly?
3.	—	—	Do you talk too quickly or too slowly?
4.	—	—	Do you sound nasal—as if you are talking through your nose?
5.	—	—	Do you frequently clear your throat or make other irritating noises?
6.	—	—	Do you articulate words clearly, making them understood easily?
7.	—	—	Do you sound confident?
8.	—	—	Do you say words in their entirety? (For example, Do you say "goin'" for "going"?)
9.	—	—	Does your voice and manner convey a sense of authority?
10.	—	—	Imagine that you are the caller. Would you enjoy listening to the person the caller is speaking with?

If you answered "yes" to numbers 6–10 and "no" to numbers 1–5, you have an excellent speaking voice on the telephone. Work to improve the areas described in the first five questions.

Answer the previous ten questions and evaluate your own voice, as though you were a CSR. Then enter "improving voice quality" or "effective speaking techniques" in your favorite search engine. In the following table, provide responses that will inform Ms. Graeff which websites contain information on improving voice techniques. Write down three suggestions for improving voice quality and sound that you learned from your research.

Websites	Suggestions to Improve Voice Quality and Sound
1.	
2.	
3.	
4.	

COMMUNICATION SKILLS AT WORK

Project 11.3 Answering Telephone Calls

Form a small group with at least two other students, and write the message you would use to respond to the following three telephone-answering situations:

1. Assume you are working for First City Bank. When calls come in, they go directly to your phone; there is no receptionist. How should you answer each call?

    _____

    _____

    _____

2. Assume you are an employee in the registration office of a local career school. All calls are first answered by a receptionist and then transferred to your desk. How should you answer each call?

    _____

    _____

    _____

3. When your boss is not available, you answer her telephone. What should you say when she is in a meeting? What should you say when she is on a coffee break?

_____

_____

_____

DECISION MAKING AT WORK

Project 11.4 What Would You Say to a Friend?

Assume a good friend calls you on your direct line at work with the intent to chat. After you've done some catch-up on personal news, she suggests that the other reps can handle your calls for a little longer. You are starting to feel uncomfortable with what is happening. Decide how you would handle this situation with your friend by describing the approach you would take and why.

_____

_____

_____

_____

CASE STUDIES

Project 11.5 The Phone Order Fiasco

Judy Martin is a CSR who receives a call from a new customer wishing to place an order. Judy has a basketball game broadcasting very softly on the radio, and she thinks the customer cannot hear it. The customer begins to give the order, but Judy interrupts and puts her on hold because she cannot find anything to write with. Because the customer has a heavy accent, Judy has a hard time understanding and says, "Huh?" quite frequently during the phone conversation. Judy concludes the transaction by saying, "Thanks for placing the order."

What should Judy have done differently during this customer dialogue?

_____

_____

_____

_____

Project 11.6 "Anyone Can Do Telemarketing"

In the southwestern college town where Angela lives, there is a company that specializes in telemarketing sales campaigns for major insurance companies across America. As a part-time college student and a new mother of a six-month-old infant, Angela desperately needs a job with some built-in flexibility. She has been told that the telemarketing company allows workers to set their own schedules within reason. Angela wants to apply for the $12-per-hour job, but she is afraid that, because of her rather strong Hispanic accent, she might not be hired. Someone told her that telemarketing companies would hire *anyone* and that she should apply.

Form a small group and brainstorm about the following questions. Report your ideas to the class, as directed by your instructor.

1. In what ways does Angela sound like a good candidate for a telemarketing job in this college town?

   _____

   _____

   _____

   _____

2. In your opinion, do telemarketing companies hire "just anyone"? Explain.

   _____

   _____

   _____

   _____

3. What is your group's sense about the future of telemarketing in the United States, especially after the creation of the National Do Not Call Registry?

   _____

   _____

   _____

   _____

Action Plan

Based on your study of Part 3, think about the many types of communication skills that a customer service representative should practice in order to serve customers well, and then complete the following activities.

Activity 1

Divide a sheet of paper into four columns and create the following list in column 1: Questioning Techniques, Communication Style, Listening Skills, Nonverbal Communication Skills, Dress, Manners, and Telephone Communication. Label column 2 *Strength*, column 3 *Needs Improvement*, and column 4 *Method of Improvement*.

Give some thought as to how you would rate yourself on each item in column 1. How do you measure up? If there is a skill, descriptor, or technique that you are especially strong in, put an X in column 2 next to that item, showing it as a strength of yours. If it is a skill that you may need to work on in some way, place an X in column 3. Finally, in column 4, indicate how you might improve those skills you've identified in column 3.

Activity 2

As a class, assign a person to write on the whiteboard or chalkboard. Break the writing space into three areas: Listening Skills, Nonverbal Communication Skills, and Manners and Business Etiquette. Devote some class time to brainstorming about each of the three areas. When class members respond, they should use the sentence stem, "Remember to...."

Finally, each student should select from each group two reminders that the student feels have the most relevance to him or her and place those items on note cards to be posted in a workspace or at home.

Customer Service Challenges in a Global World

chapters

profile

Health Care Profile

*by Denice E. Gibson,
RN, MSN, CHPN, OCN;
Good Samaritan Hospital;
Phoenix, Arizona*

ealth Science

What does exemplary customer service look like in the health care field?

As an oncology/hematology bone marrow transplant nurse, I have worked in a hospital as a staff nurse, providing bedside patient care; in a hospice organization as a clinical case manager; and in the public education system and the community, providing information and acute medical care.

From these experiences, I truly believe that great customer service in delivering health care is the essence of any health care institution because it directly affects the quality of patient outcomes. Simple things such as making an effort to remember patients' names, not being afraid to ask, "Is there anything else I can do for you today?," or giving a client your full attention mean a lot to those we serve. When delivering health care, I think of it this way: the customer is always right—as long as it doesn't involve a safety or health issue.

What skills in customer service should a health professional possess?

Although health care professionals must be proficient and competent in delivering quality care, the other critical skill sets that have an impact on the way customer service is delivered are

1. *Being culturally compassionate.* Given the culturally diverse society we live in, health care providers must be able to interact professionally within any culture and not allow personal beliefs to become barriers when serving patients.

2. *Caring at a basic level.* Because delivering care in health institutions is increasingly dehumanized, it is essential to remember that the service rendered has a direct impact on the quality of life for the patient, the patient's family, and the community.

3. *Honoring integrity.* Moral principles are critical for maximizing the outcomes of quality and respectful care. Not only can irresponsible behavior by health care providers result in direct harm to or mistrust from a patient, the patient's family, the community, or the health care institution, but irresponsible behavior is also simply not ethical and should not happen.

Finally, nurses, doctors, and other health care givers need an outstanding personal attitude that reflects exemplary customer service to the aggregate needs in health care. If you wish to be successful in a career in health care, I would advise you to:

- Be committed to maximizing quality customer service.
- Be willing to adapt to meet the challenges and changing needs of customer service in the health care industry.
- Work collaboratively with colleagues and other professionals.
- Establish yourself as a person who is culturally compassionate, has integrity, and truly cares for patients at the most basic level.

•••••••• **Industry: Health Care**

Health Care Activities

1. Think about your total experience the last time you, a family member, or a friend received health care services and respond "yes" or "no" to the following questions:

    _____ Did the health professional customer service (HPCS) person greet you in a pleasant way on your arrival at the office, clinic, or hospital?

    _____ Did the HPCS person treat you with dignity and respect your rights to privacy?

    _____ Did the HPCS person use technology to access confidential data about you or previous visits you may have had?

    _____ Did it take an excessive amount of time to provide written information or to update your medical files?

    _____ Was your time valued by the HPCS person by not having you wait too long to be served by a doctor or nurse practitioner?

    _____ Was the HPCS person knowledgeable in providing complete answers to any questions you asked?

    _____ Did it seem to you as though your service was well managed, organized, and customer-driven?

    _____ Given a choice, would you return to that health care provider again?

    _____ How would you rank customer service at this health care facility? (1 = poor; 5 = superior)

    After studying the material in Part 4, briefly explain why you evaluated the health care experience as you did.

    _____

    _____

    _____

2. Assume you are the customer service director for a local hospital. In that role, how would you instruct the customer service department to use technology, while serving patients in a caring and considerate way?

    _____

    _____

    _____

The Impact of Globalization on Customer Service

chapter 12

Objectives

1. Understand the impact globalization has had on the world economy and call center hiring trends.

2. Discuss the reasons globalization of customer service has shifted from an offshore to a homeshore environment.

3. Describe the extent to which online services are growing and the challenges facing companies involved in e-commerce on the Internet.

4. List the multichannel communication methods used by online shoppers.

The most successful enterprises in the future will be those with the right blend of high-tech with high-touch.

—BILL GATES, CO-FOUNDER, MICROSOFT CORPORATION

I t is difficult to name a product or service that is not available on the Internet today. Consider books, health care information, movie tickets, construction materials, baby clothes, music, electronics, toys, wine, cars, education, airline tickets, antiques, and more. In today's global economy, customer service is more of a challenge, using the impersonal medium of the Internet. However, when done right, online business offers consumers the best of both worlds—the old economy's one-to-one service and the new economy's immediacy, convenience, and cost-effectiveness.

From the consumers' point of view, the ability to buy merchandise *anywhere*, *anytime*, and *any way* they want is imperative in today's retail markets. One of the greatest challenges that an electronic business, or **e-business**, faces today is how to provide truly personalized service to anyone in the world while taking advantage of the Internet's swiftness and interactivity.

Part 4 looks to the future of customer service by providing an understanding of the profound impact that new technology and improved telecommunications media are having on the globalization of customer service.

Globalization and Outsourcing of E-Commerce

Globalizing e-business means expanding current markets or opening up new ones that appeal to both international audiences and domestic multicultural groups. Implemented well, strategic **globalization** initiatives ensure that customers around the world have appropriate and useful experiences as they communicate, collaborate, and transact online—regardless of location, language, culture, or business practices.

In his book *The World Is Flat: A Brief History of the Twenty-First Century*, Thomas L. Friedman illustrates in convincing detail how the worldwide proliferation of broadband connectivity, search engines, inexpensive computers, and other trends have created a global economy in which intellectual work can be delivered from anyone to anywhere. The playing field is being leveled—or, as he puts it, "The world is becoming flat."

Globalization and outsourcing are two megatrends whose benefits most businesses cannot afford to ignore. **Outsourcing**, also referred to as subcontracting, is the purchase of labor from a source outside the company rather than using the company's own staff. But the practice of outsourcing customer service to offshore call centers is beginning to look like a classic example of a good idea carried too far. Critics of the practice point to a growing body of evidence that suggests faulty economics and customer dissatisfaction are forcing a rethinking of the low-cost service approach. Customer resistance, along with data security concerns and the unexpectedly high costs of managing offshore call centers, offset and dilute their promised economic benefits. There is already evidence that these factors have combined to slow the offshore migration. Several large firms, including Dell and credit-card giant Capital One, have shifted at least some customer-support operations back to the United States.[1]

Homeshoring

An increasing number of companies are moving customer service jobs out of high overhead call centers and into what is possibly the lowest overhead place in the United States: workers' homes. Increasingly, companies are hiring U.S. home-based call agents as an alternative to the more expensive in-house operators or less qualified offshore call centers. This work style trend is called **homeshoring**.

Homeshoring is less likely to risk the accent fatigue, cultural disconnection, and customer rage that offshoring can inspire, not to mention the mounting security fears of offshoring. Once your private data—credit card numbers, Social Security number, and medical and financial records—go overseas, they're beyond the reach of U.S. law.

According to data from the technology industry research group IDC, which specializes in market intelligence in the information and telecommunications industry, homeshoring is gaining support throughout the United States. IDC's 2005 study, entitled "Home-Based Agent 2005–2010 Forecast and Analysis: Converging Economic Forces to Drive the Expansion of Homeshoring in the United States," found that growth in the use of home-based agents is centered on the need for agents who are more productive, maintain higher retention rates, and have greater flexibility in responding to peaks and valleys of voice traffic. In 2005, there were an estimated 112,000 home-based phone representatives in the United States, a number the IDC study estimates could grow to more than 300,000 by 2010.[2]

Benefits to Agents

Customer service agents and business clients derive great benefits from homeshoring. The agents, who generally are independent contractors hired by outsourcing companies, have flexibility and the ability to work out of their homes at times convenient to them. Technology has

[1]Norm Alster, "Customer Disservice?" *CFO.com* (September 15, 2005). http://www.cfo.com.

[2]Tory Brecht, "Homeshoring Gains Support Throughout U.S.," *Quad-City Business Journal* (April 11, 2006). http://www.qcbusinessjournal.com.

allowed teleworkers to function as efficiently and effectively from home as they do in a traditional work environment.

Although homeshoring workers do not receive health insurance benefits, 401(k) plans, or other benefits, they do average between $10 and $15 per hour and can work a schedule they choose. Many have spouses with jobs that provide benefits.

Benefits to Business Clients

For a fraction of the cost, companies that use homeshoring to provide customer services get superior labor. Home agents include a large group of workers who are educated, stay-at-home moms. Many live in rural areas, cannot afford child care, or are unable to adjust their lives to the mandatory, on-site work schedules of corporate America. More than 75 percent of home agents have taken some college courses, compared to 20 percent of those working in call centers. These virtual call center workers also include members of the hidden labor force: itinerant military spouses, seasoned retirees who are looking for flexible side jobs, and computer-savvy disabled veterans, among others.[3]

Homeshoring also provides a flexible, ready-on-demand workforce. Shifts can last as little as 15 minutes, and agents are paid only for the time spent on the phone. Technology lets companies monitor worker performance accurately and efficiently. A U.S. call center worker typically costs a company $31 an hour, including overhead and training, but home agents cost only $21 and are reportedly more productive. Statistics show that home agents make a higher volume of sales calls than their call center counterparts and their customer satisfaction rates are often better.[4]

Because phone and broadband technology now make it simple for companies to forward their calls to home-based workers and allow them access to internal corporate database systems, major companies are increasing their use of homeshoring. By not having to provide work space or benefits to these employees, companies are simultaneously saving a lot of money and reporting a higher worker retention rate as well as more satisfied customers.

Providing Customer Service on the Internet

Whether you are face to face with customers in a physical store or "mouse to database" with them in a virtual environment, customer service is still a universal principle of good business, because all customers are people regardless of their shopping methods. Customers can be located anywhere, but they still need or want something. Customer service and a customer-driven orientation are not new ideas. Taking steps to improve customer satisfaction in online transactions is, however. Online or not, the goals of smart companies are still to think and feel as their customers do and to try to develop knowledge about their total customer base.

The principle of first impressions is very strong in the virtual world. If traditional customers are not immediately impressed with a company or store, they must get back into their cars and drive across town to another one; however, virtual shoppers can click out of a website in a matter of seconds. The odds are stacked against an online business unless it provides answers and solutions immediately and on demand. This can be accomplished on a well-designed website by providing a home page that loads quickly, provides security, and reassures customers that they are in the right place to find a needed product or service.

Used properly, technology offers opportunities for customer service that a traditional store does not. For instance, the doors are always open, and searching online can reveal products faster than rummaging through stacks of clothing or endlessly browsing store shelves and aisles. A vast amount of information can be found on many products, and

Millions of users around the world connect to the Internet to access a variety of products and services.

---

[3]Ibid.

[4]Michelle Conlin, "Call Centers in the Rec Room," *Business Week Online* (January 23, 2006). http://www.businessweek.com/magazine/content/06_04/b3968103.htm.

the customer can browse at will. It's a matter of businesses giving high priority to customer service delivery and applying the new technologies well to those service principles.

The Customer Service Online Experience

E-commerce clearly has changed how many companies do business. The Amazon.com paradox proves that a selling relationship with *no* human contact can still be a positive relationship. Customers love Amazon not because it offers the lowest prices (because it doesn't), but because the buying experience has been crafted so carefully that most of us actually enjoy shopping at Amazon. This is not primarily a technological achievement; it results from Amazon headquarters staff obsessing over what customers want in a fundamentally new kind of relationship, the online experience.

Few companies or industries are immune to the effects of the e-commerce tidal wave. In fact, some companies transact business only on the Internet. It has created a new channel for customers and has made land-based companies that were former industry leaders sit up and take notice. Intensified competition and new e-commerce opportunities are pressing traditional companies to build e-business models that are flexible, fast-moving, and customer-focused. Figure 12.1 lists the advantages to a business enterprise of offering e-commerce opportunities to customers.

GROWTH AND OPPORTUNITIES IN ONLINE SERVICES The uniqueness of the digital economy lies in its ability to provide choices and speed to buyers searching for what they want. In this environment, transactions are over in a matter of minutes, and customers move on to another website. It is reasonable to understand that the remarkable power shift in the world's marketplace—from sellers to buyers—is driving online companies to value customer loyalty. When companies can maintain e-customer loyalty, their sales increase.

Online retailers are changing the face of shopping—much as shopping malls did in the 1970s—and companies must master the new rules to keep customers coming back to their websites. Increasingly, companies must have readily available the same customer data across *all* channels of customer interaction and must provide consistent service throughout *each* customer experience. Customer contact points are quickly multiplying, and new technologies allow companies to reach customers

remember this ...
Business Advantages of E-Commerce

- The global market is open 24/7.
- Businesses can be accessed by millions of consumers who have an Internet connection.
- Customers can conduct price comparisons easily.
- Feedback to queries regarding the status of orders can be immediate.
- Information can be updated quickly and made instantly available to customers.
- Frequently Asked Questions pages can provide easy access to self-help customer support.
- Companies can gather and analyze customer information, and react on the basis of current data.
- Companies have new and traditional approaches to generate revenue.
- Distribution costs for information are reduced or eliminated.
- Society has a new option to create a nearly paperless environment.

FIGURE 12.1

worldwide. Today, a customer may choose to contact an organization via the Internet, telephone, e-mail, an instant message, chat room, fax, or other mobile device.

E-retailers have been good at attracting high levels of traffic to their sites but have been less adept at engaging the throngs of customers and converting them from browsers to buyers. Out of necessity, e-retailers are turning away from pure customer acquisition and are making a conscious effort to build their customer bases through improved online customer service.

Busy customers rarely describe doing business over the Internet as a warm and fuzzy experience. However, never before have businesses had an opportunity to be in such direct contact with so many customers. The Internet allows a company to be in direct communication with all customers, anywhere in the world, as long as they have an Internet connection.

Think of the Internet as a direct line to customers. Businesses can assess customers' individual needs, say thank you, apologize, ask for feedback, and suggest new products or services suited to the individual rather than to a whole market segment—all online. It's a new, exciting opportunity for any company that knows the value of listening and staying close to customers.

Shoppers are looking for easy ways to conduct their business transactions. In the online world, the customer is king in a way that has never occurred before. Consumers are increasingly making buying decisions *without* vendors exercising any formal role. Why? The Internet provides access to sales information without the aid of a salesperson. Further, shoppers tend to know exactly what they want before making an online purchase. Being truly empowered, many customers now conduct their own research and trust their own judgment. To some extent, this circumstance provides new challenges for many retailers.

CHALLENGES AND TRENDS IN E-COMMERCE Although the way companies do business is changing rapidly to stay in step with evolving technologies, the fundamentals of excellent customer service have not changed. In fact, traditional service values are more relevant now than ever before in a world where a passion for technology is growing. Ultimately, the success of an enterprise has more to do with a company's core values and a commitment to delivering quality products and services than it does with the latest and greatest business trends. Figure 12.2 lists points that are important to buyers as they shop online.

remember this ...
Online Shopping Preferences

1. Effective search tools, express ordering, and highlighted specials
2. Assurance of on-time order fulfillment
3. Order status information, or the ability to securely track their own orders
4. The ability to exchange items purchased online at a retail establishment's physical store(s)
5. The ability to buy merchandise 24/7

FIGURE 12.2

Negative experiences at an e-retail site make it less likely that the consumer will return. The top customer complaints about online shopping are slow websites, unavailable products, late deliveries, and an inability to track order status. There are two types of online shoppers, each of whom requires a different buying experience:

1. Three-click shoppers are those who know what they want to buy and want the transaction to be as quick and simple as possible.
2. Online buyers are uncertain about what they want to purchase and need a more enriched shopping experience. For these customers, the e-retailer should have a range of items and offer easy methods for ordering, asking questions during the buying process, making payments, and receiving deliveries after the purchase has been made.

The key to business longevity on the Internet is friendly and knowledgeable help, not the lowest price. Look at the dot-com graveyard: among the commonalities are inaccessibility, unfriendliness, and the age-old business philosophy of "sell something first and service the sale second." When customers return to place a second or third order online, it is an indication that they feel it is easier for them to do business with that company than with its competition. Five rules for building strong online relationships with customers are listed in Figure 12.3.

Online customer service isn't just a good idea; today, it's mandatory for continued business survival. An even bigger challenge is striking the balance between high-tech and high-touch in serving customers. Basic Internet technologies for e-commerce include a website and server, a phone system, e-mail service, and customer relationship management (CRM) strategies.

Ethics | Choices

With access to everything from school courses, professional training, and telecommuting, to buying food, clothing, and other necessities online, it is possible for people to limit their face-to-face interaction with others. Do you think this behavior will become more typical in our society? What long-term effects of this lifestyle might occur on both personal and societal levels?

Customer Relationship Management

Customer Relationship Management (CRM) is a business strategy that integrates the functions of sales, marketing, and customer service, using technology and

remember this ...

Building Strong Relationships with Online Customers

1. Excel at each stage of the customer buying cycle	Once customers have found you in the virtual world, the next step is to give them a positive experience throughout the entire buying process. Whenever possible, make the website simple and easy to navigate, and provide powerful search tools.
2. Empower customers to help themselves	Most customers like to find products and answers on their own at a time convenient to them.
3. Help customers succeed by empowering them to be in control of the buying situation	Successful sites look professional, are easy to read and navigate, and work seamlessly. Broken links can destroy the trust of consumers. A webmaster must check for active links to other websites and remove any that are no longer valid.
4. Protect the privacy of consumers	Safeguard shoppers' payment information and any confidential details gathered about them. Make instructions clear about how to access customer service and how to return items, if necessary.
5. Offer several types of free technical support	Assistance can include using an online tutorial, watching a video, sending an e-mail message, or chatting with a customer service representative. Live chats with e-reps are popular because they answer customer questions quickly.

FIGURE 12.3

wide-ranging databases of information. It is all about understanding the customer's needs and leveraging this knowledge to increase global sales and improve service in a more personal way. The overriding goal of a company is to increase its customer base and customer retention through customer satisfaction. The customer focus that CRM brings to a company is the direct result of the electronic world and the World Wide Web. Few other approaches can offer companies the unparalleled opportunity to personalize services, provide multiple choices for customer support, and track customer satisfaction.

How does the CRM system work? Rather than only collecting, analyzing, and reporting on customer information, CRM allows electronic measures to be taken automatically on the basis of analyzing customer information. For example, if the CRM system detects a customer problem, it can immediately send the customer an e-mail message, alert a CSR to call the customer and follow up on the problem, and access the billing system to set up a credit on the customer's next invoice.

Customer satisfaction and customer loyalty are quickly gaining ground as reasons to get a CRM system up and running. In an economy that sees demand leveling off, making the most of the customers a company already has

is essential. In fact, to most businesses, maintaining or improving customer satisfaction can be more important than reducing budgets.

PURPOSE OF CRM Customer relationship management is more than technology; it involves a change in philosophy and attitude. To be effective, CRM needs to be viewed by organizations as an all-encompassing business strategy— a customer-centric philosophy of doing business that affects every consumer touch point. The slogan is to do *whatever it takes* to delight the customer.

A process for managing change must be instituted to help a company move from a product-centered focus to a customer-centered one. Companies cannot be customer-centered if they ignore the foundations of the CRM experience. For example, not responding to an e-mail is saying, "Don't bother us; we're not interested." For that reason, when companies want to implement a successful CRM strategy, they need to thoroughly consider what each element of implementation means.

- *Knowledge management.* At the heart of CRM implementation is the careful and secure acquisition of information about each customer, as well as the analysis, sharing, and tracking of this knowledge.

focus on **Best Practices**

Thanks to customer relationship management software and low-cost, high-speed international telecommunications, a call center can be located anywhere in the world. While the legal issues regarding offshoring can be complicated, the business issues are generally the same.

Call centers connect an enterprise and its operations to prospective and established customers. Any high-volume consumer industry can benefit by outsourcing call center functions. These industries might include health care, automotive, retailing, consumer electronics, wireless communications, insurance, travel, and hospitality.

Because a call center can deliver several types of services that can be conducted over the telephone, an organization needs to evaluate the scope of services it requires.

CUSTOMER SERVICE AND SUPPORT Advises customers about specific information they need from the company database, such as account balances and credit information.

TECHNICAL SUPPORT/WARRANTY Helps customers solve problematic issues dealing with quality standards or product performance.

SALES, RESERVATIONS, AND CUSTOMER RETENTION Converts inquiries from customers into sales, and contacts customers when subscriptions or contracts are about to expire.

MARKETING SURVEYS AND RESEARCH Identifies and conducts inquiries about consumer preferences relative to pricing and features of existing and new products.

- *Database consolidation.* This involves consolidating customer information from any form or type of contact into a single database. The goal is to have all interactions with a customer recorded in one place in order to drive production, marketing, sales, and customer support activities.

- *Integration of channels and systems.* The essence of online service is to respond to customers in a consistent and high-quality manner through the customer's channel of choice, whether that is an e-mail message, a phone conversation, or an online chat.

BENEFITS OF CRM Customer service is traditionally viewed as an expense or liability. To keep costs down, most operations typically put customers through an escalating series of hurdles when resolving a conflict, an expensive way to do business. Companies justify their CRM investment cost by recognizing that strong, lasting relationships with customers encourage recurring revenue, which offsets the cost. CRM software is relatively simple to use, and the benefits are great, given our technology-using consumers; however, implementing it requires massive cultural changes in most organizations.

Customer relationship management software allows a company to collect information about customers, such as account history and prior questions or complaints they have had. Once that information has been collected, it can be analyzed using CRM software, and the company can more accurately gain insights into how to serve each customer better. In addition to a greater awareness of each customer's interests and problems, the biggest benefits CRM companies experience are less customer attrition and increased customer loyalty.

customer service T I P

Successful companies don't use technology to replace human relationships, but only to enhance them.

Recognizing Online Customer Service Issues

The hardest part of traditional commerce is getting customers to go in to a store and make the decision to buy. Once a customer is in front of you, wanting to buy your product, the rest is easy, or at least more controllable. If there is a problem, the customer lets you know by returning to the store, where you can solve it personally. With e-commerce, the easiest part of business is creating the website, putting products on the site, and collecting the orders. The hardest part is handling problems that might occur involving shipping to the correct address or accepting returns.

In response to growing customer complaints, many e-commerce companies are trying to make technological "fixes" to the customer service problems by investing in software and technology-based systems. Today's sophisticated buyers want answers through access to e-mail, chat rooms, instant messaging, traditional 800 phone service, Internet audio, and well-trained online CSRs behind e-services.

Multichannel Communication

As pressure increases in call center environments to provide customers with around-the-clock availability and response, enterprises are forced to upgrade customer service and develop CRM strategies. Thus the call center is evolving into a multichannel customer interaction center that integrates wired and, increasingly, wireless channels of customer contact.

Think about how a multichannel customer contact center differs from a traditional call center. In the traditional call center, customer contact is predominantly by telephone, either inbound or outbound. Customers know if they place a call, they can talk to someone who can resolve an issue. CSRs are usually well trained to talk to customers about products, services, systems, and processes. However, most CSRs are traditionally trained to handle only routine calls, referring more difficult or escalated situations to a specially trained team or lead customer service representative.

A very different situation exists when a CSR works in a technology-based multichannel **customer contact center**. Here, customers who may be working on their computers at the office, at home, or on the road (anywhere in the world), expect to be able to start and finish an inquiry very quickly and with little hassle. Online customers want to talk to a person *only if* they cannot successfully address their situations electronically. When they do need to speak to someone, customers expect those CSRs to be very knowledgeable and skilled in managing their situations and to take the time to uncover and solve their problems on the spot.

Another major difference between traditional call centers and today's multichannel contact center is that the customer expects more control during the communication. Many customers today are tech-savvy and sophisticated. They want to connect to a business's website, navigate through it easily, complete an online request, and have the solution documented for them in real time on the spot. Further, customers expect the solution to be accurate, fast, and hassle-free, because they assume no human interaction will be necessary. In fact, many e-customers are seeking to *avoid* human contact inherent in the traditional call center.

In addition to participating in regular classroom training programs that emphasize the company's products and services, CSRs now need to have skills in solving problems and in *working* the multichannel contact system. Customers who need help from a CSR expect more, because they have already covered the simpler, more basic answers and solutions on their own through the electronic avenues provided to them on the company's website. This makes it very important to keep call center agents happy on the job and well trained in the latest service technologies. As a result, in today's business world, more than ever before, it is critical for companies to pay careful attention when hiring and training online CSRs.

Hiring and Training an Online CSR

The idea of providing customers with numerous communication channels is enticing to many companies; unfortunately, less attention has been paid to the issue of how to handle the required human resources. With the popularity of wireless communication devices, e-businesses

Many shoppers prefer to complete an online transaction without any human interaction.

can now reach their customers through pagers, PDAs, cellular phones, and other telecommunication devices. Although these technological advances increase customer contact points, many companies seem to have neglected one of the critical aspects of customer service quality—the customer service representative, or the human interface between the customer and the company.

How do you find, hire, and train CSRs who can do more than just field phone calls? The ideal is to hire individuals who can handle everything a multichannel call center requires. However, the reality is that most companies are dividing the overall tasks, with one CSR group answering phones and another handling electronic communications. Few companies currently have CSRs who can handle both.

The core skills needed in most customer service positions include work efficiency, problem-solving skills, social adeptness, effective communication skills, fact-finding abilities, and professionalism. Although many of the skill requirements for customer service personnel are the same, regardless of the method by which CSRs interact with customers, there are some differences.

For online CSRs (sometimes referred to as **e-reps**), who interact with customers by using e-mail and chat rooms, good oral communication is important, but not as essential as good written communication skills. In addition, when CSRs use the chat mode to conduct real-time, text-based conversations, accurate and fast keyboarding skills are necessary. Good customer service includes responding quickly to customers without making typographical, spelling, or grammatical errors. Moreover, individuals who work in the online, real-time chat mode must also frequently respond to several customers at once; thus multitasking (a component of work efficiency) is critical.

Regardless of the industry in which a company is classified, all of its employees are in the business of customer service. If a company cannot give customers the appropriate information, response, or resolution within a reasonable time frame, service and pricing won't matter. The customer can easily find another supplier from somewhere in the world's marketplace. The key to serving online customers well is to treat them with the same respect and attention that you would offline and in person.

BUSINESS in action

STAFFCENTRIX

Since 1999, Staffcentrix, a leading provider of virtual home-based career-training programs and resources, has helped thousands of people from around the world find their place in the virtual workforce. The company is a long-standing advocate of personal growth and enhanced family bonds through professional, home-based careers.

Developed for the Armed Forces and the U.S. Department of State, the programs at Staffcentrix train participants to work from home independently as virtual assistants and home-based freelance contractors on projects they are taught to find on the Internet. The services they provide range from handling administrative needs to market research.

Almost all Staffcentrix-certified trainers are employees of the Department of Defense or the Department of State. They are dedicated to establishing virtual careers as part of the domestic and international work flow and to provide career development to service members, veterans, military spouses, and Foreign Service spouses at military bases, embassies, and consulates internationally.

Concluding Message for CSRs

The modern call center is a mix of low-tech telephony and the latest in online collaborative technology. Its capabilities range from simultaneous interactive voice and data access over the Internet to the use of a web page as a simple, but timesaving, first step in the service process. Web users who need extensive help click a callback button to have an agent call them. Customers with less complex questions use an instant text-chat feature to get answers from agents almost immediately.

At its core—and despite all our technological advances—customer service involves human interaction between the customer and the company representative.

The customer's perception of the service is directly affected by the nature of that interaction, which is directly affected by the skills of the company's customer service personnel—online or offline.

Summary

- Globalization through outsourcing and homeshoring are two megatrends whose benefits most businesses cannot afford to ignore.

- Customers increasingly make buying decisions on their own, without vendors exercising any formal role.
- Today's sophisticated buyers want e-mail, chat rooms, Internet audio, and well-trained e-reps behind e-services.

KEY TERMS

customer contact center	e-business	homeshoring
Customer Relationship Management (CRM)	e-rep	outsourcing
	globalization	

CRITICAL THINKING

1. If you were the owner of a business that needed to provide customer agents through either outsourcing overseas or homeshoring, which would you choose and why?

2. What advantages do online stores have that traditional stores do not?

3. To what extent do you think multichannel retailing is affecting the manner in which businesses operate in today's marketplace?

4. Relative to the additional skills required of e-reps (as compared with the basic skill set needed by an in-store CSR), do you think e-reps should be paid more, or is the acquisition of additional skills a normal part of most jobs?

ONLINE RESEARCH ACTIVITIES

Project 12.1 Growth of Online Global Companies

Research a number of websites and locate several articles on the globalization and growth of online product and service companies. As a result of your research, develop a simple chart showing the growth trends over the past five years. Share your charted information with the class in either a panel discussion or an oral report, as directed by your instructor.

Project 12.2 Customer Relationship Management Software

James Woo, vice president of human resources and customer relations at On-Time Technology Products, needs up-to-the minute research on the advantages and disadvantages of incorporating customer relationship management strategies and software into the company to determine if he should add those costs into next year's budget.

Enter *Customer Relationship Management* in your favorite search engine. Complete the table below with what you find from your research.

Website	Advantages of CRM	Disadvantages of CRM
1.		
2.		
3.		

COMMUNICATION SKILLS AT WORK

Project 12.3 Multichannel Communication Methods

Conduct a survey of 20 friends and family members who shop online to determine the extent to which they use multichannel communication methods when banking or shopping online.

Complete the following table by breaking out the number of users in column 2 and writing a statement relative to the implications of such usage per method in column 3. Finally, participate in a class discussion where you compare all students' findings.

Communication Method	Number of Users	Implications
1. E-mail		
2. Chat rooms		
3. Instant messaging		
4. Toll free phone numbers		
5. Wireless communication devices		
6. Internet audio		

DECISION MAKING AT WORK

Project 12.4 Homeshoring Hiring Issues

Many companies are still working through the best employment strategy to use when hiring homeshoring reps. Consider the following examples of two people who are interested in becoming an e-rep.

- RosaLee has over 25 years of customer service and administrative experience. She has a home office with high-speed Internet, a great phone service, and most everything else she needs to work from home. However, she has been fired from her last three jobs because of excessive absences due to caring for her elderly parents.
- Rick has muscular dystrophy, which robs him of motor skills and his ability to hold down his last job as a technical data clerk. His physical challenges prevent him from working outside his home, but he has excellent communication skills. He sees working as a homeshore rep as an opportunity to be productive and earn money for his family by taking customer service, technical support, and inbound sales calls from his home.

1. Given these two persons who show interest in a homeshoring position, evaluate each one's strengths and weaknesses relative to a largely unsupervised position of working at home.

    _____

    _____

    _____

    _____

2. To what extent do you think the concept of homeshoring will change the type of person who applies for these kinds of positions?

    _____

    _____

    _____

    _____

CASE STUDIES

Project 12.5 Change Is Difficult

George and Sherol, retirees in their early sixties and owners of Sun City West Golf Carts, have been approached by a computer service company to develop a website for their rather modest company. George's first reaction is that their business is fine the way it is because he and his wife enjoy person-to-person contact with their customers and prefer to oversee the sales staff personally. On the other hand, his wife Sherol thinks there may be advantages to setting up a website and having multiple channels for their golf cart sales. She thinks the Internet will make it easier in the long run for them to enjoy semi-retirement more.

1. Is George's reaction to the suggestion for a website reasonable? Should most companies, even though they are relatively small, create a web presence to promote and sell their products? Explain.

_____

_____

_____

2. What are two advantages Sherol might suggest to her husband for developing an e-commerce site?

_____

_____

_____

3. If you were advising both of them about the pros and cons of building and maintaining a website, what would you say?

_____

_____

_____

Project 12.6 Hiring the Best E-Rep

On-Time Technology Products recently advertised for an e-rep. The company hopes the new e-rep will start on the job within the next few weeks. This is a new slant on the Customer Service Department, which formerly hired only in-house CSRs. Of the ten candidates who have applied, the following three applicants have been screened as the top candidates to be interviewed:

1. Candidate A is a former two-year employee of a competitor of OTTP. She has excellent communication and keyboarding skills and a great customer attitude; however, she indicates on her application that she does not have strong technology skills.
2. Candidate B is a recent high school graduate with a GPA of 3.8 and plans to be a part-time student majoring in computer information systems at the local community college. She has taken several business courses and was in an Honors English class throughout high school. She needs this job to work her way through college.
3. Candidate C is a current CSR at On-Time Technology Products and has been with the company for three years. He has excellent communication skills and loves working with computers. It is rumored that he told others that if he doesn't get this job, he will quit and go to work for a major competitor. Over the past three months, he has received two customer complaints, one for not following up as promised and the other for shouting at a customer.

Discuss the candidates' qualifications with other members of your class. Collectively report to the class your answers to the following questions.

1. What criteria would you use to select the top candidate for the e-rep position?

    _____

    _____

    _____

    _____

2. In your opinion, who are the top two candidates? Discuss the strengths and weaknesses of each candidate relative to this job opening.

    _____

    _____

    _____

    _____

3. Which candidate would you recommend hiring and why?

    _____

    _____

    _____

    _____

chapter 13

Customer Service Technologies

Objectives

1. Describe the use of web-based technologies in customer service departments.

2. Discuss some design principles that are important to remember when developing a website.

3. Understand the advantages and disadvantages of exchanging e-mail messages with customers.

4. Describe the application of instant messaging, chat rooms, and web logs (blogs) when serving customers online.

A new idea is first condemned as ridiculous and then dismissed as trivial, until finally it becomes what everybody knows.

—WILLIAM JAMES, AMERICAN PSYCHOLOGIST AND PHILOSOPHER

The Ford Customer Service Division has a representative that fields questions from dealership technicians (internal customers) 24 hours a day, 7 days a week—without stopping to eat or to sleep. We are talking about Ernie, a *virtual* representative that fields e-mail questions on the Ford dealer website, giving answers in simple sentences, just as a human representative would do. The goal is for Ernie to be able to answer 70 to 80 percent of the questions and to refer the remaining ones to his human counterparts at the Ford call center.[1]

The software Ford uses saves the call center time because the "live" CSR receives a transcript of the online dialogue; therefore, the technician does not have to repeat the inquiry a second time. Although Ernie is an example of technology in the extreme, it is important to recognize that organizations are spending money and customizing their software to provide around-the-clock assistance and service.

Identifying Customer Service Web-Based Technologies

Many consumers now rely on the Internet for product research, daily purchases, bill payments, and communication with CSRs

[1]Donna Harris, "Ernie Is Chatty, a Know-It-All, and Ford Likes Him Like That," *Automotive News* (June 4, 2001): 22.

via e-mail. As a result, companies are increasingly deploying sophisticated customer service tools that can filter and sort e-mail messages, provide an up-to-date knowledge base, and introduce advanced call center tools that are seamlessly integrated with the web. Today, customers can chat with a specialist online or click a button in the browser and receive a call back within seconds. Some systems also allow a CSR to synchronize browsers and then walk a person through a website by pushing web pages needed to make a sound buying decision to the customer's computer.

The Internet has opened plenty of options for providing exceptional customer service. According to recent statistics released from Forrester Research, customers are becoming more comfortable using online technologies.

- In 2004, 67 percent of U.S. households had access to the Internet. The number of online-enabled households is expected to grow by 21 percent over the next five years.

- In 2004, 21 million U.S. households paid bills online. The use of this method of payment is expected to grow by almost 50 percent to 31.2 million households in 2008.

- In 2002, 28 percent of households that had Internet access applied for a credit card online. By 2004, that number had increased to 39 percent.[2]

Companies use the following web-based technologies to help service customers:

- *E-mail* allows a customer to send a message quickly and effortlessly. Companies that have a system to filter, route, manage, and respond to incoming messages are able to serve customers more efficiently than those that do not.

- *Instant messaging and chat rooms* enable a customer to engage in one-on-one, real-time text dialogues with a customer service representative by simply clicking a button.

- *FAQs* permit customers to quickly find the most common product and service issues through a list of frequently asked questions. Because the majority of the questions handled by live customer service representatives in an online environment are routine,

generic responses to these repetitive queries make a lot of sense.

- *Knowledge bases* offer current and detailed information about products and services and can be accessed instantly through a natural language query.

- *Online forums* allow users to share information and post responses to one another in online discussion groups. These discussions are not in real time the way chats and instant messages are. Instead, they are referred to as threaded discussions and may span a few days, as the need exists.

- *Voice callback* enables customers to click a button on the customer service site to receive a return call from an e-rep in a call center. A variation is IP telephony, which works directly through the computer's Internet connection as a phone call.

Website Issues and Design Considerations

E-commerce has changed the way organizations serve customers and, in general, how people carry out an assortment of business-oriented activities each day. Electronic commerce, also known as e-commerce, is a financial business transaction that occurs over an electronic network, such as the Internet. It requires a business to have a well-designed and customer-oriented website. Conducting business online eliminates the barriers of time and distance that slow down traditional in-person transactions. Business-to-consumer e-commerce transactions occur instantaneously at any time and from anywhere in the world.

Business-to-Consumer E-Commerce

A popular use of e-commerce by consumers is known as **business-to-consumer (B2C or B-to-C) e-commerce**. B2C consists of the sale of goods and services from a business entity to a consumer or the general public through its website, also known as an **electronic storefront**. An electronic storefront contains text and graphic descriptions of products and services, and a shopping cart, which allows the customer to collect purchases electronically. When the customer is finished shopping, he or she enters personal and financial data through a secure web connection to complete the sale. Selecting a delivery option and fulfilling the order are the final steps of the transaction.

---

[2]Cindy Curtin, "Customers Love Online Unteraction," *Customer Inter@ction Solutions* (March 2005). http://findarticles.com/p/articles/mi_qa3995/is_200503/ai_n13507413.

Businesses that use a B2C e-commerce model eliminate the middleman. They sell products directly to consumers without using traditional retail channels. This enables some B2C companies to sell products at a lower cost and with faster service than a comparable bricks-and-mortar business that has a physical location where consumers must go to shop.

Not only do businesses derive benefits from the online B2C business model, but consumers do as well. Consumers have access to a variety of products and services without the constraints of time or distance, and they can easily comparison shop to find the best buy in a matter of a few minutes. Many B2C websites also provide consumer services, such as access to product reviews, chat rooms, and other product-related information, to help the consumer make an informed buying decision.

Effective E-Commerce Websites

With the Internet offering such tremendous business potential, many consumers and companies are venturing into the worldwide horizon. Depending on the nature of the existing business, the approach used to establish an online presence varies. The goal of a successful website is to attract customers and keep them returning to the site for additional products. According to a recent survey conducted by Jupiter Research, less than 5 percent of people visiting a website ever become paying customers.[3] This is a statistic that businesses want to improve through providing exceptional customer service.

Figure 13.1 lists factors that lead to e-loyalty and can affect whether an e-commerce customer will return to place future orders.

The best electronic storefronts plan for convenience, efficiency, and ease of use. Consumers want to navigate quickly through a site that has clear and easy-to-follow instructions. Typically, the fewer clicks it takes for a customer to find a product and place an order, the more sales an online store will make.

In designing a service-friendly website, several questions must be asked and thoughtfully considered by an e-organization.

1. *What is the purpose of the website?* Is it simply to provide information or to support a complete line of

---

[3]Sarah Lacy, "E-Tailing: It's All About Service," *Business Week Online* (July 6, 2005). www.businessweek.com/technology/content/jul2005/tc2005076_1187.htm.

---

remember this ...
Factors That Lead to E-Loyalty

- Low prices
- Wide selection of products
- Website appearance and ease of navigation
- Accessibility of up-to-date product, service, and pricing information
- Ease of ordering
- Posted privacy policies
- Security safeguards
- Shipping choices
- On-time delivery
- High-quality customer support

FIGURE 13.1

e-commerce functions, such as marketing, selling, information, and customer service?

2. *What graphics are needed to capture and maintain customer interest?* A website should be easy to navigate and require no more than three clicks to access key data, such as company address and phone number, as well as a customer support link. Designing a website so that the download speeds of the design elements are quick and acceptable is critical.

3. *How easy is it to navigate and perform search functions?* The site should allow visitors to navigate back and forth between the current page and other pages. It should have a link to the site map and

An online purchase allows consumers to complete a transaction quickly at any time.

easy pull-down menus. These features allow the customer to go directly to the content desired or to be linked easily to other related content sites and web pages.

4. *Will customers feel secure with the buying experience?* To enhance this feeling of safety, companies should tell customers when they are in secure transactions and that transmitted data will be protected through encryption during transmission. Provide all service options, from online shopping carts to accepting credit cards, because poor checkout experiences cause people to abandon shopping in the middle of their e-purchases.

5. *Is the website fun, current, interactive, and interesting?* Stay current by updating the website with new information at least once a week. At the same time, check for any broken links and fix them immediately. Customers are busy people and dislike having their time wasted.

Service After an Online Sale

Surveys indicate that a large percentage of customers are dissatisfied with customer service at online businesses. Providing service after the sale is an important consideration for these companies. Following up with a customer after a sale generates return business and thoughtful recommendations for improvement. E-retailers can improve post-sale communication by

- using technology to activate an automatic e-mail message that confirms orders within minutes of their being placed.
- offering a list of frequently asked questions (FAQs).
- sending online surveys to receive customer feedback quickly.
- answering customer queries quickly and accurately.
- offering live chats for immediate sales assistance.
- providing a means for customers to track shipments.
- establishing return policies that allow customers to make returns and exchanges quickly and conveniently.

Many e-commerce sites use e-mail publishing to keep in touch with their customers. **E-mail publishing** is the process of periodically sending newsletters, via e-mail, to a large group of people with similar interests. For example, an e-retailer can use e-mail publishing

to offer loyal customers discounts and promotions, announce new products, or deliver industry news.

How does this work? B2C businesses create electronic customer profiles. These profiles collect buyer information by tracking preferences as consumers browse through the web pages. This individualized profile then enables the B2C business to target advertisements, determine customer needs, and personalize offerings to a particular customer.

E-Mailing Customers

The recent growth and usage of e-mail in customer service areas has been phenomenal. Businesses and customers like e-mail messaging for a number of reasons.

- E-mail eliminates **telephone tag**, the problem of trying to contact busy people who are not always available to receive telephone calls.
- E-mail saves time. Consumers are protected from the interruptions of traditional telephone calls while they are attending to other matters.
- E-mail speeds up the process of making business decisions because it allows rapid exchanges from all parties involved in the decisions.
- E-mail is inexpensive. It permits unlimited use at no more than the cost of an Internet connection.

It is prudent to mention that e-mail also has disadvantages. The following drawbacks stand out:

- E-mail is not confidential. Some describe e-mail as being as private as a postcard you drop in the mailbox.
- E-mail does not communicate the sender's emotions well. Voice intonations, facial expressions, and body movements are not a part of the message, as they are with communicating on the telephone or face-to-face.
- E-mail may be ignored or delayed. The volume of e-mail often makes it difficult for some respondents to read and act on all of their messages in a timely manner.

Figure 13.2 describes some common e-mail terms that have evolved and their appropriate use in customer messages.

✷ remember this ...
Common E-Mail Terms

Emoticons	An emoticon, also called a smiley, is a sequence of ordinary printable characters intended to represent a human facial expression and convey an emotion. These are not advised for use in business e-mail messages.
Abbreviations	Abbreviations are commonly used in electronic messages to save time as you type. For example, BTW means *by the way*. FYI means *for your information*. These casual abbreviations are not advised for use in business e-mail messages to customers.
Flame	A flame is an angry or insulting message directed at one person. A flame war is an electronic argument that continues over a period of time. Avoid starting or participating in flame wars. Certainly, flaming customers is never appropriate.
Shouting	A message written in capital letters can be annoying and hard to read, and is known as shouting. Always use appropriate uppercase and lowercase letters when typing messages to customers, just as you would in traditional correspondence.
Bounced Message	A bounced message is one that is returned to you because it cannot be delivered to the recipient. A message usually bounces back due to errors in the e-mail address. Before sending a message, remember to proofread both the message and the address.

FIGURE 13.2

> **customer service T I P**
>
> *It is much easier to offend or hurt someone unknowingly in an e-mail message than in person or on the phone. That is why, before pressing the send button, it is important to be as clear and concise as possible to avoid misunderstandings.*

The Use and Misuse of E-Mail

The use of e-mail has revolutionized the way the working world communicates. We continue to learn more about how to use it efficiently. For example, scrolling through e-mail as it arrives is a big time waster. Instead, set aside time each day to read e-mail and act on each message.

E-mail should be used to save time, not to diminish professionalism and the proper use of writing. Here are some tips you may wish to review:

- *Place deadlines in the subject line.* You grab attention and increase comprehension by putting deadlines in the subject line as well as in the body of the message.

- *Refrain from using a formal salutation.* Many writers save time with quick salutations, such as "Greetings," or by simply addressing the message to the recipient's name.

- *Frontload the main idea.* Give recipients the main idea of the message in the first paragraph. Support the main idea with details in the middle paragraphs and end with any action items or requests.

- *Use e-mail features effectively.* Organizing your messages into folders permits you to save and retrieve important messages for future use.

Ethics / Choices

What if you worked in a Customer Service Department with someone who sent instant messages to her friends while serving customers and who also speckled her e-mails to customers with smileys. Would you say anything to her or your supervisor?

Employers are learning the hard way that the massive number of e-mail messages sent every year makes up a visible and potentially perilous communication medium.

Following are some examples of e-mail communication pitfalls—both practical and legal:

- Based on incorrect assumptions of privacy, e-mail users write things they would never say aloud, much less say in a business document that may be saved, forwarded, and printed.

- Employees at all levels use startlingly candid or flippant language without realizing that "delete" doesn't mean "gone." In fact, a document can be retrieved and produced years later, if needed, because messages reside on the computer server until they are permanently deleted.

- E-mail is more conversational than face-to-face communication and is often sent in haste. Loose language, slang, and inappropriate jargon compound communication problems. Further, the send button is often pressed too quickly without an adequate or careful proofreading of the message. This results in messages that readers often interpret as improper in tone or wording.

E-Mail Etiquette and Safeguard Considerations

Netiquette, which is short for Internet etiquette, is a code of acceptable behaviors that users should follow while on the Internet. Netiquette includes rules for all aspects of the Internet, including the World Wide Web, e-mail, chat rooms, instant messaging, and discussion forums.

E-mail etiquette is a set of standards that are recommended by business and communication experts in response to the growing concern that people are not using their e-mail feature appropriately. E-mail etiquette offers some guidelines that CSRs can use to facilitate better communication between themselves and their customers. Because e-mail is part of the virtual world of communication, many people communicate in their e-mail messages the same way they do in virtual chat rooms—with much less formality and, at times, too aggressively.

One overall point to remember is that an e-mail does not have nonverbal expression to supplement the written message. Most of the time, we make judgments about a person's motives and intentions based on his or her tone of voice, gestures, and body language. When those clues are absent, figuring out what the message sender really means is more difficult.

Before clicking the send button on your e-mail, it is important to know who will be receiving the message, for two reasons. First, it encourages you to think about the tone of your writing. E-mails sent to external customers will probably be more formal and brief, whereas e-mails to an internal customer or colleague might be less formal. Second, it helps you decide whether the recipient's title should be used or whether a first name or a generic greeting is more appropriate.

Despite the fact that you may send an e-mail to someone privately, remember that e-mails are public documents. Therefore, include only statements that you can openly defend, should your e-mail message be circulated or shown to parties not intended to see it.

Three ways companies can minimize the rise of e-mail abuse and safeguard its best and highest use are to enact strict policies, educate employees and managers about those policies, and then enforce them. When using a business e-mail system, all employees should bear in mind this advice:

- The employer owns the e-mail. All messages that are created, sent, or received using a company system remain the property of the employer, not the employee.

- The e-mail system is for business communications only. Personal business conducted online is unauthorized and should be conducted at home rather than at work.

- Offensive and inflammatory messages are strictly prohibited. These actions can be grounds for termination in most organizations.

- The use of passwords does not indicate that a message is confidential or that the company will not be able to intercept it.

- Each customer who sends an e-mail message should receive an immediate reply that conveys, "We received your message, and we promise to respond within one business day."

---

customer service TIP

Make every effort to return e-mails in the same amount of time that you would return a phone call.

Other Customer Messaging Systems

Although e-mail appears to be the online communication medium of choice, other means of electronic communication also exist. Customer service representatives are increasingly using Internet Protocol Private Branch Exchange Systems, instant messages, chat rooms, web logs, and faxes to communicate with customers.

Internet Protocol Private Branch Exchange Systems

Today, low-cost call centers funnel e-mails, web inquiries, and phone calls through a single computer that blends the power of the Internet with the muscle of a corporate telephone system. At first glance, these call centers seem rather mundane, because they consist only of standard desktop computers, digital phones with small screens, and software. However, the ability of call center equipment—known as Internet Protocol Private Branch Exchange Systems, or IP-PBXs—to route inquiries automatically means that fewer customers get lost in the shuffle, and their needs are more readily served.

IP-PBXs can also redirect calls to home-office workers without involving the phone company or information technology. The most dazzling feature is a pop-up window that reveals the name and sales history of each incoming caller or e-mail message sender. This element allows CSRs to begin personalized service at the start of each customer contact.

Instant Messages

For many people, shopping alone is not as much fun as interacting with someone during the experience. Consumers are using instant messages to share the buying experience with others. **Instant messaging (IM)** is a real-time Internet communications service that notifies a person when someone from a self-created list of family and friends is online and allows that person to exchange messages or files or to join a private chat room with him or her. Instant messaging, a kind of super e-mail, allows two or more people to hold a real-time, typed conversation online. The advantage of IM for customers is that when they have questions before finalizing buying decisions, they can send messages to e-reps in customer service departments and get quick replies.

Successful online retailers have learned that live messaging boosts sales in an instant. Too many companies defeat the purpose of good customer service by not having enough reps on hand to keep impatient surfers from clicking away while waiting for responses. The essence of this new technology is simple. It consists of just two components:

1. *Synchronicity* involves the ability for two people to exchange information in real time.
2. *Presence awareness* lets you know whether your correspondent is online or disconnected. It can even inform you when that person is away from the desk or is typing you a message.

How does instant messaging help CSRs within the organization? IM allows you to collaborate with colleagues in the following ways to improve customer service:

- You can send a message to a colleague for help with a query while you are answering a customer's request.
- You can inform colleagues of an incoming call, allowing them to end a less important call.
- You can send a message requesting information to more than one colleague at a time, while serving a customer.

Ethics / Choices

In your opinion, is it right for companies to create electronic profiles that describe customers' preferences as a result of websites they visit and online forms they complete when buying merchandise?

Chats

Chats allow agents or specialists to approach customers while they are online and offer assistance. Once contacted, the website visitor may decline or accept the invitation to chat. If the visitor accepts the invitation, he or she interacts in a manner similar to that used in instant messaging, in a private, secure, one-on-one chat.

Though some businesses use chats, most are cautious and take a conservative approach toward this technology for two reasons. First, using it is expensive, and second,

focus on   Best Practices

Web software that provides a more effective way of managing pre- and post-sale customer support is in high demand in the online business environment. LivePerson, a fully integrated multichannel software package, is one such program that delivers a personalized, easy-to-implement, secure, and convenient way to communicate with customers in real time. The LivePerson software technology supports and manages critical online interactions, like e-mail, self-service knowledge base, and live chats. It also has a feature that invites website visitors to chat before they leave the site.

Consumer benefits of this service include improved customer support through access to real-time customer history; increased customer satisfaction by providing faster response times; and the provision for the customer to chat directly with service reps in real-time situations. Company benefits include greater understanding of customer needs; increased sales by reducing shopping cart abandonment; increased customer retention and loyalty; and an improved ability to convert browsers into buyers.

Blogs

Blogs, or web logs, are a growing electronic communications method that uses millions of online journals linked together in a vast network. Not only do individuals on the Internet set up blogs, but businesses do as well.

Jupiter Research, a leading authority on the impact of the Internet and emerging consumer technologies on business, reveals that 35 percent of large companies plan to institute corporate blogs during 2006. By engaging prospective customers in active web log dialogue, companies can showcase their expertise and domain knowledge, creating a forum for communication of their strategies and visions. In doing so, companies can generate buzz around their products or services, while eliciting feedback and collaboration from customers who use their products.

New research finds that blogs are currently underused for generating **word-of-mouth (WoM) marketing** opportunities. Only 32 percent of marketing executives said they use corporate web logs to generate WoM around their company's products or services.[5]

Blogs are different. They evolve with every posting, each one tied to a moment. If a company can track millions of blogs simultaneously, it gets a heat map of what a growing part of the world is thinking about its business, products, and services, minute by minute. E-mail has carried on billions of conversations over the past decade, but those exchanges were private. Most blogs are open to the world. As bloggers read each other's entries, make their own comments, and link from one page to the next, they create a global conversation.

Some view blogs as the most explosive outbreak in the information world because the Internet itself has the capacity to shake up just about every business. As shown in Figure 13.3, there are almost 9 million active blogs, with 40,000 new ones popping up each day. Topics range from poetry or constitutional law to many frivolous subjects.

The important issue related to blogs in customer service is this: Because the overwhelming majority of the information the world sees and uses every day is digital—photos, PowerPoint presentations, government filings, billions of e-mail messages, even digital phone messages—with a couple of clicks, every one of these

some customers consider being invited to chat as intrusive. Recent surveys by Jupiter Research note that from 2001 to 2005, not only did the number of users who made use of text chat when available rise, but the amount of text-chat users who were satisfied with it also climbed from 45 percent in 2001 to 58 percent in 2005.

The survey report noted that businesses can use text chat in conjunction with the business intelligence they already have, such as a customer's previous purchases, to create a better interactivity between the company and customer.[4]

---

[4]From http://www.physorg.com/printnews.php?newsid=68217856.

[5]"JupiterResearch Finds That Deployment of Corporate Weblogs Will Double in 2006," (June 26, 2006). www.jupiterresearch.com.

remember this ...
Blog Growth

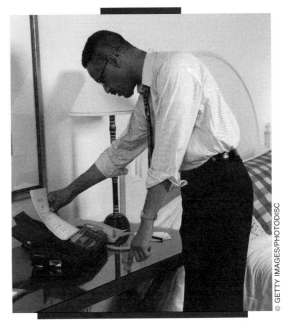

FIGURE 13.3   *Source:* Technorati Inc.

---

items can be broadcast into the *blogosphere* by anyone with an Internet hookup.[6]

Fax Documents

Fax documents can contain text, drawings, or photographs. At a time when e-mail is dominating written communication and Internet documents are replacing hard-copy forms in business, faxes can seem like a throwback to a time when everything was hardwired and nobody had heard yet of e-commerce.

What's keeping fax not merely alive, but active, in the face of competing technologies is the sheer number and pervasive use of fax machines. E-mail and the Internet probably will erode fax volume in the United States, but that's not the case elsewhere. In a global customer service economy, the use of fax machines is growing, especially in Latin America and Europe. The main reasons are that Internet access is not as readily available in those regions, and telecommunications and technology are still quite costly in some places. Today, companies in America must keep fax equipment to do business with their foreign partners.[7]

Internet faxing is an option if a traditional fax machine is not available. With this service, the Internet provider supplies the user with a personal fax number tied to the user's e-mail account. Faxes sent to that number are received as e-mail attachments to the user. Sending a fax this way is as simple as addressing an e-mail or printing a document to the fax machine's phone

In a global customer service economy, fax machines continue to transmit documents around the world.

---

[6]Stephen Baker and Heather Green, "Blogs Will Change Your Business," *Business Week* (May 2, 2005). www.businessweek.com.

[7]Bob Mueller, "Competing Technologies: No Match for Fax," *Purchasing* (February 22, 2001): 25.

number. The result is an amazingly fast and flexible personal fax system.

BUSINESS *in action*

ZAPPOS.COM

Loving the product you sell isn't as important as providing the best customer service experience in the industry. That has been the secret to success for Tony Hsieh, CEO of Zappos.com, a Las Vegas-based company that began selling shoes online in 1998 and now posts annual sales in excess of $250 million.

By intention, Hsieh (pronounced *shay*) operates his company around the clock, seven days a week, from his 77,000 square-foot warehouse. As a result of physically stocking a vast number of styles and brands rather than shipping orders from specific shoe manufacturers, Zappos is able to provide customers with guaranteed immediate delivery of shoes that carry a product return policy good for up to a year from purchase. Zappos also maintains a free shipping and return policy. Unlike other online businesses, customer service representatives are encouraged to take whatever time is needed, using chats and e-mail messaging, to help customers find the specific shoes they are looking for. Hsieh's theory is, employees don't have to be passionate about shoes, but they do have to be passionate about service.

Source: http://www.inc.com/magazine/20060901/hidi-hsieh.html.

Concluding Message for CSRs

For years, customer communications have been funneled into well-staffed and highly automated call centers with phones. Online customers, however, have changed that, and today's customer service departments are busy with e-customers.

E-commerce is evolving rapidly, if not explosively. The Internet levels the playing field, making it possible for even small companies to establish a business presence quickly in worldwide markets and to serve customers in a way not previously imagined. Service employees who have the skills to effectively communicate with customers online will be the ones who reap the most rewards now and in the future.

Summary

- Companies make available the following web-based communication technologies when serving e-customer needs: e-mail, instant messaging, chat rooms, FAQs, knowledge bases, online forums, and voice callback systems.
- The best-designed websites provide customers with convenience, efficiency, and ease of use, with easy-to-follow instructions for navigating the site.
- With e-mail being so prevalent in business communication, using proper e-mail etiquette and a clear professional writing style with internal and external customers is important.
- Although e-mail appears to be the online communication medium of choice, Internet Protocol Private Branch Exchange Systems, instant messages, chat rooms, blogs, and fax documents are also used to communicate with customers.

KEY TERMS

blogs

business-to-consumer (B2C or B-to-C) e-commerce

electronic storefront

e-mail etiquette

e-mail publishing

instant messaging (IM)

netiquette

telephone tag

word-of-mouth (WoM) marketing

CRITICAL THINKING

1. Of all the web-based technologies used in customer service departments, which two do you think are the most service-oriented from the consumer's standpoint? Explain.

2. Why do organizations use the business-to-consumer e-commerce model? In your opinion, in the future, should more businesses sell to and service customers using this approach?

3. Locate two companies on the Internet that you think best follow the design principles for developing a website that were covered in this chapter. Describe the use of at least three design principles you discovered on those sites.

4. From a customer's point of view, what are the top advantages of using e-mail to send service-related messages to companies?

5. In your opinion, which technologies—instant messages, chat rooms, or blogs—will have the greatest positive impact on customer purchases over the next five years? Explain.

ONLINE RESEARCH ACTIVITIES

Project 13.1 Debate the Issue: Electronic Customer Service

Research a number of websites and locate several articles about customers' acceptance of electronic-oriented customer service. As a result of your research, role-play with a fellow student the pros and cons of companies using technology to communicate with customers.

Project 13.2 Website Design Considerations

President Collin MacGibson at On-Time Technology Products wants to develop an effective website for his company. You are among several employees he has asked to serve on the development team.

Enter *Website Design Considerations* or similar key words in your favorite search engine. Locate four technology-based websites that, in your opinion, are good examples of strong online pages. From your research, complete the following chart by listing examples and design suggestions.

Website Example	Design Suggestions for Website Features
1.	1. Use of graphics:
2.	2. Ease of navigation:
3.	3. Interest of website:
4.	4. Customer oriented:

COMMUNICATION SKILLS AT WORK

Project 13.3 E-Mail Seminar

Assume you have been asked to put together a list of seven topics you think would be appropriate to include in a seminar entitled "The Use of Company E-Mail."

Form a small group and discuss the training topics you feel should be covered in the seminar. List these prioritized topics in column 1. In column 2, state your justification for including each topic as part of the training.

Training Topic	Justification for Training Topic
1.	
2.	
3.	
4.	
5.	
6.	
7.	

DECISION MAKING AT WORK

Project 13.4 Updating Business Communications

In a recent survey, respondents compared e-mail with the more traditional forms of business communication. Respond to each of the following statements, which indicate percentages of various survey results. Do you believe the results reflect the way business correspondence is changing? Explain.

1. Eighty percent of respondents said that e-mail has replaced postal mail for the majority of their business correspondence.

_____

_____

_____

_____

2. Seventy-three percent said that e-mail has replaced faxing for the majority of their business correspondence.

_____

_____

_____

_____

3. Forty-five percent said that e-mail has replaced phone calls for the majority of their business correspondence.

_____

_____

_____

_____

 **CASE STUDIES**

Project 13.5 Online Sales Lost

A colleague brought to work the results of a recent industry report, which estimated that more than $6 billion in online technology product sales were lost last year due to inadequate customer service. Businesses lost revenue along with customer goodwill. Pair up with a classmate to discuss the report's findings and respond to the following questions:

1. Do your own research to either support or refute this statistic. Cite your reasons and sources, as applicable.

_____

_____

_____

_____

2. If this report is to be believed, why should American businesses be concerned?

_____

_____

_____

_____

3. What can you recommend businesses do to improve online sales and customer goodwill?

_____

_____

_____

_____

Project 13.6 Increasing Customer Support

On-Time Technology Products recognizes that they should do more to connect with customers after a sale. Beyond extending the product warranty on most products and maintaining a technical support line between 8:00 a.m. and 5:00 p.m., they have done little else in the customer support area. Search online for additional articles that will help you respond to the following questions.

1. What are some techniques OTTP should incorporate to improve their post-sale support?

_____

_____

_____

_____

2. In your opinion, how can the Internet more effectively provide some innovative methods to support a post-sale transaction?

_____

_____

_____

_____

3. Describe the outcome of a recent online purchase you made. Was it a positive experience? Was post-sale support offered to you by the service representative?

_____

_____

_____

_____

chapter 14

Managing, Training, and Rewarding Superior Customer Service

Objectives

1. Explain the role of management in setting customer service standards.

2. Describe the working environment and basic duties for most customer service representatives.

3. Identify reasons companies should train, empower, and reward service professionals.

4. Discuss the qualities that a good customer service manager should possess.

Do less than customers expect and service is perceived as bad. Do exactly what customers expect and service is perceived as good.... But do more than customers expect and service is perceived as superior.

—JOHN TSCHOHL, CUSTOMER SERVICE STRATEGIST

Looking to the future can be exciting and fun. Companies that attribute their success to exemplary customer service do so as a result of setting realistic and forward-looking goals and standards that serve and value customers. These companies give more than just words to the importance of training, empowering, and rewarding customer service representatives; they stake their reputations on it.

Setting Standards in Customer Service

Successful companies are made, not born. Setting standards, or benchmarks, in customer service doesn't just happen; they are painstakingly conceived and delivered with care. **Standards** tell workers what is expected of them, in both the quality and quantity of their work. In successful companies, the employees appear to be a cut above others because they are courteous and always seem to be smiling. In addition, service professionals in these companies never fail to ask whether they can be of assistance and always seem to be having a great deal of fun doing their jobs. These employees achieve a higher level of productivity for their employers. Were their employers just fortunate to have many happy and enthusiastic people apply for the jobs? Assuming that is not the case, how did it happen?

The Role of Management

A customer-oriented business culture starts at the top and is consistently reinforced throughout all levels of management. Good managers are responsible for hiring employees with great attitudes. These managers must work very hard to create a workplace environment where service employees are satisfied. By the same token, it might also be surmised that to arrive at this core group of enthusiastic employees, companies have hired and fired numerous employees who did not meet their expectations.

There are two keys to an organization's success: solid customer relationships and trusted performance. These cornerstones to success are not new; they have been around for many years. What has changed is this: Technology has increased the speed of information and production. It has also brought efficiencies and has heightened customer demand and requirements. Today, company mission statements, specifically with regard to customer service activity,

- articulate what the customer service department is expected to contribute to overall company's goals.
- furnish guidelines for the behavior of various departments involved in customer service situations.
- provide a sense of identity, continuity, and pride in customer service representatives.

Customer service departments also need direction and usually write their own mission statements. Departmental goals should always align with those of the organization. An example of a strong mission statement particular to a customer service department follows:

> The mission of the Customer Service Department at On-Time Technology Products is to establish, maintain, and improve the company's position in the marketplace through developing strategies for customer retention and new account growth and to provide high levels of service to customers, prospective customers, and the general public.

The overriding purpose of customer service departments is to satisfy customers. According to study results published in the *Journal of Retailing*, satisfied customers are pleased with an organization's delivery of service in five areas: tangibles, reliability, responsiveness, assurance, and empathy.

1. *Tangibles* are the physical aspects of a service experience, for example, the appearance of the facility and staff, as well as any written communication such as letters, e-mails, flyers, and advertisements. In short, this is the image that an organization projects.

2. *Reliability* means performing the promised service dependably and accurately, keeping promises, and doing it right the first time.

3. *Responsiveness* refers to the timeliness of service and the willingness of service personnel to help. The loyalty factor is set in motion when an organization responds to a customer's need before he or she even realizes that a need exists.

4. *Assurance* is the knowledge, courtesy, and professionalism of the service specialist, all of which build a customer's trust. Ensuring that customer service representatives are knowledgeable requires that an organization invest in effective training initiatives on a continuous basis.

5. *Empathy* is the caring and individualized service that make a customer feel valued. Acts such as remembering customers' names and their likes and dislikes build loyalty.[1]

> ### customer service T I P
>
> *A simple secret to serving customers is this: Find out what they want and how they want it, and give it to them just that way!*

Standards for Customer Service

Exceptional customer service must be a primary business goal and core value of an organization. This commitment is reflected in company policies, procedures, and standards. When organizations have a baseline of service performance standards, they deliver, regardless of who the customer is or how much he or she spends.

Although every customer service operation is unique, all customer service centers need to measure the same key areas to gauge how well they are doing and to assess the specific areas they can improve upon. Figure 14.1 explains how companies measure and calculate certain performance standards.

---

[1]Roger H. Nunley, "Customer Service Doesn't Cut It Anymore," *Journal of Retailing* (Spring 2001): 12.

● remember this ...
Calculating Performance Standards

Performance Measurement	Calculation of Standards
Operations management	Determined by calculating service statistics • Cost per call or cost per minute • Earnings per representative
Service level	Determined by • How well x percent of calls are answered in y seconds • The percent of calls abandoned
CSR quality and productivity	Determined by • Quality—measured when monitoring calls and checking data accuracy • Productivity—measured by tracking calls per hour and amount of dollars received per sale
Employee satisfaction	Determined by calculating • Employee retention rate • Employee survey results
Customer satisfaction	Determined by calculating • Customer survey results • First-contact resolution rates • Customer retention rates

FIGURE 14.1

Effective customer service standards reflect an understanding of what customers need, want, and are willing to pay for, as well as what the competition is offering. The best way to evaluate and write standards is by looking at service situations from the customer's point of view. To have meaning, standards must be stated in numbers and be measurable. Words such as *excellent* and *superior* are good motivators, but they need to be translated into specifics of performance. Here are some examples of measurable standards in customer service:

- Ninety-eight percent of online customer inquiries will be answered live within five minutes of their receipt.
- Credits on product returns will be posted to customer accounts within two working days.
- Complaints involving $500 or less will be resolved within three working days.

customer service T I P

Effective job performance can be measured by customer satisfaction levels.

Understanding the Evolving CSR Position

HELP WANTED. Individual of high intelligence and personal charm, capable of working under extreme pressure with frequent interruptions, resourceful and flexible, cheerful and even-tempered. The individual selected for this position must be completely trustworthy, as he or she will be entrusted with millions of dollars of the company's business, and must be able to represent customers' best interests with the company while remaining completely loyal to the company. Must be a self-starter with high initiative and an excellent team player. Must be willing to work long hours in a confined space under less than ideal conditions. Must be willing to work for low pay with little opportunity for advancement. This is a nonexempt clerical position. Equal opportunity employer, M/F. Apply Box 4050, Anytown, U.S.A.

As this fictitious, but only slightly exaggerated, classified ad suggests, most companies expect a great deal from their frontline customer service representatives. However, besides the usual benefits packages, many companies don't always give a great deal in return. Formal training is often sketchy, and the general company-wide perception of CSRs as low-grade clerical workers is compounded by a perception that they are also troublemakers.

The reason for this perception is that CSRs show up in other departments only when there is a customer service problem that cannot be handled. Mix these elements with the typical pressures of the customer service environment, and it is not hard to understand that problems of morale, stress, burnout, and turnover are common to the customer service function in businesses. The following sections examine CSRs' duties, working environment, promotion opportunities, and certification.

Duties and the Working Environment

CSRs perform a variety of duties that require them to communicate effectively and to work under limited direct supervision, but in cooperation with others. Typically,

Customer service begins with hiring the right people.

they work inside comfortable offices or cubicles between 35 and 40 hours per week, with occasional overtime, night, and weekend hours. Often, they work under stress from angry or upset customers.

The physical job requirements call for CSRs to sit for long periods while using their arms, hands, and fingers. They need to speak, hear, and see well. To carry out their duties, CSRs use the telephone, calculator, and computer to produce correspondence, invoices, e-mail messages, and other product information for customers.

Promotion Opportunities and Certification

Promotion opportunities for CSRs tend to be limited. However, this entry-level job is a good opportunity to learn solid business skills and often leads to administrative and sales positions within organizations.

Certification is becoming the mark of professionals in many career fields. In the world of customer service, CSRs can pursue professional certification sponsored by the International Customer Service Association (ICSA). The ICSA Professional Certification Program is a self-paced, 30-hour training program consisting of six coordinating modules. CSRs who take specified training and participate in extracurricular customer service

activities receive points toward the designation of CCSP (Certified Customer Service Professional).

Retaining CSRs and Other Loyalty Issues

Employees working in customer service areas should be recognized and rewarded for their everyday efforts. Although too often they are on the lowest rung of a company's pay scale, CSRs' contributions to an organization's bottom line are invaluable. Customer service employees know they are valued and appreciated when companies train, empower, and reward them.

CSR Training

An April 2005 *HR Magazine* article reported that companies today are building talent internally, spending training dollars on different areas than they have in the past—areas that have a clear, bottom-line impact on the business. Training is expanding to support business in areas such as knowledge transfer, customer education to sell more products, and frontline sales techniques.[2]

Customer service training begins with the way in which an employer screens job applicants. With today's new generation of workers and accompanying new attitudes about the role of customer service, training is taking on greater importance. For example, when pre-employment assessment questions on customer service were examined, it was determined that, of those applicants surveyed,

- 45 percent said they believe that customers should be told when they are wrong.
- 46 percent said customers have to follow the rules if CSRs are going to help them.
- 34 percent said they would prefer to work behind the scenes rather than with customers.
- 13 percent said they believe that if customers don't ask for help, they don't need it.
- 10 percent said they do not feel it is necessary to help a customer if the request falls outside their area of responsibility.[3]

---

[2]Kathryn Tyler, "Training Revs Up: Companies Are Realizing that Enhanced Performance Requires a Bigger Training Engine," *HR Magazine* (April 2005). http://findarticles.com/p/articles/mi_m3495/is_4_50/ai_n13656555.

[3]Brenda Paik Sunoo, "Results-Oriented Customer Service Training," *Workforce* (May 2001): 84.

These survey results pose great concerns in business today. For better or worse, companies are most often judged by the performance and perceived attitude of their frontline personnel. There is a tendency to blame poor service on poor training. Many corporate executives spend a fortune on advertising, inventory, and capital improvements, while essentially ignoring the importance of employee training. Ongoing education is necessary for quality customer service representatives. Companies that say they can't afford the time or money to give their CSRs regular training sessions end up paying far more for the lack of training than they would have paid for the training itself.

When companies make the investment to train their customer service employees, they show that they value them and their work. One estimate is that a good training program has a value of at least five times its cost, because employees who feel valued are more motivated and more productive.

Employees who are not trained to provide good customer service find themselves frustrated in their attempts to deal with rude, difficult, and irate customers. If they are trained in how to defuse complicated situations, there is a much greater chance good workers will stay, because they will be better prepared to handle the job.

Ethics / Choices

Quality versus quantity is a common issue in business. Suppose you work with someone who boasts taking 100 customer calls per day when the average is 75. You and other co-workers do not feel her approach with customers is one of quality. The results she produces are usually less than acceptable when helping customers. In your opinion, how does quantity of calls taken measure against quality results? Further, what effect does quantity have on repeat customer business?

TRAINING CURRICULUM According to Customer Service Consultant John Tschohl, companies should provide at least 40 hours of training each year and establish clear objectives, so that employees know what they should be able to do once they've completed that training. To be effective, training must be consistent and continuous and must involve everyone in the organization. Training is especially important for frontline employees whose knowledge and behavior influence clients and customers to return with additional business.[4]

What should a curriculum that teaches good customer service skills look like? It should emphasize developing phone skills and interpersonal communication that foster a teambuilding environment. Further, the curriculum should include training on the latest customer care technologies, such as live interactive chats, intelligent e-mail response systems, telephone services, and robust self-service search engines. A critical training goal is to make sure CSRs are knowledgeable about the company's products. When employees are unable to answer a customer's question about a product or service, credibility suffers and the consequences can result in lost sales.

TRAINING METHODS The secret to effective learning is to match the delivery to the learner's receptive style, provide enough hands-on training to reinforce the concepts and, if needed, test to "real business" situations. For example, classroom training emphasizes facts that need learning, such as corporate policies and processes. **Coaching**, on the other hand, emphasizes practice, the critical "learn by doing" that turns information into knowledge and then into experience.

Role playing, using customer scenarios encountered in the real world, is one of the most effective methods for training CSRs. It helps CSRs learn how to talk with customers and how to make sales. By acting out situations, employees learn how to eliminate on-the-job shyness, prevent intimidation, extract personal information from shoppers, handle irate customers, overcome objections, and share product knowledge. Working on awkward customer scenarios and handling difficult customers are good topics for role playing.

Rehearsing in this way helps employees eliminate verbal fillers, those awkward "ums" and "you knows" that can creep into our speech when we are uncertain about what to say. But role playing is not the easiest type of training to do. Some employees are reluctant to participate because the thought of acting in front of an audience—even a tiny group—makes them nervous. To be effective,

[4]John Tschohl, "Employee Training Offers Bottom Line Benefits," *Service Quality Institute* (November 19, 2000): 4.

One of the best training methods to use with CSRs is to role-play customer situations.

the training technique requires a safe learning environment and dedicated time. The benefits gained from role playing, however, are worth the time and effort, because they boost employee confidence and overall performance.

Ethics | Choices

Suppose you overheard a co-worker say, "If you need seven layers of management to sign off on every minor customer decision, what's the point of having a customer service center?" What is your reaction to this statement? Do you agree? Explain your position.

Empowering CSRs

Empowerment is an enormous employee motivational tool that can give a business the competitive edge it needs to survive. Empowering employees gives them the authority to provide exceptional customer service. That means bending—sometimes breaking—the rules to achieve customer satisfaction.

Without empowered employees, it is difficult for service to reach the customer level. With little or no service, customers are not likely to return to a business. CSRs should be given the authority to handle customer complaints and concerns on the spot and allowed to use that authority to win customer satisfaction without fear of repercussion.

When managers do not empower or delegate responsibility for getting the job done, employees tend to react in some fairly predictable ways:

- Often, they become apathetic, developing a "so what?" attitude. Energy declines and productivity slows down.
- When people are unable to exercise their talents, those talents waste away. Without challenges, no new talents are acquired to move the organization forward.
- Employees who are not given responsibility hear the message, "You're not good enough to take control of this job." This leads to the employee being less motivated or less likely to take responsibility at a later date.
- Employees with limited responsibility tend to break rules, be absent more often, or increasingly show up late for work.
- Employees feel their hands are tied in the absence of managers, because no one is trained to think independently. This creates problems of succession and poses threats to the longevity of a company.

Reward CSRs

Well-trained customer service employees who feel they are valuable members of the corporate team create the magic inside the business that keeps customers coming back. Customer service employees know they are valued when companies use positive reinforcement and public praise. Workers need to know that their contributions are noticed and appreciated.

It's unfortunate, but too often top *sales* performers earn sizable bonuses or expensive prizes, whereas top *service* performers go unrecognized or are recognized on a much smaller scale. It is unwise for companies to send the message that service is *less important* than sales. Even small successes should be celebrated because they give companies the opportunity to recognize employees on a regular basis.

A recognition event doesn't have to be extravagant. A pizza party, a small gift, a gift certificate, a balloon bouquet, or a special parking spot often does the job. Some companies use a system called "Stories of Success" coupons that works like this: A coupon is awarded each time a manager sees or hears of a CSR performing one of the following behaviors:

- Demonstrating teamwork
- Offering to help someone

- Taking ownership of a problem
- Making a suggestion for cost savings
- Having perfect attendance for the month
- Teaching someone something that improves results
- Going above and beyond the call of duty
- Providing excellent customer service
- Making a suggestion that increases productivity
- Finding a potential problem and fixing it

Most coupons are worth one point (one point = $1). The CSRs collect the coupons and can trade them in for a merchandise gift certificate, a restaurant certificate, or a cash payout at the end of each month.

Other Loyalty Issues

Customer service centers are notorious for high turnover, but that doesn't mean organizations should accept turnover as a given. When employees leave, it's not just about money. Certainly, money matters, and if employees are not compensated fairly, good employees will leave. Research shows that certain motivators have an impact on employee retention and loyalty.

- *Organizations that provide meaningful work.* Having work that is meaningful keeps people excited about their jobs. If CSRs feel their work isn't meaningful, managers should spend time with them, brainstorming how to make their situations better. Sometimes that simply means helping CSRs view their jobs differently.
- *Organizations that provide good bosses.* To most employees, a good boss is one who shows respect, demonstrates genuine caring, gives good direction, is receptive to ideas, and shares information in a timely fashion.
- *Employees who feel they are part of a team.* Employees need to feel as if they are part of something bigger than themselves, that their individual contributions make a difference to a greater whole.[5]

Staff loyalty is critical to a company's success because turnover costs businesses money that is better spent growing the customer base. Research suggests that replacing a key employee costs between 70 and 200 percent of his or her annual salary. That doesn't take into account the costs of losing key customers who leave

---

focus on Career

A customer service manager must understand the content and requirements of customer service, as well as possess excellent people management skills. The person in this position must skillfully coach his or her CSRs to facilitate communication between customers, staff, and the sales team. Managers need the ability to create, control, and manage their operational areas while directing their CSRs. Although customer service managers come to the job with many of these skills, they often do not have all of them.

For that reason, customer service managers frequently attend professional off-site training seminars that provide them with current breakthrough strategies and techniques they can apply to ensure extraordinary customer service. Typical seminar topics include meeting service levels consistently, forecasting the workload with accuracy, developing accurate schedules, and setting the right performance objectives. The most popular management training seminars, conducted by the American Management Association, Fred Pryor, Career Track, and SkillPath, are available in many of the major cities around the country.

---

because their favorite CSR is no longer at the company.[6] That is why it's necessary to view retaining CSRs through a reward system as a critical business strategy.

Managing a Customer Service Department

Some of the best managers in an organization are promoted up through the ranks. Good managers are comfortable assigning tasks to CSRs because these managers know the job inside and out. They are good at facilitating cooperation between departments as well as with

---

[5]Sharon Jordan-Evans, "The Four Reasons Employees Stay in Their Jobs," *Customer Service Manager's Letter* (April 15, 2000): 2–3.

[6]Michael Lowenstein, "Securing the Service with a Smile," *Customer Loyalty Today* (October 2000): 6–7.

customers because they've "been there, done that," as the saying goes. Valuable leaders of customer service departments know how to motivate and monitor CSRs, as well as how to resolve conflicts that inevitably arise in any organization.

Motivating CSRs

A strong leader works hard to understand and motivate workers. Customer service managers must be well organized and capable of helping the department organize itself to accomplish its goals. One of the strengths of a good leader is the ability to see a better future for the department than what currently exists. Managers who create an environment that works for the customers and staff set the stage for customer service excellence. Figure 14.2 describes five effective methods managers can use to motivate CSRs.

Monitoring CSRs

Internally, managers need to watch out for attitudes among CSRs that paint the customer in a negative light. What may start out as harmless talk about customers can wind up becoming a company culture that pits CSRs against customers and can ultimately result in low customer retention. Two ways a manager can determine the quality of service reps' customer relations are presented here:

- *Review e-mail for consistency and core values.* Gather all e-mail and written correspondence from CSRs. Review them for grammar, misspellings, effectiveness of presentation, and politeness. Also, scan the documents for common words and decide whether those are truly the most fitting words or statements to describe the company.
- *Monitor customer service calls.* Listen in unobtrusively to customer service calls. Pay attention to the tone and manner the CSR uses to discuss various situations with customers.

Resolving Conflicts

Managers who never experience conflict on the job are rare. All workplaces suffer from conflict periodically, and several factors may be tied to its cause.

One factor is our increasingly diverse workforce. Sharing ideas that stem from a variety of backgrounds, experiences, and personalities probably leads to better problem solving, but it can also lead to conflict. Another factor is the trend toward **participatory management**, the

♦ remember this ...
Motivation Techniques

Method	Examples
1. They generate a spirit of service by	• Encouraging laughter, humor, warm greetings, smiles, and compliments. • Demonstrating belief in people through positive words of encouragement. • Casually visiting with staff, seeking their input, and incorporating that information into observable actions.
2. They build trust by	• Keeping people informed of change. • Demonstrating flexibility and interest in the personal situations of employees. • Sharing information about the organization. • Defining boundaries and providing reasonable expectations for all workers.
3. They develop people by	• Providing timely feedback through effective coaching. • Adapting communication techniques based on the needs of each employee. • Rewarding successes and addressing problems promptly.
4. They lead through example by	• Practicing the behaviors and ethics expected of frontline workers. • Giving direction in a respectful manner. • Listening attentively and responding to feedback from staff.
5. They stay focused on customer needs by	• Recognizing individuals for giving great customer service. • Implementing employee suggestions that improve service.

FIGURE 14.2

practice of empowering employees to participate in organizational decision making. In the past, only bosses were expected to resolve problems, but as employees are making more decisions, they have to deal with conflict more frequently on their own. Working together harmoniously involves a great deal of give and take, and conflict may result when people feel they are being treated unfairly.

To be good at resolving work-related conflicts requires a lot of practice. Interpersonal relationships with people at work may cause tension that you are not aware of. For example, if someone who is normally upbeat and friendly toward you suddenly begins avoiding you, there is probably a reason. If a coworker is cheerful with everyone except you, chances are a conflict exists. In such instances, use your best communication skills to address the problem through the following nine-step process:

1. Make an effort to determine whether there is, in fact, a problem.
2. If there is a problem, set up a private face-to-face meeting to discuss it with the other person.
3. In a nonconfrontational manner, explain what you think the problem is.
4. As you talk, ask for feedback. Do not attack the other person with accusations.
5. Try to listen to the other person with an open mind.
6. Respect others' opinions.
7. Attempt to determine the root cause of the problem.
8. Aim to work out a compromise that pleases both of you.
9. Find a way that both of you can walk away feeling like winners.

The goal is to reach a compromise that both of you can accept. Regardless of the type of conflict managers may face, there are general guidelines service professionals can follow to bring harmony back into the workplace. To review the rules for disagreeing diplomatically, refer to Figure 14.3.

Handling a difficult person requires skill, but more importantly, courage and time. Most of us avoid conflict because we think we don't have the time, emotional strength, or energy to put into a confrontation. Unfortunately, when difficult people are ignored, they tend to repeat their bad behavior because it works for them. Being firm, assertive, and using the proper techniques will help defuse the situation by coping with it rather than withdrawing from it.

BUSINESS in action

SIX SIGMA

Today's demanding business environment requires that customer service managers rethink the value of their current performance standards and customer contact operations. Strategic planning and design decisions must be grounded in a set of guiding principles that are based on facts and analysis—not assumptions. Six Sigma, the manufacturing theory used by Motorola and Xerox, has re-emerged in the customer service area. The increasing competitiveness of our global economy has forced organizations to begin focusing on areas that have been neglected in the past: customer satisfaction and service.

Six Sigma is a highly disciplined, project-based methodology that helps companies focus on developing and delivering near-perfect products and services. Its processes use data and statistical analysis to measure and improve an organization's customer service performance by identifying and eliminating defects in service-related processes. To attain Six Sigma, a process must not produce more than 3.4 defects per million opportunities. A Six Sigma defect is defined as anything outside of customer specifications. The application of Six Sigma performance standards in business is popular because it improves customer responsiveness, reduces errors, streamlines processes, and—if properly applied—delivers consistent, high-quality customer service.

Concluding Message for CSRs

There was a time when customer service meant hiring an individual to sit behind a complaint desk. Today, customer service is much more comprehensive. It requires employers to hire the right employees, create a customer service culture, and train employees on certain technologies without sacrificing the human touch.

! remember this ...
Rules for Disagreeing Diplomatically

Rule	When You Say	It Really Means
Reflect your understanding of the other's position or opinion.	"If I understand you, ..."	"I am listening to your opinion and take it into account before I state mine."
Let the other person know you value him or her as a person, even though your opinions differ.	"I understand [appreciate, respect, see] how you feel that way."	"I hear you and respect your opinion."
State your position or opinion.	"I feel [think, want]. . . ."	"I don't agree, but I value you—so let's exchange ideas comfortably, not as a contest for superiority."

FIGURE 14.3

Knowledgeable, courteous, and effective employees bring in and help retain customers. Advertising brings customers in the door, but poor service turns them away and points them in the direction of a competitor. Consumers are more knowledgeable and have higher expectations than ever before. When a company improves its service delivery, the satisfaction bar is raised. The challenge for businesses in the twenty-first century is not just serving customers, but also

- understanding customers as people.
- being prepared to serve customers right the first time.
- helping angry customers immediately.
- asking customers for information the right way.
- listening to customers with empathy.
- being responsible for their actions when a customer calls.
- living up to their commitments and always following through.
- being memorable by going beyond what customers expect.

- surprising customers with unexpected acts of kindness.
- striving to keep customers for life.
- getting unsolicited referrals from customers regularly.

Summary

- Setting standards for performance that tell workers what is expected of them, both in quality and quantity of work, is a conscious effort and involves direction from customer service managers.
- Typically, a CSR works inside comfortable offices or cubicles between 35 and 40 hours per week, with some occasional overtime, night, and weekend work.
- Four factors that encourage loyalty on the job are meaningful work with appropriate rewards, opportunities to learn and grow, having an effective supervisor, and inclusion on a team.
- Good customer service managers generate a spirit of service, build trust, develop people, lead by example, and stay focused on customer needs.

KEY TERMS

coaching   role playing
participatory management   standards

CRITICAL THINKING

1. Why is it important for managers to use measurable customer service standards? Cite two examples of measurable standards.

2. List the pros and cons of a typical working environment for customer service representatives.

3. What is the incentive for companies to train, empower, and reward service professionals?

4. Name two recognition and reward programs you would like to participate in and describe what you like about each one.

5. What skills do you possess that would make you an effective customer service manager? Describe in a short paragraph how you would apply your managerial talents in a customer service setting.

ONLINE RESEARCH ACTIVITIES

Project 14.1 CSR Job Qualifications

Search a number of career-building websites and locate several job descriptions currently available for a CSR. As a result of your research, develop a list of the top eight qualifications and job skills that employers are seeking in the customer service representatives they hire.

Present your findings to the class using a visual aid, such as a PowerPoint® presentation, flip chart, or overhead transparencies.

Project 14.2 Managing a Customer Service Department

Mary Graeff is moving out of state and the company must advertise for the position of Customer Service Department Supervisor.

Enter *customer service manager* in your favorite search engine. Locate several open positions and find the qualifications those jobs require. As a result of your research, complete the first table with seven of the most important job requirements for a customer service manager. In the second table, list at least three reasons that On-Time Technology Products should consider filling Ms. Graeff's position from within the organization.

Job Qualifications	Three Reasons to Promote from Within
1.	1.
2.	
3.	2.
4.	
5.	3.
6.	
7.	

COMMUNICATION SKILLS AT WORK

Project 14.3 Communicating Standards to Customers

You have been asked to put together a chart that will be used to train new CSRs in performance standards, accuracy, and production at On-Time Technology Products. Using the information from this chapter and other sources you locate relative to this project, recommend a standard (method or action) that a CSR can demonstrate to perform each listed characteristic.

Benchmark Characteristic	Method or Action to Meet the Benchmark Characteristic
1. Value	
2. Communication	
3. Attitude	
4. Reliability	
5. Empathy	
6. Exceptional service	

DECISION MAKING AT WORK

Project 14.4 Career Advancement or Job Security?

At a recent customer service conference, there was a debate among customer service managers as to whether it is best to hire a CSR who is more concerned with job security or one who is more interested in career advancement. Be prepared to participate on either side of the debate by preparing a defense for the following two statements.

1. **Defend:** When hiring a CSR, it is better to offer stability and longevity on the job over any other factor. Doing so will get you a better employee.

_____

_____

_____

_____

_____

_____

_____

_____

2. **Defend:** When hiring a CSR, it is better to offer advancement through a career path and promotion opportunities over any other factor. Doing so will get you get a better employee.

_____

_____

_____

_____

_____

_____

_____

_____

CASE STUDIES

Project 14.5 Cost of Nonservice

A woman was mistreated by a salesperson in a store where she had been shopping once a week for three years. As a result of the poor service, she began shopping elsewhere. Twelve years later she returned to the store and told the owner what had happened. He listened intently, apologized, and thanked her for coming back. Back in his office, he estimated that if the woman had spent only $25 a week in his store, he would have had $15,600 additional revenue over the past 12 years. He had lost her business to nonservice.

1. In your judgment, to what extent does nonservice affect businesses today?

_____

_____

_____

_____

2. What methods can companies use to prevent this one incident of poor service from causing an economic disaster?

_____

_____

_____

_____

Project 14.6 Customer Service Fallacies

During an interview for Mary Graeff's position, an applicant made the following two statements. Most of those on the interview team recognized that these statements represent two common customer service fallacies that exist in business today. Argue the statements as false during a class discussion.

1. Improving customer service means adding more people to the payroll.

_____

_____

2. You must pay people more money to improve customer service.

_____

_____

Action Plan

Based on your study of Part 4, think about the many types of communication skills that a customer service representative should practice when serving customers in a globally connected world, and then complete the following activities.

Activity 1

Divide a sheet of paper into four columns and create the following list in column 1: Understand the Challenges of Serving Global Customers, Possess Computer and Internet Skills, Create Written Communication with Customers, and Appreciate Industry Standards. Label column 2 *Strength,* column 3 *Needs Improvement,* and column 4 *Method of Improvement.*

Give some thought as to how you would rate yourself on each item in column 1. How do you measure up? If there is a skill that you are especially strong in, put an X in column 2 next to that item, showing it as a strength of yours. If it is a skill that you may need to work on in some way, place an X in column 3. Finally, in column 4, indicate how you might improve on those skills you've identified in column 3.

Activity 2

Working together as a class, assign a person to write on the whiteboard or chalkboard. Break the writing space into two areas: Navigating Websites and Messaging with E-mail and Chats. Devote some class time to brainstorming about each of the two areas. When class members respond, they should use the sentence stem, "Remember to...."

Finally, each student should select from each group two reminders that the student feels have the most relevance to him or her and place those items on note cards to be posted in a workspace or at home.

glossary

A

active listening Listening with your whole mind and body—not just your ears.

adversity quotient A precise, measurable, unconscious pattern of how people respond to adversity.

aggressive communication style A style of communication in which the person is closed-minded, listens poorly, has difficulty seeing another person's point of view, interrupts other people while they are talking, and tends to monopolize conversations.

alternative choice questions Questions that provide specific choices for the customer to select from.

American Customer Satisfaction Index (ACSI) Established in 1994, tracks trends in customer satisfaction and provides valuable benchmarking insights of the consumer economy.

Amiable personality The personality type that wants to build relationships, give others support and attention, values suggestions from others, and fears disagreement.

Analytical personality The personality type that is systematic, well organized, deliberate, values numbers and statistics, loves details, and tends to be introverted.

assertive communication style A style of communication in which the person uses active listening, states limits and expectations, and does not label or judge people or events.

assimilation The process of becoming part of a larger group.

B

Baby Boomer Generation Born between 1946 and 1964, this generation is idealistic, competitive, questions authority, desires to put their own stamp on things, and challenges institutions.

baseline standard The minimum level of service it takes to satisfy customers under ordinary circumstances.

blogs A website where entries are made in journal style and displayed in reverse chronological order. Also referred to as web logs, they contain text, images, and links to other blogs or web pages, and are part of a wider network of information.

blue rules Customer service rules that can be bent or modified, based on the circumstances.

body language Nonverbal messages that include tone of voice, eye movement, posture, hand gestures, facial expressions, and more.

burnout The state in which a person feels psychological exhaustion and decreased efficiency resulting from overwork and prolonged exposure to stress.

business etiquette The rules of acceptable behavior that identify the application of correct or polite manners in a general business situation.

business-to-consumer (B2C or B-to-C) e-commerce A type of electronic commerce that involves the sale of goods and services from a business entity to a consumer or the general public through the Internet.

C

call center A location where groups of people use telephones to provide service and support to customers.

closed questions Questions that usually elicit "yes" or "no" answers.

coaching A training method that emphasizes learning by doing and turns information into knowledge and experience.

communication The successful exchange of information when there is shared understanding between two or more persons.

conflict To be in variance or opposition to another. A conflict with a customer can jeopardize productivity, relationships at work, and dealings with customers.

contact center In an organization, an area, similar to a call center, that typically uses more technologically sophisticated devices when interacting with customers.

contact points Situations when customers are served, which can occur in person, on the phone, through written communications, or online.

culture A system of shared values, beliefs, and rituals that are learned and passed down through generations of families and social groups.

customer contact center A technology-based multi-channel work setting where CSRs serve customers through multiple channels using online call centers as well as other types of customer contact, including e-mail, website inquiries, and chat rooms.

customer economy A description of a type of economy that defines the power shift from companies to their customers.

customer expectations The ideas and beliefs that a customer has before a transaction occurs.

customer perceptions The opinions that are formed by the customer during and after a business transaction.

customer profile Demographic information that is collected about customers, explaining who the customers are and what they want in terms of service.

customer rage An expression that describes an increasing number of frustrated consumers who are taking out their anger on customer service representatives.

customer relations policy A company policy that is the foundation for maintaining customer goodwill and which lays out the guidelines for communicating with customers and for handling customer complaints.

Customer Relationship Management (CRM) A business strategy used by companies that integrates the functions of sales, marketing, and customer service, and uses technology and wide-ranging databases of information to improve service to customers in a more personal way.

customer satisfaction The state of mind that customers have about a company and its products or services when their expectations have been met or exceeded.

customer self-service (CSS) A proactive approach to customer service that empowers customers to go to a company's website and find answers to most of the queries and functions that normally go through a call center.

customer service The process of satisfying a customer, relative to a product or service, in whatever way the customer defines his or her need.

customer service representative (CSR) The frontline person who deals with customers on a day-to-day basis.

customer-centric service A service strategy that puts the customer first, demonstrating a service-oriented commitment.

D

decoding process A step in the communication process that occurs when the receiver's brain filters the message and gives it a unique meaning.

direct questions Open or closed questions that are posed as instructions and use the name of the person being addressed.

disability A condition caused by an accident, trauma, genetics, or disease, which may limit a person's mobility, hearing, vision, speech or mental function.

Driver personality The personality type that wants to save time, values results, loves being in control, and does things his or her own way.

E

e-business An electronic business that allows customers from around the world to buy merchandise via the Internet, from anywhere and at anytime they choose.

electronic storefront An online business (website) a customer visits that contains text and graphic descriptions of products and services.

e-mail etiquette A set of standards recommended by business and communication experts in response to the growing concern that people are not using electronic mail appropriately.

e-mail publishing The process of periodically sending newsletters, via e-mail, to a large group of people with similar interests.

empathy The ability to understand another person's position without getting emotionally involved.

e-rep A term used to describe a customer service representative who services customers online using e-mail, chat rooms, and other technologies.

empowerment The act of giving a CSR the necessary power or authority to make administrative decisions based on corporate guidelines.

encoding process A step in the communication process that occurs when a message arrives from a sender; the senses pick up the message through signals and then relay it to the receiver's brain.

ESL (English as a second language) Used to describe customers who have studied English and generally comprehend it, but who may have difficulty speaking it for several reasons.

exceptional customer service The type of service that provides customers with more than they expect in a business transaction.

Expressive personality The personality type that values appreciation, enjoys social situations, likes to inspire others, and is extroverted.

external customers People outside of an organization that purchase and use a company's products and services.

F

fee-based 900 number A premium telephone number whereby individuals or businesses provide information and services that are billed directly to the caller's local telephone bill.

feedback A step in the communication process that occurs when a message is transmitted back to the original sender.

filter A screen or frame of reference that can depend on one or more factors and affects a person's perception of situations.

filtering The tendency for a message to be watered down or halted completely at some point during transmission, which can result in deflecting or stopping the listening process.

first-call resolution (FCR) The process in customer service of resolving customer calls to service reps on the first call or contact.

G

Generation X Born between 1965 and 1981, this generation is resourceful, self-reliant, distrusts institutions, and is highly adaptive to both change and technology.

globalization The process by which a business or company becomes international or starts operating at an international level.

H

help desk A location where customer service representatives answer customer questions by phone, fax, e-mail, and the Internet.

help desk software Software that automates the help-desk function and is used to quickly find answers to commonly asked questions about particular products and services. Typical functions of this software include call management, call tracking, knowledge management, problem resolution, and self-help capabilities.

homeshoring The practice of domestic companies hiring U.S. home-based call agents instead of more expensive in-house operators or less qualified offshore call center operators.

I

inbound telemarketing A marketing technique used by companies primarily to take orders, generate leads, and provide customer service.

inclusion The addition or presence of somebody in a group. An approach, relative to diversity, that embraces and leverages differences for the benefit of the organization.

instant messaging (IM) A real-time Internet communication service that notifies you when one or more contacts you have designated are online and allows you to exchange messages or files in a real-time typed conversation.

internal customers People within an organization that rely on colleagues to provide the support they need to serve their own internal and external customers.

K

knowledge base Computerized data compiled by CSRs and used to resolve problems with customers about service issues.

L

leading question A question that confirms information and helps speed up interactions with people who find it difficult to make a final decision.

M

Mature Generation Born prior to 1946, this generation is patriotic, loyal, fiscally conservative, and has faith in institutions.

messaging on-hold A system that plays a pre-recorded program for callers to listen to while they are on hold.

Millennial Generation Born after 1981, this generation is confident, ambitious, technologically sound, can be impatient, and gets information quickly.

mirror principle A business concept that says a company's employees will not treat customers better than the company treats the employees.

mixed message A single message that contains two opposing meanings. Typically the verbal part of the message is positive, while the nonverbal component is negative and contradicts the verbal part.

moment of truth An episode in which a customer comes in contact with any aspect of the organization and thereby has an opportunity to form an impression.

mystery shopper A third-party person who anonymously and objectively evaluates a business for the purpose of analyzing customer service, product quality, store presentation, and other elements of the customer experience.

N

National Do Not Call Registry A list created by the Federal government to give consumers the choice of whether to allow telemarketing calls to their homes.

negative language Language that conveys a poor image to customers and may cause conflict and confrontation where none is necessary or desired.

negative stress A type of stress that comes from a person worrying about things he or she has no power to change.

netiquette Short for Internet etiquette, this is a code of acceptable behaviors that users should follow while on the Internet.

O

open question A question asked in a way that requires a fuller answer than a simple "yes" or "no."

outbound telemarketing A marketing technique used by many organizations because of rising postage rates and decreasing long-distance phone charges.

outsourcing The purchase of labor from a source outside the company rather than using the company's own staff; also known as subcontracting.

P

paraphrase The communication technique of repeating back what has been said, using other words for clarification.

participatory management The practice of empowering employees to participate in organizational decision making.

passive communication style An indirect communication style in which a person agrees externally with others in order to avoid expressing his or her true thoughts and opinions, although privately disagreeing.

passive listening One-way communication in which the listener does not give the speaker feedback in the form of either verbal or nonverbal responses.

personal digital assistant (PDA) An electronic device that assists a person in organizing a busy schedule.

ping-ponging The process of a customer being passed from one employee or department to another while he or she is trying to resolve a problem or concern.

positive language Language that projects a helpful, encouraging feeling rather than a destructive, negative one.

positive question A question phrased in a non-threatening manner so that a person is not afraid to answer.

positive stress A type of stress that can be channeled into productive results that motivate and energize a person rather than making him or her anxious and frustrated.

post-episodic surveys A satisfaction-type survey that gathers information from customers after they each complete one business transaction.

proactive problem solving The process of anticipating and resolving problems *before* they occur.

probing question A question that uses information already established to clarify points and elicit more details.

problem-solving process A systematic five-step process used to solve a wide range of problems.

procrastination The act of putting off completing an activity until a later time.

R

reactive feedback A type of communication exchange that affirms the speaker's message.

red rules Customer service rules that are very prescriptive because they have to be followed exactly as specified.

reflective feedback A type of communication exchange that mirrors content and intent.

relaxation A state of being that is self-initiated and provides relief from physical and psychological efforts.

responsive feedback A type of communication exchange that characterizes the listener's feelings.

role playing A training method where learners use customer scenarios to act out situations encountered in the real world.

S

script A document used by CSRs when conversing with customers that states consistent responses to common customer problems.

selective listening The process of hearing only what you want to hear—filtering out what you think is not important or not of interest to you.

self-talk The voice inside us that affects our attitude—positively or negatively.

service animal Any animal that has been individually trained to provide assistance or perform tasks for the benefit of a person with a physical or mental disability.

service recovery A gesture of compensation, specific to the situation, that is offered to the customer who feels betrayed and not well served.

soft skills Also referred to as people skills, these include punctuality, positive attitude, and cooperation.

softening techniques Positive approaches that service professionals use when interacting with customers, for example, an open posture (no crossed arms) and kindhearted eye contact (no rolling of eyes).

standards A baseline description of service performance guidelines that tells workers what is expected of them, in terms of both the quality and quantity of their work.

stereotyping The tendency to categorize individuals or groups according to an oversimplified and standardized image or idea.

synergy In teamwork, the effect of combined efforts of many individuals that is greater than the sum of their individual efforts.

T

telephone tag The process of telephoning back and forth between individuals who repeatedly miss each other's calls and must leave multiple phone messages for each other.

tiered service system A customer service approach in which the service level increases or decreases proportionally to the amount a customer is spending.

time management The conscious act of using time in the most effective way possible.

tone In written communication, a manner of expression that reflects the writer's attitude toward the reader and the subject of the message.

W

word-of-mouth (WoM) marketing An expression used, especially with blogs, to describe activities that generate personal recommendations as well as referrals for a company's products or services.

index

Note: *f* indicates figure on page.